BATTING ON THE BOSPHORUS

Angus Bell is a Scotsman with a first-class degree in English, Flying Saucers and Space Studies. He has visited 40 countries, and has written for the *South African Sunday Times*, *Inside Sport* in Australia, the *US Student Traveler*, *Cricinfo* in India, and *The Wisden Cricketer* and *Fat Controller Magazine* in the UK.

He now plays cricket in Montreal, Canada, where he lives with his girlfriend Candy and his pet rabbit Usagi. For more articles and photos from his travels and misadventures, visit www.angusjjbell.com.

Author photo © Andy Barr

BATTING ON THE BOSPHORUS

A SKODA-POWERED CRICKET TOUR THROUGH EASTERN EUROPE

ANGUS BELL

CANONGATE

Edinburgh · London · New York · Melbourne

First published in Great Britain under the title *Slogging the Slavs* in 2006 by Fat Controller Media Ltd, 4th Floor, Sunco House, Carliol Square, Newcastle Upon Tyne, NE1 6UF, UK

This paperback edition published in 2008 by Canongate Books Ltd, 14 High Street, Edinburgh, EH1 1TE

1

Copyright © Angus JJ Bell, 2006
The moral rights of the author have been asserted

Photos copyright © Andy Barr, Jason Barry, Angus JJ Bell, Borut Čegovnik, Vladimír Chudáčik, Ruslanas Iržikevičius, Ivo Scepanovic, Richard Scott, Andrej Souvent, Ed Symes, 2006

British Library Cataloguing-in-Publication Data
A catalogue record for this book is available on request from the British Library.

ISBN 978 1 84767 290 2

Typeset by Cluny Sheeler

Printed and bound in Great Britain by Clays Ltd, St Ives plc

www.canongate.net

CONTENTS

When a Psychic Tells You You're Going to Do
    Something, You Do It   1

Batting in the Baltic   8

The Batsman Who Would Be King   40

It Was Like a Stephen King Novel   52

Fielders Without Fingers   60

The Village that Beat Poland   76

The Worst Coaches in the World   98

The Lost Tribe of Mežica   109

Sex on the Wicket   142

On the Trail of Torvill and Dean   169

The Spy Who Left Cricket Cold   185

The Cricket and Kickboxing Club of Bulgaria   202

Midnight Express   212

A Man on My Chest   220

Transylvanian Toothache   227

Trotsky Was a Ukrainian Cricketer (of Sorts)   242

Inspector Morski   261

Pummelling the Poles   277

Psychic Revisited   290

"If Stalin had learned to play cricket, the world might now be a better place to live in."
Dr R Downey, Bishop of Liverpool, 1948

"My grandfather used to say cricket is like sex. You wait in the pavilion all day for your chance. And when you finally step up to the crease you're out for a duck."
Lenny Henry

1

WHEN A PSYCHIC TELLS YOU YOU'RE GOING TO DO SOMETHING, YOU DO IT

The Psychic Expo building in Old Montreal

"You there! Young man with your arms folded!" shouted the psychic, waving his free hand feverishly in my direction. "Can I give you a message?"

I looked down. My arms were folded. I was a young man. "Me?" I asked dumbly.

"Yes! Can I give you a message, from the spirit world?" There was great urgency in his voice. I shrugged and nodded.

I was at a psychic exposition in Old Montreal with my girlfriend Candy, whose family runs a chocolate factory. Around the hall were turbaned seers, crystal balls and workshops on travelling in the astral plane. Overseeing the most popular booth, according to her banner, was a 'TV-famous' psychic dwarf. She wore orange and black striped stockings and pink kids' sunglasses.

Candy and I had pushed through a housewife scrum to the forum's rear, where a bearded man – a dead ringer for George Lucas – was winding down a stage demonstration.

"For the last few minutes, I'm going to do some clairvoyance," he had announced by microphone, closing his eyes. Candy and I had taken seats.

"You have this big idea that's taking up all your time!" said the psychic. "At the moment you're putting it out there, and it's being thrown back in your face every time! It's some kind of media idea. You're *pretty much* at a final draft, but you have to look at doing it another way. It's very important for your career."

It was true; I so badly craved the life of a media slut, without the cocaine. Was this prophet talking about my four-year search for a book publisher? He was onto something, I decided. I sat still, not wishing to give away clues.

"You're beating yourself with a cat o' nine tails!" he squealed. "And you're *not* doing everything you can do to get it out!"

And I thought consulting the dead was the end of the line.

The psychic looked to the ceiling and placed a palm on the wall. "I'm afraid to say your job here in Montreal is only temporary," he said, adopting a tender tone. "You're going to be finishing sooner than you think. You're going to be leaving North America and going back home."

This provoked mixed feelings. My job was a minimum-wage, part-time, Mafia-money-laundering operation under the guise of magazine publishing. My boss told investors he was selling 80,000 issues every quarter. In my first week alone this brought him $1.5 million(US). Then I discovered the magazine hadn't sold an advert in four years, and had no readers. They printed 5000 copies once a year and locked them in a garage. After a three-month job hunt, this was all I could find. I needed to stick it out.

"The way I see it, you're a man on a mission," said the psychic. "Your travelling is *not* over. In fact, you're going to be doing a *lot more* travelling. Pretty soon it's going to be your *job* to travel."

I had travel-writing ambitions all right, but given the current career trend this could mean I'd be a pizza delivery boy.

"I don't know what you do in life. I don't know if you're aware of it, but you're going to be putting together a book, or a movie . . . and this time it's going to get accepted. Your interest in the paranormal is not by coincidence either. This feels to me like an interview."

The psychic skipped across the stage.

"You have a contact . . . *Not* in the physical world, but in the *spirit* world. This would be someone from your mother's side of the family, like an uncle. He died an infant death, around the war. Every time you're sitting there and an idea pops into your head from nowhere – and you feel it's something you have to do – it's him putting it there. He's living his life *through* you. That alone is a good idea for a book, or a movie."

So, I could blame this infant ghost for every bad decision.

"He will come to you through meditation, if you choose."

The psychic placed another palm on the wall. "Someone else is going to help you in this project. I get the feeling his name is Jason, but that he *changed* his name. In other words, he dropped the kid's name and took up Jason. He's in media, and appearance is very, very important to him."

I had no idea who this Jason was.

"Lastly, you're going to be coming back here to Montreal. You're going to be seeing me again. I'm not an immigration officer, but you'll need to complete a lot of paperwork in order to work here again. Any questions?"

I drew a deep breath and exhaled slowly. The audience stared at me for verification. Candy looked rattled. What do you ask the man who can see the future? I wondered.

"Yes, there's one burning question. Are there such things as Neanderthal ghosts?"

The psychic looked at me incredulously. "*No*! They've all reincarnated into higher beings."

*

Back in Candy's apartment, the psychic's words played heavily on my mind. There were enormous consequences if what he was saying were true, and not just about Neanderthal ghosts. People go on about nature versus nurture, but could it be an infant ghost was deciding my fate? Was it his fault I disliked Marmite, yet found fascination in my own earwax? Were my travel manuscripts his works? Did *he* bring me here to Montreal, in -40°C, to live with Candy and play French Canadian cricket? Where training started at 11 on a week night, with a Coke bottle as stumps? Where, out of 46 teams, I was the only white guy?

I phoned my mum in the Scottish Borders.

"There's only been one infant death in the family," she said. "Your great-uncle Ivor from Wales. He died of measles, aged two, before World War One. Why?"

This phantom now had a name. *Ivor* would come to me through meditation, if I chose.

The following week, my money-laundering job came to an

abrupt end when I was made redundant, along with the entire staff, after just six weeks. "Go try get a job at McDonald's," they told me. I said I couldn't. I was vegetarian.

Back in the apartment, I scoured newspapers and websites for jobs. Openings in the travelling-media/pizza-delivery industries looked thin that week, like every other. The Montreal papers only advertised six jobs: all telesales.

"LIKE TRAVELLING?" screamed the classifieds. "Call centre staff needed now!!!"

I sighed. I'd been topping up my earnings by participating in psychological experiments for cash at a university. Now these were drying up.

As the days went by, I branched out to PhD ice-cream-flavour surveys at $10 a pop. But my bank balance continued to be whittled away as fast as my chances of serious employment. Either I used my experience from Candy's family's chocolate factory, and baked cakes to sell on the street, or . . .

Damn it, the psychic was right. This wasn't the time to be in Canada. I almost laughed at the idea now. Heck, my visa would be expiring shortly.

When Candy returned from the chocolate factory one evening, we discussed moving to Scotland. The next day, I brought my return flight forward three months. Candy, with her Belgian citizenship, would come with me. We'd make a success of it in Glasgow. Just for a year, and see how it went. Would I have been doing this if it weren't for the psychic? Sometimes you just need that little shove, don't you?

*

A fortnight later, I was propped up at the computer in my dressing gown, unshaven, a bowl of Cheerios on my lap. It had been a late night, with Montreal cricket training finishing at a record 1 a.m. As I slouched in my chair, drifting through cyberspace and munching my breakfast, two words popped into my head: cricket and Ukraine.

What the hell does 'cricket and Ukraine' mean? I wondered, sitting upright. I typed them into the Google box and clicked on 'Search'.

The first results appeared incoherent and silly, and there were a few about insects in the Crimea. But with little better to do, I ploughed through every search page, sensing there was something I had to find.

On the sixteenth page, I spotted a link that made me stand up and spill my Cheerios. Here was a website about a cricket league at the Odessa State Medical University. Students had formed 16 teams. *16 teams.* A psychic talking to the dead about my future, I could understand, but 16 teams at a former USSR university?

I searched again, this time for cricket in Bulgaria. Yes, they had a team, in the capital, Sofia. I tried Romania, and stumbled onto the European Cricket Council website. In their contacts section they listed cricket clubs across Central and Eastern Europe, from Belarus to the former Yugoslavia. Estonia, they announced, was developing cricket on ice.

I could hardly draw breath. How had these Slavs, Latins and Finno-Ugrics, never colonised by the British, come to play the Englishman's game? In private schools? Was it cloaked behind the Iron Curtain? Did they spend their winters watching Sky Sports? Had they ever pulled a sickie from work for a game? Did they fight over Cadbury's Mini Rolls and Jammie Dodgers at tea break? Where did they buy their whites? Were they ever beaten up on the street and called gay for wearing them? Or did they, like village idiots in Britain, sport chinos? This, I believed, merited serious investigation.

Every time you're sitting there and an idea pops into your head from nowhere – and you feel it's something you have to do – it's him putting it there.

There was no doubt in my mind what I had to do. The decision was made in a flash. My mission, as the psychic foretold, and the ghost of my great-uncle Ivor was making clear in that moment, was to travel around the former Soviet bloc, playing cricket. I would uncover the story of the Slavic game, and put it in a book. Could I, a keen Scottish player with a fetish for Eastern Europe, succeed on this level? Where better to boost my batting average and score that elusive first century?

2
BATTiNG iN THE BALTiC

A streaker interrupts the Ice Sixes final. At -15°C, he's a brave man

Here's a fact you probably didn't know: forget Bangladesh, Estonia has the worst international cricket team in the world. At 105th in the (unofficial) rankings, they fall far short of Sierra Leone (joint 51st with Switzerland) and 74th-place Sweden (sandwiched between Panama and Venezuela). Still, this EU-accession country can be proud. Many nations, such as North Korea, don't even make the prestigious list.

It was January. I was spending Burns Night under my coat on the floor at Stansted Airport, with a stranger's vinegary feet in my face. While a typical off-season tour might mean a month in Sri Lanka or Australia, here I was preparing to board a budget air carrier for Estonia's capital, Tallinn. If all went well, my week-long foray into the icy world of Finno-Ugric cricket would set me up for the season. Everything was falling into place. Even my Glasgow call centre had laid me off on Christmas Eve.

As the planeload of testosterone-charged stags swooped over the Baltic, touching down by a string of frozen vegetable plots, I struggled to picture Estonia's cricketers touring 75th-ranked Venezuela.

At arrivals, to my astonishment, a petite blonde stood waving a sign with my name on it.

"I'm Liina, your chaperone for the week," she explained as I approached.

"Great. I didn't know . . ."

"Jason sent me," she said. "He is Estonia's cricket captain. He heard about your trip and wants to meet you." I was impressed. If it had been Scotland I'd have expected to be met with a mugging.

Liina whisked us into a waiting taxi and coped commendably with my machine-gun questioning. She was Jason's accounts manageress and spoke better English than half of Glasgow.

"No," she said. "I have never played cricket . . . Basketball is the national sport of Estonia . . . I have no idea how you play cricket on ice . . ."

Our taxi zipped through the snow, passing casinos, 'striptiis' bars and megalithic former Soviet meat and vodka factories.

"What's the building makeover for?" I asked.

"More nightclubs," said Liina, grimacing.

My preconceptions of Estonia had been of babushkas and rotting tower blocks. But Tallinn was a city with chic, new constructions at a snip of the price of our Millennium Dome and Scottish Parliament.

"We were quick after 1991 to change the communist look," explained Liina.

Saabs, Volvos and blacked-out Jeeps roamed the streets. Where were my beloved Trabants running on two-stroke fuel mixed by hand? Only one came into view. The dog on the driver's lap appeared to be steering.

Our taxi pulled up opposite the port terminal, overlooking four Finnish booze-cruise liners. I inspected the ships' sides for vomit stains, but everything appeared freshly painted.

"This is your hotel, owned by the Saku brewery," said Liina. I stopped in my stride. A chaperone, now a hotel owned by a brewery? It was like walking into a Carlsberg advert.

"Check in and I'll take you to meet Jason," she said.

I approached the desk. A tight-topped receptionist issued me with free beer coupons. A sign on the wall read: 'Hotel for hard working people'. Did they screen their clients? I wondered.

Entering my room was like being beamed into a work of science fiction sponsored by easyJet. I could hear Boney M's 'Rasputin' piping down the corridor. My keycard slotted into the wall, powering up spotlights. They revealed orange walls and a framed portrait of David Bowie in heavy make-up. The door-hanger read: 'People working hard. Do not disturb. Piss off!'

I flicked every switch three times, marked my territory with a slash and rejoined Liina by the bar.

Along a close at the edge of the old town, we slipped into the mysterious Jason's office. Again, it looked as though the room had been decorated by a Swedish smack addict. The walls were a splurge of pink and lemon, dotted with posters of Scottish castles. There were bookshelves stocked with brandy and enough computer cable to stretch to Vladivostok. Most pleasing of all were the cricket bats and beer crates for Saturday's ice tournament.

Liina introduced four American-accented, sexilingual girls on the staff – all part-time students. "There's not many grants here, so when you're not studying you have to work, or you don't eat," said one.

I was drawn to a framed photograph on the wall of a Philip Schofield lookalike driving a London taxi. "Is that . . . *Terry Wogan* in the back seat?" I asked.

"Yes," said Liina. "He came here to present the Eurovision Song Contest. Jason gave him the office and drove him around in the taxi . . . Here he is now."

I spun around. The half-English, half-French, silver-haired Jason was no ordinary man. A marketing whizz and captain of Estonia's cricket team, he breezed in wearing a dark Russian overcoat, greeting me with a crunching handshake.

"Great to hear about your trip," he said in a BBC broadcaster's accent. "We're very glad you could come and play us. If there's anything I can do to help, anything at all, let me know."

I'd never met the captain of an international cricket team before. I thought about asking for his autograph.

We sat on a sofa in the centre of the office, distracting the girls and sipping Tetley tea. Not only was this Leicester athlete running five companies (travel, recruitment, design, internet and marketing), he was the brother of a yeti hunter in the Himalayas. He was the player-coach of Estonia's national hockey team, too. A dual internationalist. Few people achieve that sporting accolade. *And*, I learned, Jason had played cricket in quite a number of places. In fact, a *world-record* number of places.

"One hundred and twenty-eight countries and territories so far, and I plan to do another 100 next year," he said.

I felt like cancelling my trip then and there. This visionary had beaten me to it.

"I've only done some Eastern European countries," he put in hastily, seeing the curl in my lip. "Many years ago now. Poland, Czech Republic, Slovenia, Russia . . . I was arrested at Moscow Airport for teaching cricket to Georgian refugees by the toilets."

"Is that a crime in Russia?"

"No, but I broke a window and set off the sprinkler system. But what you're doing is different. You've got to go through with it. Just don't get any ideas about beating my record, or I'll cut the ice from under you on Saturday."

We both laughed.

"Only joking. But once you start, it's like a drug. You won't be able to stop."

"I have a girlfriend in Scotland," I said. "She's not the biggest cricket fan, being Québecoise, and all. My relationship wouldn't last another five minutes if I took up cricket full-time. And you can't bat without a partner."

"True," conceded Jason, who then revealed he'd been engaged once. "I was cricketing in Australia. I proposed to my girlfriend after three days, in the car. I gave her a Hula Hoop as a ring."

"What did she say?"

"'Yes!' But then I found out her father was a Nazi war criminal on a ventilator in her basement. The relationship fell to pieces after that."

I could see Jason's mind spurting forth extraordinary memories. On the sofa, chatting about cricket, he had the air of a man getting the world off his chest. It must have been a struggle relating his cricket tales to Estonians. I couldn't get enough of them. My pen raged across my notebook. Jason ran to retrieve a box of photographs.

"Why did you decide to go around the world playing cricket?" I asked.

"*Groundhog Day*. That film with Bill Murray. I couldn't face a life like that, going through the same mundane tasks each day."

Jason handed me snaps of cricket fields in China, Chile and France.

"Ten years ago I decided I wanted to play cricket in 50 countries. A friend in the pub bet me 50 pounds I couldn't do it. My girlfriend at the time said, 'You'll never do it.' So I thought, right, I'm gonna show you. I left in 1996, in a sponsored Peugeot, playing cricket and raising money for local charities. The tour was called One Man and His Bat. It lasted four years. I had to mortgage my house to keep going."

And I thought *I* was loopy about cricket. This clinched a world record.

"Did you ever play against 75th-ranked Venezuela?"

"Didn't get the chance. I went to Colombia, though. The guard at Bogotá Airport slit down my new cricket pads with a knife. 'What did you do that for?' I shouted. 'Checking for drugs,' he said. 'You think I'd smuggle drugs in my cricket pads?' I said. 'Oh, so you're smuggling drugs, are you?' That was it. They led me to a room and gave me the rubber glove. Two fingers. Have you seen the old town yet?"

We drained our tea, wrapped up warmly and wandered into the UNESCO-protected cobbled streets. The snow was crashing down in avalanches from the rooftops. Jason said Tallinn's multicoloured, swollen walls and medieval doorways were prize property for house-hunting Finns. There were beams you could hang rival nightclub owners from.

We entered the fairytale, trapezium-shaped Raekoja Square. Once a venue for executions, it now hosted jousting tournaments and an annual parrot-shooting contest. Jason led me to Europe's oldest pharmacy in one corner and talked about the history of cricket in his adopted land.

Estonia's cricket roots began in 1998, when an Indian restaurant owner, Anilmal, and an Estonian back from holidaying in Australia, Little K, formed a club in the centre of a horsetrack. "Money and women didn't help his cricket," said Jason of Anilmal. "He used to appeal before he let the ball go."

Estonia had two grounds now – the newer one in front of a Bank of Estonia manor, with three trees in the middle.

"One's at mid-wicket, one's at square leg, and the other's at cover," said Jason. "They're the best fielders we've got. It'll be a shame to lose them. Forty-eight per cent of Estonia is covered in forest, yet it took us six months going through the Ministry of the Environment to get permission to clear them. The minister said we have to move them. 'But they'll die,' I told her. 'I know,' she said."

"Who makes up the team?"

"Initially, it was the odd expat. Now we've got a squad of 18: six Estonians, plus players from Finland, Sweden, Zimbabwe, Australia, South Africa, Britain and one Dutchman – although he's disappeared . . . "

"How did you become captain?"

"I came here as part of my tour in 1999. The bank offered me a job after the game. I only had £200, so I decided to stay. As for becoming captain, I, umm, sort of appointed myself. But I did put four grand into Estonian cricket last year."

We stopped beside a faux-wooden cart and bought hot cinnamon nuts from a man dressed in a sack.

"What's it like being the worst international team in the world?" I asked.

"We love it," said Jason. "It's a great marketing tool. When we've won, it's been embarrassing. We just want to give touring sides a good run, let them win, and hope they enjoy it enough to come back. Otherwise we'll have no one to play."

"Have you ever won?"

Jason chuckled.

Estonia's greatest (and only) victory came on tour to Finland. Invited by another Indian restaurateur and his team of waiters, Estonia discovered the silver-service men to be serious cricketers.

"They smashed 80 in 6 overs," said Jason. "'What on earth are we doing here?' we thought."

Astonishingly, Estonia won with two balls to spare, and the waiters went berserk. "Why was he bowling then? Why was he fielding there?" they shouted. Their captain, feeling outnumbered, called his boys, who arrived with clubs and beat his team, it was alleged. After a speech about the spirit of cricket, Jason and the Estonians made a swift exit. Next day, Finnish immigration was tipped off, and two illegal immigrant player-employees were deported – all for questioning their captain's bowling selection.

"Imagine if they'd run him out," I said.

"I tell you, India versus Pakistan in Finland is World War Three."

After dodging some costumed monks, I asked Jason if any Estonian had scored 100.

The highest knock to date was 99, he said. "It was against Sir Tim Rice and the Heartaches. The bastard caught me on the boundary, one-handed, over his shoulder. He'd dropped me three times that afternoon."

On top of Toompea Hill, Jason and I admired the onion domes of the Alexander Nevsky Cathedral, named after a man who, appropriately, had led a battle on ice against the Germans nearly eight centuries before. Of greater interest to me, though, was the solitary, high-tech, Swedish-built toilet. Local newspapers had reported it cost two million Estonian kroons (almost

£90,000) to build. When I put my coins in the slot, the door wouldn't open.

"Who else do you play against?" I asked, trotting back to Jason without relief.

"Latvia . . . the odd touring team from England. This summer the Netherlands are coming."

"They're 14th in the world! They've played in two World Cups!"

"I know! They must've confused us with someone really good, like Australia. But I have a plan. The Dutch are used to drinking out of short glasses with lots of head. We'll give them full half-litres and take them out drinking three nights on the trot till seven. We'll get them completely sozzled, then play will start promptly at 11. For the toss, I'll use a small coin, which their captain won't see, and we'll still lose."

"Though a win over the Dutch would propel you up the rankings and save you from touring Sierra Leone," I pointed out.

We reached Jason's rented attic apartment beside the British ambassador's residence. It overlooked the old town's spires and the Gulf of Finland. "The last occupant fled because it was haunted," Jason said, ducking under a beam. He picked up his cricket bat and rehearsed some pull strokes.

Hearing his exploits, seeing the flags, photos, shirts and caps decorating his apartment, I was overwhelmed. I had no idea *Groundhog Day* could do that to a man. Having lost both his parents by the age of 19, forcing him to forgo university, Jason had gone on to make an impact on a great many people. He hadn't had it easy, and was dutifully modest about the whole thing.

"When I looked back at the videotapes of my tour," he said, "I thought, 'You're a wanker'. Now I'm just a semi-wanker who's not particularly good at anything."

"Will you ever move back to the UK?"

"No reason to. I couldn't do what I do here back in England. Estonia's one of the few countries where I can run our companies. In the office we've got 16 fully serviced computers on broadband for £40 a month. The workforce is highly educated, affordable and has first-class ideas. And, as you may have noticed," he rolled his eyes, "the girls! Fast food hasn't arrived in Estonia, unlike in Finland. That's why everyone's so fit."

"And what about the technology?"

"Estonia's one of the most advanced IT countries in Europe. The Finns use it as a test ground. Thanks to a system invented in Estonia, called Skype, I get free phone calls worldwide through my PC. When you park your car here, buy a pint in the pub or a can from a vending machine, you pay by text message. The phone is now your bank."

I was gobsmacked. Estonia was fooling the world with a mock, ye-olde-Sunday-carvery image in the streets. Hell, its oldest pub only opened in 1993. It was a technological super-state; the world's largest, most exclusive Ikea showroom, with no one in the car park.

Pinnacle of invention Estonia may be, but after leaving Jason to return to work, agreeing to meet in a pub later, I stopped at a cash machine. Getting 600 kroons seemed simple enough. I entered my PIN, the desired amount, selected 'Yes' then 'Receipt' when offered. Out popped my card, a receipt confirming my withdrawal – and no cash. After five minutes it still hadn't appeared, and I began to think it wasn't going to.

I glanced around the corner and saw that the bank was shut. Oh dear. I had three pounds left in my pocket. Granted, it might buy a two-course meal with wine, but it wouldn't last the remainder of my stay.

I hailed the next passer-by. He spoke immaculate English and had a mobile phone one-third the size of mine. "I have never heard of this happening!" he exclaimed. "I will call my wife. She will know what to do."

The wife's answer was not to panic. She said I should see the bank in the morning and they'd sort it out. The man suggested I try again. With a different card or a different bank, I figured – which produced better results.

Both of us tarted up in shirts and smart shoes for the evening, Jason led me from bar to bar, where armies of genetically screened waitresses hovered to meet every request. The decor was always lavish. White PVC cushions covered the walls. Silver stereos, lava lamps and personal beer taps on the tables provided further entertainment. Even the chrome urinals belonged in an art gallery.

From his perch on a leather bench, Jason pointed out business acquaintances in long, dark overcoats. They approached us to shake hands.

"He was probably carrying a gun," whispered Jason, when one departed.

"How'd you know?"

"I slapped him on the back in the toilet once."

The next heavy-set man to appear was a strip-club owner. He'd hired Jason to coach his girls. "They sat on the office floor. I gave them a seminar with a flip chart on what to expect with English clients."

The conversation came round to cricket again. I wanted to hear more One Man and His Bat tour disasters.

For the first game of his trip, Jason arrived at the British Embassy in Brussels. The captain he'd been coordinating with wasn't there, nor was his team. "He'd been reposted to Mauritania and hadn't mentioned it. That was embarrassing," he said, sipping his G&T.

Against Monaco, Jason broke his ankle taking a quick single. "My leg was purple to the knee. I drove to Switzerland after the game. At two in the morning I parked in a lay-by and slept. When I opened the door next morning there was a 2000-foot drop beside the car."

"What about the ankle break?"

"I only found out about it two and a half weeks later."

In which time he'd run many more singles.

Next, in Italy, Jason encountered a one-armed umpire. "His team fined him for every incorrect call. Each time it was a wide, he signalled no ball; and every six, he gave as byes."

After another round, courtesy of the house, Jason lamented the sad demise of cricket in South America. "I found a 78-year-old opening the batting in Argentina. He looked like he needed to be carried to the wicket in a wheelchair, but he was scoring 50s against 18-year-olds. I asked him why he was still playing. He answered, 'Women!' He said there was no one else to play any more. The woman is king in Argentina now. They don't want their men dressing up in white and running around a paddock all weekend."

As the next strong tonic took good effect, Jason did his best to fight off a slur.

"In 1998 I travelled to Tel Aviv. They said at the hotel, 'We have a lovely apartment for you!' just as 200 guests were checking out. We went to our room and turned on the TV. It showed a map of Israel and pictures of gas masks being handed out. Saddam was reported to be launching Scuds. 'No worries,' I said.

"My Norwegian girlfriend was taking photos on the balcony when Special Forces burst in. 'What are you doing?' they shouted.

'We're here to play cricket,' I explained. They said, 'Don't point your camera on the balcony! That's the American Embassy next door.'

"So I called the BBC for a phone interview. I was sitting in a deckchair on the balcony, wearing my cricket sweater, sipping a cocktail. I said, 'We're staying to the end and hoping to have a game of cricket.'"

Jason next recounted the story of his doomed tour to Ghana. He arrived at the airport expecting a grand welcome and visa from the Minister of Tourism.

"The trouble was, he'd gone off on a fishing weekend. 'No visa, no entry,' said customs.

"So they threw me in with a roomful of detainees. I could see the guards peeping through a hole, waiting for someone to become agitated and pay up. I thought, I'm gonna sit here and do my crossword. Eventually, they called me through. I was to be put under house arrest for two days at my hotel, and they wanted my passport. As I was getting into a taxi on the street, I remembered I'd left $1000 in my passport. I sprinted back. The chief was just eyeing my passport on the desk, thinking, what's in there? His hand was reaching for it when I grabbed it, whipped out the cash and ran out again. You should've seen his face!"

"A lucky escape," I said.

"It got worse. When I got to the hotel, I learned my house in England had been repossessed. The bloke staying there hadn't been paying his rent."

From these stories I could only conclude cricket is a very dangerous pastime.

Jason adopted a serious expression.

"There'll be times when you think, why do I bother?" he warned. "People out there will be jealous of what you're doing and will put you down for it. You'll need to prepare yourself."

"How do you mean?" I asked.

"Remember I said I was raising money for charities? A journalist told me last year, 'I just spoke to Save the Children. They say they've never heard of you.' I told him, 'It was five years ago. Don't you think their staff might've changed?' He didn't care. He'd got his quote."

"Any other examples?"

"I was doing phone-ins on David Gower's Radio 5 show. I got in a taxi outside Broadcasting House. I could hear myself on the radio. 'What d'you reckon about this guy?' asked the driver. ''E's got the life of Riley, and 'e's shit!' That was funny."

I sat back, wiping Le Coq beer from my chin and giving my notepad a rest. The pages were almost in flames. But a vital question remained unanswered, one that hung over my thoughts like a heavy spectre. Was this Jason the man the Canadian psychic had spoken of 10 months earlier? The man who was going to help me in my quest? He already had. My beers were on his tab. He was in media, like the psychic said. He'd written for magazines, worked on radio and TV, and was a part-time BBC correspondent.

"Would you say appearance is important to you?" I asked, hesitantly.

"Course. I'm totally vain. In fact, I'm debuting as a male model tomorrow. The cheeky bastards said they wanted someone in the 45–50 age range. I said, 'Why you picking me? I'm 39.'"

"Is your real name Jason?"

"No. My real name's Charles. But there was another kid at school called Charlie, so I changed it."

A lump formed in my throat. Jason leaned forward, wondering where this was going.

"Umm, this may sound a bit strange, but . . ."

I told Jason everything the Canadian psychic had said. He sat looking relaxed, probably thinking, How the fuck can I get out of here? But no alarm bells were evident in his response. In fact, he'd had a psychic experience himself.

"It was at the Nottingham Goose Fair when I was 18. The bloke said I'd be a married millionaire by the time I was 30. I went back when I was 31 for a refund."

Jason sat back and furrowed his brow. "I can't believe you have a ghost friend who knows a ghost friend of mine! Six degrees of separation and all. I wonder who it is?"

We both thought about it for a while, but couldn't come up with an answer.

The paranormal link didn't end there. Jason, it emerged, once saw the ghost of his dad on the cricket field.

"I was turning back to my bowling mark at my home ground in Leicester. I saw an old man in a blazer, hands on hips, standing away from the pavilion and spectators. There was something really odd about him. Then I realised it was my dad. He had the same stance, the same dress. No one else would wear that gear. I looked up again and he was gone. There was nowhere he could've walked unseen."

I was tucking myself into bed at the hotel when the door swung open. A man in a gamekeeper's cap, a red scarf, spectacles and a wax jacket filled the frame. I leapt onto the floor.

"Ah, Mr Bell," announced the figure, examining me in my boxer shorts.

"Julian?"

"The very one."

Julian was a fellow Slavophile and co-architect of the upcoming ice tournament. After our brief chats on the phone back in the UK, I hadn't imagined we'd meet like this. But as we were going to be sleeping together for the next four nights, it was best we get cosy right away.

"Time for a quick drink?" he enquired.

I re-dressed and we staggered back out into the snow.

Julian ran Baltic Adventures, a London-based travel company that specialised in unusual activities in the Baltics. He had tapped into the top end of the stag market, organising fighter-jet flying weekends, axe throwing, secret agent shooting and rugby in the snow in Latvia.

We made our way, hunched over, nostril hairs turning to icicles, towards the old town. We passed Jason's London taxi, in which he'd chauffeured Terry Wogan. It sat on a plinth outside a hotel.

Julian and I made a circumference of the city walls, seeking an opening. Round, red-tiled towers, including 'Fat Margaret's', stood out majestically, and Julian drew my attention to a fourteenth-century prison for prostitutes.

We walked through the city's crumbly medieval gate and stepped into a smoky karaoke club. Atop the bar shone taps of Beamish Red, Foster's, Newcastle Brown Ale, Guinness and Tennant's. Having expelled the Russians, Tallinn was suffering a Western invasion.

"The last thing I want is to see this place trashed by thugs," said Julian. "We've got to be quite careful with our clients."

"Just like the Saku Hotel," I put in, which confused him.

"Most pubs here are run by Scots," he continued. "When Scotland came to play football here in '96, Estonia didn't turn up, because the floodlights weren't working. Scotland kicked off without the opposition and still couldn't score. Half the Tartan Army stayed behind."

"Whit ya ofter, pal?" asked the tattooed barman in a string vest.

"Are you fae Scotland?" I said.

"Och. I've been asked that every night for the last nine years!" he spat.

Julian ordered four vodka shots in Russian.

"Where d'you learn that?" I asked.

"I was at university in Ukraine, in Dnipropetrovsk."

"What was it like?"

"Communism had collapsed, but if there was a queue you joined it, whether it was for your monthly bar of soap or toilet paper. There was a missile factory in the city, which now produces frying pans and trolleybuses. And there were big rumours of a secret underground base with a hundred-thousand-strong workforce."

"Any cricket?"

"Yeah. I remember Indian exchange students playing outside their halls."

"It must have been strange."

"Yeah, people made conversation about the price of bread, like we talk about the weather. And everyone used warm water to rinse their mouths after brushing instead of cold."

"That is strange."

"Salt and pepper shakers were the opposite way around too. The salt shaker had lots of holes, while the pepper shaker had one."

We got chatting about Saturday's ice tournament. There were six teams: Estonia's national team, divided into two, and four UK squads – a mixture of Cambridge students, stag weekenders, London civil servants and strangers. Estonia's arch-rivals, Latvia, 41st in the world rankings (one behind Mozambique), turned down the opportunity to play. They were keen until they heard the tournament was to be played on ice. For the Latvians and their purist ideals, that was just not cricket.

"We were due to play on the Baltic," said Julian, "but, as you can see, it's the warmest winter for 50 years and the sea hasn't frozen. We would've played on the Olympic Marina, where you could bowl from the Olympic Flame or Nunnery Ends. We're on Plan B. The matches'll now be held on an ice rink inside a former Soviet missile factory."

We each drained another vodka.

"What are the rules?"

"It's six-a-side, six overs each innings. Play is always ongoing. We want to encourage people to run. The wicket has been marked, and we've had hockey players scuff the field to give a better grip. There are bicycle helmets for anybody who wants one."

"Will the bowling be that quick?"

"Oh, there is one special rule," Julian added, his face betraying a sinister grin. "As stated in this month's *Wisden Cricketer*, which you may or may not have seen, we've made a rule that Scotsmen *must* play in kilts."

"Lucky I've brought mine along."

At three o'clock, screaming erupted at one end of the bar. A teenage American, part of a touring throng, shouted, "Hey, what the fuck, man? This dude just tried to take my fucking wallet!" He thrust a finger at a stone-faced Russian on a bar stool. "You're an asshole! Hey, everyone! He tried to take my fucking wallet!"

On the opposite side of the room, the karaoke host made an announcement. Julian nudged me. "You're up, Angus! I put your name in the hat."

Applause rippled around the room. I could hear the American still cursing the Russian.

"I can't sing!" I said, panicking.

"The announcer's calling you," said Julian. "You get to sing in *Estonian*. It'll make a good story for your book."

"Songs in the Finno-Ugric-Korean group aren't my forte . . . I'm like an untuned piano missing two-thirds of its keys."

The audience became restless. The announcer pleaded I step forward. Everyone began a countdown, in Estonian. I lowered my head and glanced over to the Cold War confrontation at the other end of the room. The Russian had left his stool and was walking out of the door. I hoped the audience would mistake him for me. The barman rushed after him and half-nelsoned him on the street. Boos echoed all around. Julian left for the toilet, sniggering.

In an act of mercy, a goth girl stood up and took the microphone. She began singing 'A Whole New World' from Disney's *Aladdin*, in Estonian. During the chorus, the barman tumbled back inside the door, locked in arms with the Russian.

"He tried to take my fucking wallet! Get him!" shouted the American, stamping his foot. The brawl rolled across the floor, knocking glasses from tables. Ashamed at my cop-out, I turned to look at the TV.

Cricket was showing. Steve Harmison was running in to bowl in striped pyjamas. No one blinked an eyelid.

*

Over the next 48 hours, Tallinn's cricketing population soared as players flew in for Saturday's tournament. Julian had arranged a day of rally karting in the lead-up, allowing our team to bond and size up opponents.

We travelled by minibus while a foot of snow fell. I felt a tinge of concern when I saw there was no way of distinguishing the road from the front gardens. But then I relaxed, imagining a satellite-guided pilot up front.

Our team, Baltic Adventurers, was a mixed bag of Antipodean and British strangers, drawn by the coveted Baltic Ice Trophy. Our line-up included two London money-laundering investigators, a Sydney business analyst-cum-DJ, a South African Muslim working in the NHS and a New Zealand electrician. One of the money-laundering investigators, it turned out, I'd met before. We'd stayed in the same hotel-from-hell in Sydney, five years earlier. It was a part of our lives we'd never forget.

"You were in the heroin addicts' dorm," I said.

"That's right," said Richard. "I ran away after three days, because of the cockroaches. How long were you there?"

"Four months, until eviction. I wrote a manuscript about it."

There was more coincidence. Our Kiwi electrician's wife, Soggy, mentioned she'd started working at a London employment agency.

"Is it Hudson?" I asked.

"I'm not gonna say."

"Do you know Marc?" I asked.

"How the hell do you know that? He works beside me." She looked shaken.

"When I lost the timesheets for my Glasgow call centre," I said, "I phoned a guy in London called Marc. He worked for an employment agency and he sounded like he was from New Zealand."

"God, that's freaky."

I dared not tell Soggy, nor my other teammates, that I had an infant ghost pointing out these links.

The minibus stopped and we entered a hut beside a birch forest. A man with silver teeth gave us blue boiler suits, lime-green helmets and plastic goggles. We went over the afternoon's rules in Estonian, then in English, then in Estonian and English again. The key point was not to race off-track and crash into rocks or people. This would incur heavy penalties unlikely to be covered by Estonian cash machines. Unfortunately, we couldn't see the track, only a four-foot bank of snow.

With us strapped inside the karts, testosterone levels soared with each rev of an engine. We ploughed blindly in figures of eight, drawing on Scalextric experience.

"I hope there are fewer crashes in your fighter-jet flying," I said to Julian.

At swap-over time, an impromptu game of piggy-in-the-middle started up in the paddock beside the hut. When the volleyball landed in my arms, the game dissolved, without warning, into full-contact rugby. Five opponents charged me. As the last piled on top, a knee clocked my right eye and a boot cracked my head. I tried to scream, but my lungs were squeezed empty and my mouth was full of snow. The ball was rucked clear and I struggled to my feet. The snow and the sky were now coloured with luminous yellow dots.

I wandered away from the action and tripped on a hidden tree root. It sent me rolling to the foot of a steep-sided ditch. When I realised what had happened, I attempted to stand, but the ice beneath the snow gave way. Cold, thick, stagnant ooze surged up the insides of my trouser legs. I clawed at the collapsing ditch sides for snow to apply to my rapidly swelling eye.

After the final race, I sat silently on the minibus on our return home. How could my afternoon go so horribly awry? I had the face of Quasimodo. There was this business with the bank too. It was getting near to closing time and I might now miss the last chance to find my 600 kroons. I picked chunks of muddy ice from my trainers and held them to my face. Then I realised I'd forgotten to take off my boiler suit back at the hut. We were now entering Tallinn.

It was a ridiculous scene in the bank shortly before closing. I stood there, with a freakish swelling on my face, smelling of something long dead, in a shit-smeared boiler suit. I held a cricket bat in one hand and applied a melting snowball to my face with the other.

"And the money never came out," I explained. "Is it possible I can be recredited, please?"

"Hmmm . . . ," replied the clerk, unimpressed. "It seems your bank has not provided enough information on the receipt. You need to ask them what happened. We cannot help."

I felt like Michael Douglas in *Falling Down*. I swivelled around and marched back to the hotel.

The next morning we arrived in two minibuses at the four-storey, crumbling Jeti Hall, former Soviet missile factory. It was a monstrosity Stalin and Glasgow city planners would have been proud of. That the Estonians had converted it into an international sporting venue deserved great credit.

"You'd have been shot for prowling round here 15 years ago," said Julian, as we stepped out of the minibuses.

Inside, concrete walkways and rusting girders criss-crossed above four ice rinks. It was -15°C (colder than outside), but the music of Jason Donovan soon had us dancing. Scandinavian and Baltic flags hung from the roof, illuminated by a string of lamps over the pitches.

"You wearing anything under that kilt?" asked the former drummer of D:Ream, himself in tartan trews.

"You bet," I said.

We gathered on the ice pitch. Even in spikes it was like walking on oiled glass. Estonia's captain Jason announced the draw and went through the rules.

"If you hit the roof – don't," he began. "It's not very stable."

We all squinted up to see a number of brown windows, and a great many more missing their glass.

"Wides will be generous," he continued, "depending on what team you're playing for."

Everyone chuckled.

The scoring rules were complicated, even before we'd started drinking. Jason drew our attention to the beer crates, Stoli vodka, French cognac and Crimean 'champagne' stacked behind the barrier.

"The toughest challenge will be keeping the tea urn from freezing," he said. "Now let's get on with it."

In thermals and ski jackets, our team, the Baltic Adventurers, took to the field against stag side Kelletino's Warriors. Waiting squads looked on from behind the barrier, swigging booze and preparing to warm their fingers in a sauna.

Oscar Wilde said he never played cricket because "it requires one to assume such indecent postures". He would know, of course, and when our captain handed me the plastic ball wrapped in duct tape, I did too. Trying to propel it, dressed in a kilt, scarf and gloves, was no easy task. I trotted three paces, threatened to do the splits and looped the ball down the wicket. With no cracks to exploit or fall through, it plopped down pathetically. The batsman, wearing one pad, poked at it with undue respect.

The next part of play, before a second ball was bowled, took place in slow motion. After 10 seconds, a fielder waddled over from cover to gather the stationary ball. He tripped and sent it to a far-off, empty corner. Half the Adventurers set out in low-speed pursuit, during which time our opponents scampered five runs. But just as the batsmen were gaining confidence, they collided with the stumps, our wicketkeeper and umpire Jason and his clipboard.

Baffled Russian curlers and Estonian ice-skaters shuffled in to spectate. Each graceless pirouette and *Home Alone* flip prompted Nordic "ooohs", which boomed across the hall, shaking the roof.

Every player hungered for victory. The inaugural Baltic Ice Trophy was as prized a possession as we were ever likely to lay hands on. We hurled ourselves across the ice like frozen beef carcasses, cutting off runs and, fortunately, not fingers. My knees cracked off the surface with every pick-up. Holding back our tears, we restricted the Warriors to 74 in their 6 overs. Our team talk at half-time was about how Estonia had chased more against the Finnish waiters.

The skiddy accuracy, leg theory and comedy of the Warriors strangled our reply from the start. They cut off our straight drives – shots which had proved so lucrative for them. With my sporran for a box, I chipped 40 of the most pelvis-damaging runs of my career. Slipping resulted in four run-outs in our innings, from which not even Australia (or Estonia) could have recovered. The burly stag men looked like they'd cruise through the group, into the final.

We huddled behind the barrier after our gubbing. It was the first time I'd seen frost, instead of sweat, on pads. The skipper made us swear we'd make Estonia's elite pay in our final clash, which began immediately.

Being short and bearded, with a little Courvoisier coursing through their veins, the Estonians were at a considerable advantage on ice. They wore whites so they could hide in the field. Despite their physical qualities, we had built a commanding 93-run platform by half-time. My own contribution with the bat this time was minimal. I lasted a single ball. I'd flown more than 1000 miles and failed to score against Estonia. It was the final ball of the innings, however, and I managed to keep my wicket intact.

The Estonians came out fighting in reply, as you'd expect an international side to do. They spanked my grenades and hot-footed singles like a team who'd been practising. Their innings progressed at an alarming rate, until pea-rollers forced them to fall on the self-destruct button. Baltic Adventurers, with no training other than a few shared pints and some rally karting, bowled out Estonia for 70, proving that we could compete on an international level.

Our tournament over, it was time to thaw in the sauna. Our chaperone led us down a dark, half-kilometre-long, concrete corridor. To the team's disappointment, the chaperone hadn't been hired to strip off and join in.

There was no such playtime for me. If the psychic's prediction was to come true, I had a media show to organise. I'd bought a MiniDisc recorder and a microphone to piece together a radio pitch. I fiddled with leads and warmed my batteries in my underpants in preparation for interviews.

Then I had to repeat the exercise with Julian's camcorder for a TV pitch. After that, I would have to take photos and notes for magazines. I had no training and no idea, but I was fucked if I was going back to a call centre for the rest of my days.

Assisted by my South African Muslim teammate Ibraheem, I shot 20 minutes of shaky footage. As Group Two of the tournament fought it out, we went to film the building's exterior. During one of these takes, three drunken Russians surrounded me. One pulled out an open bottle of beer from his cheap leather jacket and handed it to me, while the other two put their arms over my shoulders. They tried to coax me towards a waiting van across the car park. My spikes dug into the snow.

"Umm, what are they doing?" asked Ibraheem, filming the abduction from 10 yards away. The Russians yelled at him to turn off the camera.

There's a story in Tallinn about a group of Russians who took a van tour to Germany. They consumed so much vodka en route that one member died. A debate was held about what to do. It was decided, as they'd paid for their holiday, they should continue. At the borders, they pretended the corpse was a drunk, nodding his head and presenting his passport for him. At the end of the week, they returned with the corpse in the van. Seeing these three Russians and their van, I could believe that story and momentarily pictured myself as the corpse. I freed myself from their grip and scampered inside the hall.

Group Two of the tournament was more closely contested, with each of the three teams recording a win – even Estonia's second entry, which surprised them most of all. Estonia's chairman, the dangerous Kristjan Kogerman, took more wickets in his twirly-armed two overs than in the previous five years – an achievement that earned him a bottle of Crimean 'champagne'. Alas, it wasn't enough to see a home side make the final. A superior run tally handed Cambridge's students a place against stag side and Group One winners Kelletino's Warriors.

Captain Jason played DJ in the announcer's box while the finalists took a warm-up lap around the ice. It was a nervous showdown. The Cambridge bowlers charged in from the barrier, hoping to blast out their opponents with pace and bounce. Their tactic backfired, as more than once the ball flew directly from the bowler's hand into the crowd. The stag men piled on 103.

The loudest cheer of the day came in the second innings, when our New Zealand electrician, eager for a role in the final, jogged naked across the pitch. Play resumed after two minutes' delay, and the Cambridge students subsequently crumbled to 86 all out.

Without quite knowing how, Kelletino's Warriors became the first Baltic Ice Champions. "They'd have thrashed us outdoors," admitted their captain. "I guess the ice is a leveller. And that streaker in the middle must have rattled them."

Extraordinary scenes followed. More than one team posed for a winning photo, while some of Estonia's cricketers were still unaware they'd won a game. No one doubted the success of the inaugural sixes. It prompted the announcement of a second tournament in March, to which Sweden and 50th-placed Finland would be invited. Sure beats orienteering. There were also giddy talks of an Ice World Cup.

"Send over the Scottish team to play on this," said the Estonians, "and we'll make them mincemeat, or haggis."

By that evening, each of my legs had three kneecaps. I was thankful the temperature in the former Soviet missile factory had prevented greater swelling.

We were gathered for a pre-feast drink in our hotel lobby. A deep Soviet voice called out, "Angus! Father of all nations."

I turned to see a spectacled lady in a red cardigan, looking like she'd been raised in a pine forest. I stepped closer and she grabbed my shoulders. Her eyes widened almost to a point of no return.

"I am a witch from Saaremaa," she said, "the largest island of Estonia. I have been taught the mysteries of the gypsies. Welcome to my nightmare . . . Sit." She forced me down. "I will read your palm."

"Wait one second," I said, rising. "I'll just get something from my room."

"Lookin' for a condom, mate?" cracked my Aussie teammate from the bar. "You've pulled."

Back in the lobby with a beer, I sat beside my first Estonian witch friend. She took my right palm and stroked it. Her mitts were sweaty and her fingernails filthy. I wondered if she could match the accuracy of the Canadian psychic.

"Your hands are shaking," I said. "What's wrong?"

"My nerves," she replied hoarsely. "My money was stolen."

"Tonight?"

"No. Many times. Every Russian in town knows my PIN code. I know who it was. An evil, evil Russian . . . Now, let me see . . ." She traced a line with her bony digit. "You have a worker's hands, but . . . too soft, too soft to touch a woman's body."

How could hands be too soft for a woman's body? And how could a worker's hands be soft?

"That's just my opinion," she said. "I am an old lady."

She was 32.

"My heart is like a rrred, rrred rrose," she continued. "Yeats. I know it off by heart . . ." She looked at my palm. "You're more with your feet on the ground. You don't want to fly, like me. It's not for us. We are fairies. We *really* are."

I nodded, though I believed fairies did fly.

"Where did you learn palmistry?"

"From the gypsies in Lithuania. In 1999, after the sun went down, at the end of the world . . . Nostradamus. You know? Nostradamus . . . So, we are in the future already. Heaven has come on earth."

She wafted her arms above her head, then flexed each of my fingers back. "Wow! Wow! Wow!" she cried at each turn. "You're like a s-nake. Mine are rri-g-id, rri-g-id, rri-g-id. You play piano, yes?"

"How d'you know?" I said, feigning amazement.

"It's just a game for me!" She cackled. "It's very irrational. Because my aunt's son used to be a piano player . . . and *he* told me."

I was getting odd glances from the cricketers. "Do you live in Tallinn?" I asked.

"Yes. In the suburbs."

I didn't want to be rude, but I wondered what she was doing in a hotel, stroking a foreign man's hand.

"My money was stolen, for the first time . . . I *know* I'm free now. I can fly . . ."

Oh fuck.

"So, good hands, good hands," she said. "But do more physical work . . . Prayer and Benedictus."

"I'm an atheist."

"That doesn't matter. It's good for anybody. Also physical work, or 'sport', as you say in England."

"Cricket?"

She laughed. "Oh, the English!"

"Estonia has a cricket team."

"I know, but it's not interesting to me . . . Sportsmen are very good people. They don't think of anything . . . perverted."

I nodded. "So you've heard of cricket?"

"Of course. I have read *Alice in Wonderland*."

How appropriate.

"That's croquet," I corrected.

"There is a difference?"

"Cricket is more like baseball."

"I know baseball! *Catcher in the Rye*. Simply, simply holy."

She examined more creases in my palm. "This is love. Wow! Real love. Just dream, dream. Dream and she'll come . . . But don't waste yourself!" she chastened.

"What does my palm say about the future?"

"How do *I* know?" she shrugged. "Avoid sex or . . . use a condom. It's the highest rate of AIDS here. More than Russia."

"I'm a good boy."

"I know, but tell anybody you see."

There was a call from my teammates. We were due to leave

for our post-match feast. I would need time to wash off the dirt and sweat.

"Thanks for your guidance," I said, standing up.

"Where are you going?" She looked upset.

"Dinner."

She towered above me and closed her eyes. "Govinda jia, jia, govinda jia, jia. Govinda jia," she sang, swivelling her hips and waving her hands above her head. Everyone looked on. When she had finished, she clasped her hands round my neck and pulled me in. I feared she was going for the snog.

"Angus," she whispered, her lips moistening my ear. The smell of her BO was nauseating. "When you are trouble, always, always pray, pray, pray. Go down to the tree by the sea and sing. Sing on. Dream. Do your magic things, and you will be free. Welcome to Estonia."

Remarkable, I thought. Even the witches in this country are friendly.

*

Tallinn Airport was filled with a cloud of the previous night's and that morning's booze. I knew the smell would become more concentrated in the plane's air-conditioning. Troops of stag weekenders, in matching straw hats, were arriving straight from the strip clubs. It was possible for them to head immediately for the waiting lounge, as Tallinn Airport had automatic check-in machines.

It was easy to set the cricketers apart from other groups. Although some had achieved their goal of wild hotel sex after last night's medieval feast, in public we were still gentlemen on tour. Kelletino's Warriors proudly displayed their prize – a silver trophy containing the incinerated bails, inside an ice-filled wine cooler.

I was one of the last to board the plane. A skinhead in a pink girl's vest and Calvin Klein underpants lay spreadeagled across three of the few remaining seats. He waggled his tongue like in *The Exorcist*. "Wanna sit next to 'im?" asked his Essex mate, coarsely, with a grin.

I could see 20 in their group – all ugly bastards with crew cuts, prematurely balding. They wore matching polo shirts and necklaces. They were the sort of people who believe wearing Lynx deodorant makes you desirable. The only variation among them was a fatter head.

"I think the gentleman behind me's interested," I mumbled, looking for a seat beyond.

I sat at the rear of the group, beside a scar-faced ex-con who looked like he'd wake and vomit on me. The thug in the pink vest stood up and slipped on his polo shirt. 'Stag', read the back. One of his cohorts leaned into the aisle. 'Dodger', read his shirt. Though I couldn't see my neighbour's, I imagined it read, 'Scum'.

During take-off, Scum woke and, determined to lose his voice entirely, shouted, "Come on, son! Come on!" while the plane rocketed along the runway.

"Go on, son!" the rest of the lads yelled in crescendo.

"Get that fat bastard down the front up 'ere so we can fly!" screamed Scum. "Get up 'ere! You know who you are! You know who you are! Come on, son!"

As soon as the seat-belt light was off, Dodger pushed his assistance button.

"Yes, sir?" asked the stewardess.

"Sandwich. Cheese. Two," he demanded.

"Water," added Scum, before closing his eyes.

Thankfully, they'd slipped into comas before the sandwiches arrived. Two blissful hours passed, all the other passengers believing they'd got off lightly. I reflected on the silliness of beating an international cricket team, and thought forward to more success in the summer. I'd have to start sketching out my season.

But then Stag regained consciousness and thought he'd rouse the others. He whipped his cock out and slapped it on Dodger's forehead six times. When that failed to wake him, Stag tried a headlock, which resulted in a swift blow to the balls.

Next was Dodger's neighbour, one of the fatter ones. Stag bashed him with the safety card for 15 minutes, screeching like a banshee after every swat.

Stag approached Scum next. He licked a cigarette paper, leaned over me, his fruity breath making my stomach churn, and poked it in Scum's ear. Scum remained with his head on the fold-down table, and flicked a hand blindly after each tickle.

"Oi, fuck off!" he hissed, sitting up. He summoned the stewardess again.

"Get me tissues."

"They're in the toilet, sir."

Scum said, "Cheeky bitch. Who she fink she is?"

There was some good news about their 48-hour piss-up. It was clear the only sex they would've got was the kind you paid for, but, according to Stag, they were so paralytic in the brothel all weekend they couldn't even manage that.

When disembarkation began at Stansted Airport, a wonderful opportunity presented itself. Stag was perched at the top of the slippery steps; no one was below. I stood directly behind. One little shove, I thought, and I could do his bride-to-be and any other medieval city he threatened a great service.

3
THE BATSMAN WHO WOULD BE KING

The Škoda

Back in Scotland I got a job in Glasgow's most notorious methadone clinic. On the first day the doctor said I needed a hepatitis injection in case a patient bit me. I ran the switchboard, sorted the mail for six practices and guarded the key to the incontinence cupboard. I sold onions, broccoli, grapes and powdered baby milk from a trolley beside the phone. Yes, onions – part of the NHS healthy-eating campaign. I suggested they reopen the internal market and make fruit salad and punch from the unsold produce. The idea even proved popular at Friday's alcoholics' clinic, but not among the administrators. Hence, the

NHS fruit-and-veg box continued to run at a loss, not helped by rampant thievery.

By day, I dealt with shell-suited man-beaters and pregnant 14-year-olds that mixed their baby milk with custard. By night, I planned the forthcoming cricket season. I stayed up all hours in the flat, firing off emails to Belarus, Serbia, Slovenia and Ukraine, pleading they let me come and play. Often emails were unreturned. I wondered if the recipients didn't understand them, or feared they'd given up the game entirely. Poland was a model citizen. I'd have invited them to be the best man at my wedding. They always replied to my emails within 10 minutes, positively. Shortly, my first summer game was inked onto the calendar: Poland versus 'Pakistan from Warsaw or Berlin', May 24.

One of the peculiarities I discovered in my midnight researches was that Eastern Europe had missed several tricks in developing its cricket. In pre-World War One Riga (then part of the Russian Empire) the authorities got word of a local expat cricket club. Believing cricket might be dangerous, the authorities sent a policeman to investigate. Not grasping the concept, the policeman stood in the centre of the field and was struck on the head by the ball. He reported back to his superiors that cricket was a lethal sport and it was banned as a result.

The second setback was in 1920, when former England cricket captain CB Fry narrowly missed out on becoming king of Albania.

There could be no finer role model for Slavs and Turks than CB. As a student, Fry broke the long-jump world record. England's cricket team never lost under his captaincy, and his party trick was to leap backwards onto a mantelpiece. He was an entrepreneurial prodigy, who endorsed chocolate bars and barley water, and in his leisure time translated hymns into Greek. In 1901, he represented England at football against Ireland, and the following year played full back for Southampton in the FA Cup Final.

Fry's chance at Albania's throne came while he was working at the League of Nations in Geneva as a substitute delegate for India. The previous Albanian king, Wilhelm of Wied, had gone on holiday to Germany in 1914 and never returned. The Albanians appointed a Christian bishop (a spitting image of Fry's former teammate WG Grace) to seek a replacement – specifically, "an English country gentleman with £10,000 income a year". They went to find him in Switzerland.

Fry wrote a speech that drove Mussolini from Corfu. So impressed was the Albanian bishop by this that he approached Fry's boss and former England batting partner, Ranjitsinhji, to arrange an interview. (Ranjitsinhji himself was a famous maharaja, once accused of setting fire to dogs in the night.)

In his autobiography *Life Worth Living*, CB recounts how he hired "the largest salon in the Hôtel de la Paix" for the reception. (By 'salon' he meant a hotel suite, not a hairdresser's.) Ranjitsinhji even lent CB his servants in full Nawanagar dress. It was a boozy interview, in which the bishop repeatedly fingered his beard and downed tumblers of whisky.

Like his three attempts at running for Parliament, CB didn't win the seat. Maybe it was because he didn't have the money; perhaps it was because he was no-balled nine times in a row for throwing in a county match, and the Albanians were seeking a better bowling coach. Ranjitsinhji consoled CB by reminding him he'd been saved from a life in a lonely castle and spared a bullet in the ribs. Who knows where Albania would be in the world rankings had CB Fry sat on their throne?

Slowly, welcome replies from across the bloc arrived in my inbox, and a mouth-watering itinerary began to shape up; one,

I was sure, that would hand me my first 100. It would take me 8000 miles to the Bosphorus and back, through Slovak villages, over the Slovenian Alps and across the Polish plains. It would also cover some of the same ground as my previous travels.

Three years earlier I'd driven through Central Europe to Bosnia with my younger brother. It was a trip that saw us escape from a Polish brothel in the night (innocently, of course) and survive a jaunt through a minefield.

A year later I travelled solo by overnight train and donkey across the countries bordering the Black Sea and Russia. I suffered a mugging on a Bulgarian beach and was forced to get a job in Transylvania. They were stories destined for a travel book, but there'd never been a linking thread until now.

With the tour fixtures looking set, I feverishly penned them down on the milkman's calendar.

> *May 24 – Lubuskie, Poland*
> *June 4 – Prague, Czech Republic*
> *June 7 – Hajske, Slovakia*
> *June 18 – Mežica, Slovenia*
> *June 19 – Velden, Austria*
> *June 25 – Zagreb, Croatia*
> *July 2 – Vis, Croatia*
> *July 9 – Zrenjanin, Serbia*
> *July 7 – Sofia, Bulgaria*
> *July 13 – Istanbul, Turkey*
> *July 19 – Bucharest, Romania*
> *July 30 – Kyiv, Ukraine*
> *July 31 – Gomel, Belarus*
> *August 2 – Vilnius, Lithuania*

Such a venture this time, I decided, perusing the map, would require a vehicle. There could be no finer choice than my Škoda

Felicia hatchback, now in its tenth year. It had a chip in its windscreen and a key scratch along its flank. It was a hardy beast that had survived Balkan car-jackings and explosives. It could deliver large volumes of donated cricket equipment to where it was most needed. On the hard shoulders it could double up as a sandwich bar or bed. And if there was anywhere I wanted to break down, it was the Czech Republic. The Škoda was ideal; though I confess, in the pit of my stomach, I feared this might be elephants'-graveyard time for it.

Commuting to my methadone clinic in the Škoda was invaluable practice for Eastern Europe. There were steel plates over the houses, potholes in the road and broken glass sprinkled across every car park. The parallels between Glasgow and Sarajevo were uncanny.

The only snag in my otherwise flawless plan was that I couldn't afford the proposed trip. At six pounds an hour, my receptionist-and-greengrocer post was the highest paid job I'd ever had (except for my day as a lollipop man), but it wouldn't cover the rent, let alone a two-month high-risk road trip. My overdraft was spiralling out of control. I would have to cut out lunch again, and buy fruit and veg at the clinic. This made me queasy. I saw patients pick their 'red, itchy scawbs', then finger the fruit until it was beyond selling. It was enough to put me off my baby milk.

A TV documentary deal was out of the question now. There was more chance of Estonia winning the World Cup. I continued to spend my weekends at BBC Scotland, shaping the ice material for radio. Unfortunately, when the friendly producer there pitched the idea of a cricket travelogue in London, the commissioning editor said, "I don't like cricket." And the BBC wonders why it lost sport to its rivals.

The initial dip into the freelance writing pool had proved rewardless too. Every UK broadsheet and magazine turned down my Estonian features. Within weeks the same people I'd contacted were booking trips to report on the next tournament. I was on the verge of giving up entirely when my luck swung. A glossy magazine stole my article. This was fabulous. Now I didn't even have to approach editors and they'd publish my work. What a turnaround!

I realised if I was to fund this trip and hand out equipment then I needed sponsorship. After two days in the library I sent a carefully crafted letter of appeal to 100 cricket fans listed in *Who's Who*, including Sir John Major, Sir Clive Woodward and Heather 'The Weather'. The ploy pulled in £47 after deducting postage costs, a dog-eared photo of Mark Nicholas and a signed hanky from Channel 4. I didn't know whether to stick the picture on my mirror and blow my nose with the hanky, or flog them both on eBay. Was this what the psychic had meant when he said pretty soon I was going to be paid to travel?

Whether I could afford the journey or not, I was going ahead with it. I would sleep in hedges if I had to. The story had to come out.

Then the Scottish Arts Council stepped in. They would contribute £1,500 to the project. I thanked my psychical stars. Given the choice I would still sleep in hedges, though. It made for better material.

I was sitting at my computer desk in the flat; Candy was still at work. I had just lost my job at the methadone clinic. They gave me two hours' notice. There was no send-off gift, not even a goodbye; such is the life of the office temp.

There was dispiriting news in my inbox from Poland, too. Their wicketkeeper-captain would be away on the weekend of our match, and they asked if I could reschedule. This minor hiccup was easily resolved. I fired off an email, and Poland would now switch to the final game of the tour, on August 6.

As I ate a banana and pondered the economics of the clinic fruit box, the words 'cricket' and 'communism' popped into my head. Was this another call from the ghost of great-uncle Ivor? I wondered. I was beginning to sound like a patient from the psychiatric clinic. Bananas were always a popular seller among them.

I decided my redundancy was for the best. It was an opportunity to throw myself into some serious research. I googled 'cricket and communism', and the search returned a site entitled 'Cricket versus Baseball as an Engine of Growth, by Howard J Wall'.

Mr Howard J Wall was from the Department of Economics at Birkbeck College, London. Here was his paper outlining some distressing fiscal findings.

In the late nineteenth century, it said, a classical economist called Marshall declared that the pursuit of sport produced a productive labour force, thus in turn fuelling an economy's growth. He proposed that sports that "involved the carrying, and sometimes the tossing, of a ball; and the frequent collision of opposing bodies" made the biggest impact on economic growth.

Then, in 1908, two economists, Russell and Whitehead, refined Marshall's theory. According to Wall, "they found the necessary, but not sufficient, conditions for a sport to be an engine of growth are (1) that it uses an ash implement to strike a round object; and (2) that at any time the majority of players spend their time standing idly in an expanse of grass, or sitting on a wooden bench doing nothing".

I don't know about Russell and Whitehead, but whenever I'm waiting to bat or standing in the field, I'm thinking about the game in hand. Not doing nothing.

The paper explained how rival schools of thought had developed, split by the Atlantic. There were those who believed cricket to be the most effective financial booster, and those who backed baseball. All debate ceased in 1952, when a Frenchman called Le Point rubbished the idea of sport's influence on an economy. He said, "There is a fine line between playing baseball and standing in a pasture dressed like an idiot". I couldn't agree more.

"So powerful was Le Point's attack," wrote Howard J Wall, that "later editions of Keynes [*The General Theory of Employment, Interest, Money and Cricket*] do not include the original twenty-fifth chapter on the role of cricket in ending the Great Depression".

Cricket ending the Great Depression! I'd have paid more attention in school if they'd included that chapter.

Wall, in his bid to resurrect old arguments, had drawn up a formula "using data from 95 non-communist, non-OPEC countries", including their "growth rate of real capita income between 1960 and 1990". Who were these 95 non-communist, non-OPEC countries playing cricket or baseball in that period? And would Estonia's modern-day squad of 18 really sway their economy?

The results were damning. Cricket-playing caused an economy's growth rate to tumble by 43 per cent. On the other hand, baseball-playing caused countries to experience growth rates "80 per cent *above* what they would have been if the countries did not play baseball, and 123 per cent above what they would have been if they instead played cricket!"

Wall's conclusion was iron-fisted. "For emerging countries without a history of cricket or baseball, baseball instruction and subsidies should be an immediate priority."

And up to now I'd been sending food parcels.

"With the help of international institutions like the World Bank and the IMF, baseball aid should flow from the baseball powers, the US and Japan. The difficult problem is devising a plan to eradicate the cricket-induced malaise of the cricket-playing countries. Clearly this is a task of herculean proportions, rivalled only by the economic reform of formerly communist countries. Like communism, years of cricket have polluted the very souls of these countries . . . "

Jesus! I didn't want to go now. The whole trip looked like it might spark financial ruin, and not just for myself. There was no way I could change it to a book about baseball. I didn't want to stand in a pasture dressed like an idiot all summer. I decided the only thing to do was to write to Mr Howard J Wall and see if there was an alternative solution. A quick Google search revealed he had become Assistant Vice-President and Regional Economics Advisor at the Federal Reserve Bank of St Louis.

To: Howard J Wall
From: Angus Bell
Subject: Cricket versus Baseball as an Engine of Growth

Dear Mr Howard J Wall,

I recently came across your paper Cricket versus Baseball as an Engine of Growth. Congratulations on your exhaustive research, insight and style. As a Scottish cricket–lover with an A-level in economics and politics, I'm fascinated by your findings, and I'd like to know more.

How is it, do you suggest, that cricket burdens an economy? Do you see the economic divide between cricketing and baseball countries worsening today? I noticed for your formula you looked at 95 non-communist, non-OPEC countries. Can I ask which of these countries played cricket and which played baseball? Was there ever a clash? If so, how did this affect the economy?

I'm intrigued, too, about the missing 25th chapter of Keynes's *The General Theory of Employment, Interest, Money and Cricket*. I would dearly love to get my hands on a copy, and I just can't find it in the library. Just what was the role of cricket in ending the Great Depression? Is anyone compiling a modern book on baseball's fiscal effects?

The statistics put me in a bit of a quandary. I'm taking a trip around 12 former Warsaw Pact and USSR countries, playing cricket. I'm aiming to encourage youngsters to take up the sport, and provide equipment that will allow them to do this. Do you think, as your paper suggests, I'll be doing more harm than good? Should I be coaching baseball in these countries instead?

Best wishes,
Angus Bell

To: Angus Bell
From: Howard J Wall
Subject: Re: Cricket versus Baseball as an Engine of Growth

Dear Angus,

Thanks for your interest. Before providing an answer, I have to ask a question of my own. You do realize that the paper was meant as a joke, right? And that most of the references, including the Keynes one, are fictitious? The empirical section was, however, authentic.

Regards,
Howard

Howard J Wall
Assistant Vice-President and Regional Economics Advisor
Federal Reserve Bank of St Louis

Well, thank Christ for that. The US economy was in safer hands than I thought. Now I could go ahead with my plans. All I needed was a car insurer.

For a month I combed the internet for a broker who would cover me in the event of my hitting a Belarusian donkey. Without a green card certificate, and short of a $100 bribe every time, I wouldn't be able to enter half the countries. But on each occasion I phoned a broker, they hadn't even heard of these countries.

"But people drive from Beijing to Paris!" I told my mum a fortnight before my scheduled departure. "People drive to Cape Town! They all have insurance. But every company's telling me Ukraine, Belarus, Serbia and Montenegro are absolute no-nos. It's only a Škoda!"

In a last-ditch effort I called my final broker. Within 15 minutes they were back on the phone. "We'll do everywhere except Newbain," said the lady.

"Where?"

"Newbain. Didn't you say Serbia and . . . Newbain?"

"It doesn't exist, but that's fine."

"The cost is £760."

"That's almost as much as the car!" I squealed. " . . . No problem. Please just send the green card to my parents' house as soon as possible, thanks. I'm leaving this Sunday."

"You'll have it by Wednesday."

On Thursday the green card still hadn't arrived. Candy and I vacated the flat in Glasgow, and I whisked her to the airport for her return to Montreal. Though I liked to think Candy was passionate about cricket after our year and a half together, she didn't share my enthusiasm for the trip.

"You know I don't like cricket," she said, "but I understand this is what you have to do. Just promise me you won't do anything silly, like pick up hitchhikers. People get killed . . . See you in Montreal in a few months."

I moved back in with my parents.

"Angus, have you cleaned your whites?" screamed my mum.

"They're fine," I said.

She dug them out from my bag. "No, they are *NOT*! No son of mine is going to Eastern Europe with dirty cricket whites! Put them in the machine *now*!" She stamped her foot.

"Yes, mum," I conceded quietly. My dad laughed in the background.

After completing my laundry, I phoned the car insurance broker again. "The green card's on its way first-class," they assured me.

On Friday the green card still hadn't arrived. "I need this!" I pleaded down the line. "Can you at least send a fax, please?"

The fax arrived as an utterly illegible black smudge. A Belarusian border guard wouldn't have seen fit to wipe his bum with it. "Give me strength!" I howled.

Finally, on the last postal day of the week, my documents arrived. Everything looked set for the road. My whites were clean, my bat was oiled; the car was serviced and loaded with kit. A last-minute email check caused no undue alarm; my 10-week itinerary looked foolproof.

Or so I thought.

4
IT WAS LIKE A STEPHEN KING NOVEL

Avoiding a bouncer in the Harz Mountains

I boarded the ferry at Newcastle docks and climbed up from the car deck to my cabin. My confidence dropped the moment I opened its door. It smelled like a dirty hamster's cage on the other side. Snoring on my bunk was a Hell's Angel in leather underpants. Below him was an AWOL Latvian marine. On the third bed, in his own words, was a "German orthopaedic shoemaker master". He was carrying a ferret.

"They just increased the ferret quotas between Britain and the Netherlands," he informed me.

I nodded. Why passengers would be taking ferrets to Amsterdam for the weekend, I didn't want to think about. I made a swift exit for the bar. There I hoped to scoop up a hitchhiker.

We hadn't left port and a force of 800 had gathered in the pub lounge, skulling jugs of Stella. I felt my way through a cloud of cheap European cigarette smoke and sat alone at the back. My fellow passengers comprised earringed, beery British darts players, hens in matching rabbits' ears and Dutch schoolkids in shell suits and bumbags. Their fake tans glowed strangely in the light. "Man-U-Man-U-Man-United!" everyone sang in unison.

The introduction of bingo settled the crowd. "Two little ducks, 22. Quack, quack," said the host Dutchman on his microphone.

I made a cross on my sheet. I hate bingo, I thought. What was I doing?

At the conclusion of the sixth round, I tore up my sheet and tossed it in an ashtray.

Soon after, the host began singing the first of five 'Happy Birthdays'. The crowd countered each time with "Hey-hey, baby! Ooh! Ah! I wanna know-o-o-o if you'll be my girl!" and waved their arms.

"Stay around, folks," said the host. "We've got the electric ballet coming up."

This signalled an invasion of the dance floor. Every passenger bopped as though they'd coordinated their dance actions on Newcastle docks. To my horror, I was dragged into the conga, and I snaked around the room before splitting the dance floor.

I'd regained my seat by the start of the electric ballet. It was a moving performance, beginning with Michael Jackson's 'Thriller'. The lead dancer leapt around the stage in a hairy rubber Halloween mask. When *Beauty and the Beast* followed, Jacko's werewolf costume was again used for the Beast. The spectacle ended with a Europop cancan, at which point I skulled the dregs of my watery Stella and decided I'd take my chances in my stinky cell.

In the morning I drove off the ferry ramp in IJmuiden, west of Amsterdam, and set out across a flat landscape. The Škoda was quickly unleashed on the German autobahn, reaching 85 miles per hour on the rare downhill stretches. Mostly I kept to the inside lane as BMWs rocketed past, shaking the Škoda. I sang along to pirated MiniDiscs and practised my Czech cover drives in my head.

It would take two days to cross Germany and reach Prague. To break up the monotony of the wind farms, I decided to stop for a night in the Harz Mountains. Google, instrumental as ever in this trip, had provided me with the address of a pension in the Harz National Park.

After eight hours of motoring, I slipped off the autobahn and wound through misty, wooded mountain villages. The houses looked as though they were made of gingerbread. I parked outside my peaceful pension and walked to the door. A thin man in a greasy shirt greeted me, cigarette in hand.

"You're the only person 'ere!" he said, knocking me back with a Lancastrian accent. "Ah was gonna lock up and go. You're lucky. Better coom inside now."

I sat in silence in the nicotine-stained lounge, my rucksacks leaning against the wall. My host handed me a cup of coffee, then stood a few yards off, looking into space, nervously puffing away. I recognised the signs of cabin fever. My coffee drained, I cleared my throat of tar and broke the ice. "So, does anything *unusual* ever happen here?"

The proprietor thought about it for a minute, then answered, "No. Noothing unusual ever happens here. In fact, noothing ever happens at all." I was saddened. I made a note to scrub the Harz Mountains from the book.

After the eighth cigarette, the Lancastrian said, "D'ya fancy going for a cheap Korean?"

We were at the pub after our Korean dinner, which comprised burnt tofu masked by the taste of mein host's cigarettes. Around us now in the antique pub were five others, each with a trucker's shirt and a mullet. No one said a word. I ordered a beer and the barman gave me two. Mein host sat quietly opposite.

Once he'd got a few Cokes under his belt, mein host began opening up about life in the village. It surprised me to learn that, out of a population of 300, 50 per cent were having multiple affairs. "They're always in-house," said mein host mysteriously. "No one ever marries an . . . " – he glanced from side to side – " . . . an 'outsider'."

I took a long draw from my glass and asked mein host what his part in all this was.

"Me proper girlfriend, she's in South-East Asia. At the moment, ah'm on me third girl from round 'ere . . . Ah swear, the first time ah didn't know this girl were married. Ah knew 'er husband, as well. 'E were in the guest-house regularly, like. But this girl ah'm seeing now, she's pissing me off . . . " He stubbed out his fag and reached for another.

"Oh?"

"She's messing around with a coople of oother blokes. That's why ah'm not there tonight."

And I had thought it was the exhilarating nature of my company.

"So this girl, what's she like?"

"Well . . . " He seemed stuck momentarily. "She's the ex-wife of the ex-owner of me guest-house . . . 'E, by the way, now lives next door with his *new* girlfriend. The both of them cause me a lot of trooble . . . "

"Like what?"

"The ex-owner, 'e stares through the window of room number five each day for two hours with 'is face pressed to the glass. 'E threw a brick through it a few weeks ago, and then 'e came round and poonched me."

"Shit!"

"'E's been caught on camera throwing eggs at the houses in the night, and supergluing people's doors shut . . . Ah 'ad to get an ex-French Legionnaire from the village to go threaten 'im . . . "

I nodded. A tingling realisation was creeping into my thoughts. There was something very, very wrong with this village, and I might have to flee tonight and sleep in the car. But I looked down and saw that I'd already drunk too much. My only option was to increase the dosage and hope I slept through any troubles. I sensed even darker secrets lay beneath the surface.

"Why is there a straw witch hanging in the corner?" I asked.

Mein host looked up. "Every year the village celebrates witch-burning," he said. "This year, for the first time, we didn't have a witch. Everyone were talking about it. Joost after the flames were lit, they all came round to me guest-house asking that me girlfriend coom out. They reckoned she were a witch, you see. She's a bit weird, ah suppose . . . A bit gothic, y'know?"

I was now extremely worried. How would they have treated my Estonian witch friend?

"And right up to the witch-burning this year," he continued, "we had a haunting in the guest-house."

The colour in my face drained as quickly as the froth in my glass.

"There were a lot of screaming coomin' from room five – the one the ex-owner stares into every day, if you remember."

"Which . . . which room am I in?"

"Ah can put you in four, if you like."

"I'd like that, please."

"A lot of guests in five 'ave told me they've 'ad this dream about an old woman coomin' in the night and lookin' under their bed. Ah 'ave this reoccurring dream about a blonde woman hanging . . ."

My fingernails dug into my palms.

Mein host continued. "Recently we 'ad taps left on every day. We 'eard footsteps and doors were opening by themselves. A few weeks ago ah came downstairs in the mornin' and the dryer had steamed up the window to the garden. There were a drawing on there."

He took my notepad and made a sketch. It showed a crying face, a bush and a tree with a hand coming out from beneath it. He drew a bird on a branch.

"It had a little worm coomin' out its mouth. Every day since then, ah've seen that little bird from the drawing in the garden in real life, with a little worm coomin' out its mouth."

"Who did the drawing?"

"Ah've no idea. No one were staying there. Ah clean the windows every week. Ah scrubbed the glass with alcohol that mornin', and when ah came down next day the drawing were back again."

I needed something stronger. I ordered a double Scotch. "D'you think it was someone playing a trick?"

"No!" yelled mein host. "The guest-house's ruining people's lives! A woman broke her ribs! A man were hospitalised for six weeks staying there!"

"D'you think it was the blonde woman hanging who made the drawing?"

"Maybe," said mein host pensively, lighting up again. "You know, ah've started digging under the tree . . . for a body."

Oh fuck. This was *The Tommy-Knockers* meets *The Shining*.

"Ah've gotta go deeper. Ah'll show you tomorrow, if you like."

I considered excusing myself and evacuating via the pub's toilet window, but just as I was about to get up, a head with a hand attached to its throat landed on our table. The locals in the bar, who up to this point had said nothing, were now engaged in a violent brawl. The barman, alert to the situation, tottered over to the door and locked it.

"Shit almighty!" I whispered.

A human tug-of-war whipped around the room; men with mullets on each end, girlfriends sandwiched between. I cowered in a corner with mein host, Scotch in hand, laughing.

"Probably another affair," said mein host coolly. I fiddled in my pockets for my camera, but as I pulled it out, mein host put his hand over it.

"No, no! They might kill us!"

The fight rolled around the room as though we were in a wrestling ring, and the barstools quickly became weapons.

After 10 minutes the screaming died, and we were allowed to return to our seats. The guilty participants shuffled around, apologising to everyone individually.

"Keine Probleme," I said, shaking their hands.

Then round two was unleashed.

At the conclusion of round three, the barman evicted one baseball-capped fighter. He continued to loiter on the doorstep, peering through the glass, baiting his partner. The partner fought to be let out. None of us were going anywhere.

I was still laughing when Starsky und Hutch arrived in leather jackets to note everyone's names in the Bad Boys' book. Mein host, after a brief statement, downed his Coke and suggested we return to the safety of his haunted guest-house.

Noothing unusual ever happens here. In fact noothing ever happens at all, I recalled as I crept to bed.

I slept that night with the door to room four double-locked and placed a pillow over my face. In the morning, mein host hadn't forgotten about the previous evening's offer.

"Fancy coomin' to the garden when yer finished yer breakfast?" he said. "Ah'll show you that hole ah've been digging."

I followed him outside.

As promised, a large hole had been dug under the tree, beside the bush. "I agree. You ought to go deeper," I said.

"Ah'll maybe get round to it this week." He lit a cigarette.

As I set off once again in my Škoda for Prague, I was confident he'd find his corpse.

5
FiELDERS WiTHOUT FiNGERS

The Czech container

You know you're in Central Europe when the first man you see is selling two-stripe tracksuits labelled 'Abidas' through car windows.

A capitalist take-off was in full display between the road and the forest in the Czech Republic. Stalls were offering garden gnomes and plastic mermaids by the thousand – just what you need when going on holiday to Prague. Every 20 yards I saw wigged hitchhikers, fumbling with fish-net tights and lipstick. In the towns, pole dancers glanced furtively from sauna-bar windows, causing many a rear-end bump.

I checked my mirror to overtake a lorry crash. Looking at me there was a transsexual with shoe polish plastered on her face. "Come over here," she beckoned with a finger, "and we'll go mess around in the bushes."

Motoring through the Czech Republic required considerable caution. When Estonia's captain Jason came here on his world tour, a policeman spotted his foreign plates and pulled him over. He wanted $200.

"No," said Jason, who was then thrown into jail in Prague.

Jason's words came to me now, as I spotted a sniping police car. "I was in there for two days," he'd said. "They issued me with an 'illegal parking ticket', even though I was driving through the countryside at the time."

After seven hours at the wheel I merged with Prague's evening rush hour. Diesel fumes poured through my air vents. I had no map, no local currency and little idea where I was going. Apart from an infant ghost, my sole guide was the Prague cricket captain's address, scribbled down in haste that morning from the internet.

I looped around the city's ring road twice, and when, after two hours, I could take no more, I exited and drove down tram-lines towards the centre. As though great-uncle Ivor himself was guiding me from the passenger seat, the unmistakable sight of a cricket field came into view. It was here, among all the detritus, that Prague's cricketers battled it out each weekend.

Captain Leo's flat was a few blocks away, up a hill in a wealthy suburb dotted with villas. I parked and waited till my clothes had dried out, then sounded the door buzzer. A tall 20-some-thing in a baseball cap appeared in the frame.

"Ah. You're lucky I was in," announced Leo. "I didn't know when you were coming. Welcome."

"Thanks. Is it safe to leave my car here?"

"Yes . . . though we did have ours stolen last week," he said rather too confidently. "They broke into the house and took our DVD player, laptop and CDs. Then they found our car keys. I saw the guy jumping out the window and heard him driving off."

I now had reservations about living here for a week.

"You look a bit worried," said Leo.

"Yeah. I had my car broken into here three years ago. They took my photos, my tent and my boxer shorts."

Leo grimaced.

"There's one thing I hate more than a thief, and that's a crap thief," I said.

"Better take your cricket gear inside. I'll give you a hand."

That evening, as we walked out to get some food, Leo talked about his job. He'd moved from Wiltshire to work for his dad's marketing company, introducing UK firms to the Czech Republic. Once, he changed jobs and worked for the Czech Mafia.

"They drove me around and around so I couldn't identify the place," he said, as we entered a pizzeria. "It was a call centre, with women in bikinis in the office. My job was to phone people who'd clicked on pop-up ads asking them to invest $10,000. I had to say, 'Do you *have* $10,000? Are you *sure* you have $10,000? Can you *guarantee* you can get $10,000 to us today?' If they said 'yes', the money was wired to a Latvian account and never seen again."

"People who click on pop-up ads and enter their personal details deserve to lose $10,000," I said. "Did you get any sales?"

"No. I was only there for one day. We had this Jewish guy and his kid working in the office. The dad used to snog the girls in bikinis in front of us. Anyway, a few months later I saw them on the FBI's Most Wanted."

Two pizzas the size of car wheels arrived, along with tall, frothy measures of Staropramen. I asked Leo about his cricketing experience.

"I played a game for Chile after university," he said. "And this season I landed the Prague CC captaincy. It's an exciting time. We just launched our national league."

"How many teams are there?"

"Four: Prague CC, the Indian Embassy, Prague Bohemians and Hradec Králové – that's a city east of here. Sometimes DHL provides a friendly fixture."

"Do you ever get touring teams?"

"In the past we got pissheads coming over from London. We'd arrange the matches six months in advance, then an hour before play they'd phone up and moan, 'Aw, shit. We feel sick. We've gotta cancel.' So now we're doing our own thing."

Leo confessed he knew little about the history of Czech cricket. "All I can say is we're like nineteenth-century missionaries out here. We poach a lot from softball. They come around when they realise there's a better alternative."

I nodded and smiled.

"You'll get more stories from the others at nets tomorrow."

Next morning, Leo left for work and I set out by tram for the city centre. Half the passengers were lugging guitars, cellos or harps. Prague was a city of wannabe musicians and writers. I had come to the right place, I decided. Then I stepped out and heard Robbie Williams blasting from every boy racer's car.

Starting in the Castle District, I poked through people's medieval doorways, sniped photos from under painted arches and zigzagged down the cobbled streets to the river. Few walls were untouched by Prague's graffiti artists. Even the boarded-up Mafia buildings had been targeted.

Across a park full of kilted bagpipers, I came to the John Lennon Wall. It was here, under communism, that Prague citizens stole out each night to scrawl their protests. Every day the authorities painted it white again. The Czechs say the Beatles saved their lives under communism, in much the same way that David Hasselhoff saved the East Germans.

Near the banks of the Vltava I spotted the legacy of the 2002 flood. The watermark reached above the first-floor windows. In the deluge even the Charles Bridge had been threatened. The Czech army tried to save it by dropping bombs from helicopters upriver to sink barges. They employed four tanks to hold a floating restaurant, whose owner was away on holiday. Cranes on the bridge fought to clear trees and a sea lion which had escaped from the zoo. Even a hippopotamus broke loose and had to be executed.

By midday, the weight of 10,000 tourists was threatening to topple the Charles Bridge. I wanted a flawless photo of its soot-smudged towers and statues. This looked unlikely amid the carnival on top. There were struggling and juggling artists, sketches of Harry Potter and friends, Nigerian sailors in Popeye suits and hand organists, who'd have fared better with monkeys on their shoulders. The only way I'd get my photo, said the tourist office, was by hiring the bridge, for $10,000, between four and eight in the morning.

Over the warbling organ pipes I heard an unmistakable, clipped English accent. I turned to see Michael York in a blazer and shades. Leo had said we were one short for Saturday. I thought about asking Basil Exposition if he fancied a game, but a Chinese horde cut me off, screaming, "Austin Powers!"

"How extraordinary," said Michael York.

Beyond the town square and its astronomical clock, I dodged a horse and carriage and slipped into an internet café. After a browse of the menu, I chose the cheapest item available – toast. The waitress looked at me as though I'd spat in her face.

"Are you going to order butter with that?" she asked scornfully.

I gulped and glanced at the menu again. Butter was indeed a separate dish. It cost three times as much.

"Please," I said.

The waitress stared at me for an awkward moment as I reached for my money.

"SIT DOWN!" she screamed.

Everyone in the café swivelled and gave me a glare. I turned pink and my heart fluttered. I shuffled to a lonely chair in the corner and, for a second, thought about running.

In the 20 minutes I waited for my toast I leafed through a copy of *The Prague Post*. With nearly 40,000 Americans living in the city, I wondered what they were all doing, apart from writing for this weekly paper or teaching English. Why weren't more friendly Americans running the Czech Republic's catering industry?

I browsed the classifieds section and saw freelance masseuse was a popular career alternative for Westerners inescapably drawn here. "Beautiful women significantly younger than you for serious relationships", read one advert.

I'm only 24, I thought.

"Linda, 22, pleasure time", read another.

Sad as it is to admit, it got me thinking about an afternoon's cricket, scoring my first 100.

The most serious downside of Prague's US invasion was that cricket had a battle on its hands. Leo and his teammates were struggling to compete against the booming softball and American football leagues, which got regular write-ups in the press.

My slabs of butter arrived on top of a wilted salad. The waitress dumped a slice of burnt toast on the table.

"Děkuji," I said.

The waitress hovered over me while I hurriedly buttered my toast with a teaspoon. Then she lifted the remainder of the butter and salad and whipped it away, probably for the next customer.

My meal finished, I left a handsome tip and moved over to one of the café's computer terminals. The moment I logged in and opened my inbox, a backpacker walked across.

"Are you gonna be *long*?" he asked rudely in a North American accent.

"There are 10 other computers," I said, pointing them out along the wall.

"Yeah, but the one you're on is free if you only use it for a few minutes."

I sighed.

"I'll be 10 minutes," I said.

"Good."

He sat down beside me and read over my shoulder.

There were no new messages in my inbox, so I logged off and took comfort in the fact I wouldn't have to pay. I stood up and the prat in the baseball cap jumped into my seat.

"That'll be 30 korunas for 15 minutes!" the waitress shouted to me.

Leo and I travelled by tram, metro and bus for over an hour to reach nets that evening. We stepped onto the street among rows of decaying grey tower blocks in the suburbs. "This is where all the Czechs live," said Leo a little sadly. "You wouldn't think that when you see the centre."

Clutching our kit bags, we threaded between blocks, over scraggy strips of grass. "Watch out for dog crap," warned Leo.

"I've never seen so much dog crap as in the Czech Republic. Especially on the cricket field."

We reached the British International School and approached four teenagers on the steps. "These guys have formed their own school cricket team," said Leo as we neared. "They organise it all themselves."

We shook the kids' hands. They were Macedonian, Russian and Czech. "We're playing the girls' school team next week," said one to Leo, "but we're still six players short. Any ideas?"

Leo said he'd have a think and we entered the school. Crappy artwork hung on the walls and the smell of cleaning fluid took me back 10 years. Leo and I stopped by the gym. There were hoops and bars, a horse block and a piano, and a cupboard full of cricket equipment.

"It reminds me of Cubs," I said. "I see you've broken a few windows. This is perfect."

"No, we're just here to pick up the kit," said Leo. "Nets are outside. We play here in winter. This is where we held our tsunami benefit match."

Leo and I strode outside to the AstroTurf pitch. Pheasants were getting frisky around its fenced perimeter. Soon Czech players began arriving in a mixture of whites and jeans. Each handshake was a memorable one, as it produced an electric shock from the AstroTurf.

"This is our national coach and captain of Prague Bohemians," said Leo. "Scott from Australia. He also repairs bats for the region."

"If you meet anyone in Eastern Europe with a broken bat," said Scott, half taking me aside, "send it my way. I'll give you a price list later."

The formation of Prague's National League seemed to have caused slight fractions among certain players. Leo's team, Prague

CC, had been depleted as players broke away to create the new Prague Bohemians. But Leo had his eye on the broader Czech game, and ran nets without bias. At his instructions three batsmen from separate clubs began padding up in a goalmouth.

While the cricketers set about top-edging sweeps into British classroom windows, I roamed the nets, searching out some of the Czech Republic's 15 home nationals. "Pěkná rána," they called after every classy shot, meaning "good blow". Their national squad included a half-Greek, half-Czech hospital porter and a pure-blood travel agent, hooked since seeing cricket on Dubai TV. They were all equally surprised to hear their team floated between 92nd Iran and 105th Estonia in the rankings.

One Czech showed particular promise. Magda, a left-arm seamer and opening batswoman, found herself snapped up by Somerset while studying at Bath University.

"I take cricket so seriously," she said between creaming my full tosses. "I cried for six hours after dropping a catch in Munich two weeks ago."

She should be an England wicketkeeper, I thought.

Fielding in Munich was tough, though. One boundary was on top of a six-foot grassy bank, and there was a sandpit and an athletics track to negotiate.

Training ended and seven of us set out for the pub to rehydrate over prize Czech beer. The café was typically old-style, said Leo. Its clientele looked thin and ill. The air was heavily blanketed with cigarette smoke, and the mustachioed waitress had a scowl that could curdle milk.

"If you come to the Czech Republic, you *have to* try this," insisted Leo, selecting from a greasy-fingered menu. "It's a national dish, and it's sooo good."

Our dinner of deep-fried, breadcrumbed cheese arrived, looking like a Findus Crispy Pancake. It went a long way to explaining why Czech men die nearly five years below the European average. That and their marvellous, frothy beer.

To combat the effects of this dietary disaster, the Czech cricketers had drawn up a constitution which forbade smoking and booze consumption on-field. The benefits, they claimed, had been reaped. In the previous year's tri-nations versus Poland and Slovakia, they recorded two wins out of two.

"That puts us top of the Twenty20 rankings ahead of Australia," announced national coach Scott. "We've come a long way since our first game against Poland in 2000. We scored 172 and won, yet *nobody* in the game made double figures."

"How?" I asked.

"I scored 131; the next top score was Magda with 9. None of the Poles made more than 7."

I turned to the three Sri Lankans at our table to ask about the conception of cricket in Prague. After a painful 10-year lay-off from the sport, they had sparked it all off by convincing three Czechs to join them in a game in 1996.

"We thrashed about between the Technical University and a metro station," said one, gleefully. "We used tennis balls on concrete."

Team totals back then peaked at a heady 15. "We did much better on the tram heading home, playing with an apple and a knocking-in mallet."

The players could not have known then how their efforts would develop, culminating in an unofficial 'Test' versus Slovenia within a decade.

"It was a timeless Test but the players had to return to work after two days," said Leo, making everyone laugh as we got up to leave.

*

Friday arrived and Leo turfed me out of bed with some unpleasant news. "We've gotta go in 10 minutes," he said. "We have to cut the cricket field."

Official Czech groundsman Lukas was waiting downstairs when I staggered in. Broad-shouldered Lukas was a softball convert and a fan of Surrey CCC. He was the Czech Republic's highest run-scorer and their only centurion to date.

"I have to study for my exams today," he said. "So I can't cut the pitch. I'll drive you and Leo and the lawnmower down there."

During the car ride I asked Lukas where Czechs got their whites.

"I got mine from my mum," he said. "She's a doctor at the hospital."

Lukas deposited us at the ground and left for a cram session. Leo unlocked a blue container and wheeled out a second antique lawnmower.

"The drive function doesn't work, so you'll have to push," he said.

"I bet Shane Warne never had to do this," I replied, tugging the start cord.

"Don't worry. We'll get paid from the match fees."

One boundary was covered in pylons and intersected by the number 22 tram. Opposite stood ash trees and thick rhododendrons. I looked to the sky and saw this was one of the few grounds in the world where a jet, landing behind the bowler's arm, could hold up play.

"Sometimes the games stop because of gypsies on horseback in the covers," said Leo.

Leo and I began a three-and-a-half-hour mowing session. I adored the smell of fresh grass cuttings and petrol. It signalled the start of the cricket season and the happiest time of the year. As fumes and heat went to my head, I envisioned myself moving to Prague and earning my keep as assistant groundsman. Then Leo pointed out that not all was rosy with the job.

"I had to clean sick off the wicket last week."

By the time Lukas returned from his studies, the ground was no Lord's but it would do for an Eastern European international.

"So, tomorrow's game," said Leo, turning to me. "Prague CC versus the Czech Republic. You're playing for the Republic. Nervous?"

"Always."

*

Match day arrived. After a week of blistering sun, Prague CC versus the Czech Republic was a washout. I didn't even have to look out of the window to know.

"We've called it off," said Leo, looking glum as he emerged up the stairwell. "If the ground's wet, we just can't use the plastic pitch. It's lethal. I'm really sorry."

The cruellest part, I explained, was that we played through conditions like this every week in Scotland.

"Well, my dad's going to look at some houses out of Prague, if you're interested. I'm gonna get on with some work."

Leo left and I took up the offer of a tour of abandoned farmhouses. Leo's dad, Simon, was president of the Czech Cricket Union. He drove through the drizzle while his Czech partner, Katerina, sat in the back.

We left the outskirts of Prague and, after a brief scout around some bargain holiday villas, visited a garden centre. It was in an Edinburgh garden centre much like this that my mum purchased my first pair of cricket pads. They were actually called 'My First Cricket Pads'.

At under-12s boarding-school practice I had to hide the packaging carefully. Though no one ever saw the brand, every teammate laughed whenever I produced the pads. Owning crap pads meant I was a crap player. It just so happened that the captain and vice-captain's pads, bats and gloves were the best, simply because they belonged to the captain and vice-captain.

The straps on my pads ripped and fell off after a week and I had to reattach them with safety pins. The thought of a teammate discovering this caused me many a sleepless night in the summer term.

During one match, while waiting to bat, our wicketkeeper, Oliver Holt, ran across and kicked me just because I was wearing my crap pads. It bruised my shin and left a permanent dent not only in the padding but also in my psyche. Both school teams and their masters laughed so hard that there followed a five-minute delay in play, after which the bowlers never regained their line and length. The haunting memories which came to me only made that day's Czech washout all the more bitter.

Simon, Katerina and I drove next to Kutná Hora. It is a classic day-trip venue for those who venture beyond Prague's Irish pubs. Its most famous chapel is decorated with the bones of over 40,000 humans. A thirteenth-century abbot had returned from the Holy Land with a jar of soil for its grounds, instantly transforming this into one of the most popular graveyards in Europe. Then in the sixteenth century, a half-blind monk dug up the plague victims' bones to clear a way for new customers. A woodcarver was later commissioned to hang up the decorations. He made a coat of arms from ribs and a chandelier containing every bone in the human body. He built great pyramids of skulls in the fashion of Pol Pot.

As I stepped out of the ossuary, feeling a little queasy, Czech Cricket President Simon had some breaking news.

The Prague cricketers had been watching England slaughter Bangladesh in the first Test at the pub. The rain clouds had parted, and now Leo was on the phone summoning us back to the city.

"There's about 50 of us playing cricket!" he yelled down the phone. "We've got tons of beer! Hurry up!"

Simon stepped on the accelerator.

The location had been switched from the usual ground. Entering a football pitch within the confines of a crumbling running track, I came upon the conclusion of an exciting game of tip-and-run. There were metal dustbins as stumps, a netted goalmouth at slip, and the non-striker was brandishing a snapped plank that looked like it might impale him if he tripped. In the distance rose the enormous Soviet TV tower, now with bronze babies crawling up it, and over the hedge a rock concert raged.

The tennis ball squirted out to square leg. "Get it in! Get it in!" everyone cried. With my first touch I scooped up the ball and shied down the non-striker's end. There were drunken cheers and high fives all round. Run-outs are frequently a problem in this part of the world. The Czech word for 'yes' is 'no'. Then someone explained my side was batting, and I'd just run out my captain.

After the run-out things only got worse for my makeshift side. Like Bangladesh that day we suffered an innings defeat. Things became so desperate at one point that coach Scott, umpiring, tried to prevent an opposition catch and ended up copping the ball in his eye.

But win or lose, in the best tradition, the players headed pub-ward after the game, pointing out that Prague is the cheapest place on the planet for post-match drinks.

In the bar, plied with frothy Staropramen, I listened as more bizarre Czech tales came forth. I asked the group about odd players in the past. It emerged there had been two alleged ex-terrorists without fingers a few years back.

"I'm pretty sure they were Tamils," explained coach Scott. "They had their middle three fingers cut off so they couldn't fire rifles."

"And they still played cricket!" I cried. "That's awful! Where would the captain hide them in the field?"

"One actually held a catch," said Scott. "The batsman hit it up in the air and thought, 'This is an easy two.' But the guy bounced it with his thumbs, and clutched it to his chest."

Given the difficulties, neither digitless alleged ex-terrorist was ever required to umpire, and they never bowled spin in tandem.

After more drinks further tales emerged. "Remember that game with the prostitutes?" recalled another player, indicating I should write this down.

"An Australian turned up in a stretch limo looking for a game. He came with two prostitutes who weren't wearing any knickers."

"Yeah," said Scott. "Never have so many players and spectators been so keen to explain the rules of cricket."

The table erupted.

"The Aussie said to our 15-year-old virgin wicketkeeper, 'I've paid the girls for 24 hours, mate, so you can have your cherry picked if you want.'"

Too bashful at the time, and with his focus on the game, the youngster politely declined. The poor prostitutes got so bored by the cricket that they left within the 24 hours.

"Imagine being turned down by a teenage boy," I said. "They must've been distraught. Is the wicketkeeper panged with regret?"

"Nah, he had his cherry picked on May 1, on Petrin Hill, while fireworks celebrating EU entry were exploding overhead."

As we continued our late-night crawl into Prague's cellars, I concluded there was nothing innocent about Czech cricket.

b
THE VILLAGE THAT BEAT POLAND

Me and my hitchhiker, Chairman Lubos

Bratislava reared up like a concrete graveyard on the horizon.
I followed a Lada in on the approaches and suffered flashbacks
from my previous visit. I remembered a giant motorway on stilts
running through the centre, past the castle. Check-in at our
refurbished mental-asylum hostel had taken us an hour and 20
minutes – and we were the first in line. When I'd asked the
school matron at reception if the hostel had kitchen facilities,
she'd made some phone calls before answering, "We might do."

Yes, Bratislava. The most exciting thing to happen here was the assassination of a Mafia boss in 1997. A hitman wounded his target outside a hotel, then returned a fortnight later to finish the job. He scaled a hospital roof with a ladder and pumped 24 bullets into the guy in his bed. At the thought of this I got out my milkman's calendar, and decided to head straight for Slovakia's cricket capital.

Forty minutes later I signalled off the Slovak D1 and pulled onto a grassy verge. In front of a warped house with a wooden hayloft, a rosy-cheeked young man was holding out his thumb. As he crept round to my passenger door, he wore a look of terror.

"I-I saw car with no driver!" his voice wobbled as he climbed in. "Wh-where are you from?"

"Scotland."

His expression changed to a broad beam. "Ahhh! You here to play cricket! We all expecting you! You look for Vladimir, my neighbour, yes? I take you now!"

As fortune would have it, I'd just scooped up the 20-year-old chairman and marketing and media manager of Slovak cricket. Lubos was returning from his job manufacturing Korean computer stands. He was a supervisor, earning two euros an hour. Cricket was infinitely more exciting to him, he said. He liked nothing more than to sit down with a beer and watch highlights of the '99 World Cup. His sporting duties had seen him star on every Slovak breakfast TV show. "The presenters' breasts made me nervous," he confessed, as we entered his home village of Hajske.

Headscarved babushkas were cycling around the square, holding rakes and hoes over their shoulders. We passed a chocolate-biscuit factory, the town hall, whose doors were bricked up, and the local Co-op. Lubos got me to stop outside a large red gate. Goats were grazing on a lawn in front.

"Vladimir lives here," said Lubos, opening the gate and leading me through. On the other side stood a beautiful thatched garage and a garden so immaculate it looked to be straight out of a Homebase showroom. I could hear hens clucking and saw, over a fence, geese gobbling on grass cuttings. Lubos knocked on the door of the house. The double of a young Gabriel Byrne and a lovely-looking blonde appeared. Lubos spoke to them in Slovakian before turning to leave.

"Welcome!" burst out the couple in chorus.

"We were just getting ready for your visit," said the lady, looking a little nervous. "Please, come in."

"I'm sorry. I'm a day early. I couldn't face check-in in Bratislava."

"No problem, my friend," said Vladimir, smiling. "Please, you will stay with Anna and me."

"Would you like some tea?" asked Anna. "I can make you English tea. I'm sorry we're not more organised for your visit."

We hurried through to the newly decorated kitchen, and sat at the table under a wooden beam. Anna put a pot of water on to boil while we exchanged pleasantries.

Vladimir was a manager in a fertiliser factory. He was a fan of skiing, ice hockey, tennis, Liverpool FC and cricket. His passion for the last began in 1997, when he travelled to the village of Frampton in Gloucestershire to study English for a year. He joined the local football club, and when it came to summer the footballers turned to cricket. Anna, meanwhile, had learned English as an au pair in London, Vienna and Nice. Now she worked in envelope seals, and was secretary of the Slovak Cricket Club. She excused herself to fetch something from the garden.

"Everyone grows their own food here," she explained 10 minutes later, a little breathless, presenting me with a plateful of peas, peppers and tomatoes, and a mug of English brew.

"Thank you," I said, adding sugar to my cup and stirring.

"No!" cried Anna. "This is salt! I will boil another pot for you."

I apologised and turned to Vladimir.

"So how did cricket start in Slovakia?"

"I learned the game from the Frampton footballers," he explained. "They took me on their end-of-season tour to Majorca. When I returned to Slovakia I couldn't believe there was no cricket here! So I decided to set it up myself."

Vladimir had carved some sticks from the wood and persuaded a topless 20-stone gypsy to stand in the middle of the football field while he bowled at him.

"He was so fat you couldn't see the wicketkeeper, let alone the stumps. When he ran it was like an earthquake. There were four of us. I taught them to bowl with a straight arm. At first the ball flew 10 feet over and 10 feet wide. No one *believed* it was possible to hit the stumps, even without a batsman! Spectators were shouting at us from the side, 'Get off the field and go work in the garden!'"

In a tireless recruitment drive, Vladimir knocked on the doors of all 1300 villagers. Slowly, the numbers at training grew, as girls and boys turned out to explore this new sport, and each other.

"There were some heated meetings on the pitch in the beginning," said Vladimir. "The football officials didn't want to lend us the ground for cricket. They thought we were stealing players. I pointed out that football training was on Wednesday and cricket training was on Monday and Tuesday. In the end they saw sense."

Within three years Vladimir had forged a unit that was to topple Poland. That famous first victory came on a camping tour to Prague. "We were helped by plum brandy at drinks break," said Vladimir.

Now the village celebrated Cricket Day every May 1. One hundred and thirty fans had turned out this year, including three ambassadors.

"For the future, who knows?" shrugged Vladimir. "Tomorrow our wicketkeeper has his bus driving test, so maybe he can take us on tour to Russia."

I was staggered. With a budget of 120 euros a year, Vladimir had achieved a sporting miracle. I thought of small UK clubs spending £15,000 a year for an Aussie pro and an overseas amateur, and yet their playing memberships dwindled. Here, with an average player age of 20, Slovak cricket looked set to accelerate.

"But our cricket is still in nappies," put in Anna.

Vladimir led me through the house. He showed me a cricket bat on his bookshelf, signed by Michael Vaughan's England team. Then he led me upstairs to the guest bedroom.

"I'm afraid the lights don't work at the moment. The electrician is weird. He's my best friend, but when he fixes the power in the garage, it goes off in one room in the house. He will come tomorrow. Will candles be okay for you?"

"Perfect."

"Okay. I will let you get ready for training now."

We were assembled on the village football field, 19 of us. A revolution had occurred in Hajske. Cricket training had more attendees than football training, making it the number one sport in the village. I got the impression some of the players were there on dates.

Vladimir wheeled out a green plastic shower mat from the pavilion hut, then he and Chairman Lubos unrolled it on the grass. This Flicx pitch, awarded by the European Cricket Council, would tame some of the demons in the ground.

Vladimir lined up six newcomers and hauled me over. "If you can teach them the batting basics, I will translate," he said.

The Slovaks took naturally to gripping the bat; mainly, I guessed, because of their tree-cutting and ice-hockey experience. When the newbies were judged ready, Vladimir quickly formed a game of tip-and-run.

Though most of the villagers had never seen televised cricket, they were utterly transfixed. The batsmen worked the ball into gaps and pounded down the wicket; the fielders cheered them on. Even when Vladimir announced fielding drills there was a clap. In a place so far removed from the world game, these Slovaks carried none of the prejudice that hampered cricket's development in its homeland.

"You have a lot of left-handers," I said to Vladimir, one of the rare right-handers, as we locked the shower mat back in the pavilion.

"Yes. Seventy per cent of the squad bat left-handed," he said. "I think this is because of ice hockey."

We left the field and entered the village pub. Puff Daddy was playing on the stereo. Three silent old men looked up from the fussball table. The cricketers shuffled out the back and sat down on benches with beers and ice cream.

I asked Vladimir about the make-up of the squad. Seventy per cent were gardening and/or politics students, he said, and all were native. But the most startling statistic leapt out from the Slovak team sheet. Move over the Waugh brothers, Slovakia had four Juríčeks, three other sets of brothers and two cousins.

"Their mothers are very proud," said Vladimir.

Former Pakistan teenage prodigy Hasan Raza could take a step backwards too. The junior Juríček debuted versus Poland aged 12, making him the youngest ever internationalist by two years.

Though most of the players had passed their English exams only a week ago, it was a struggle to get anything more than 'hello' out of them. Vladimir graciously acted as a buffer, while the rest sat poised on the edge of their seats for his translations.

"These guys," said Vladimir, pointing at two teammates, "recently applied to Nitra University. Everyone must sit entrance exams unless they are a member of a Slovak national sports team. Nitra University approved their applications based on them playing cricket. But guess what. They have batting averages of two and zero. One of them has never scored a run in his life!"

The successful applicants giggled and nodded when they saw I understood. Cricket had transformed people's lives here. It gave them opportunities. It kept people in the village when they might otherwise have fled to the cities.

I asked Vladimir about his proudest moment.

"It was meeting the British minister of sport at the Embassy in Bratislava," he said. "There were gold-medal Olympians at the reception. Out of 40 guests that evening, 30 were from Hajske. I gave the British minister the ball from our first win over Poland. He said he would put it in the Long Room at Lord's."

I asked Vladimir if there had ever been any trouble in his games. Vladimir consulted with the others. After some minutes he answered, "On our first tour to Prague, we didn't have enough cars, so the village mayor had to drive us."

Everyone laughed. Another player leaned forward and whispered something. "Oh, yes," said Vladimir. "We had a match in Vienna. We started the game with only four players because the rest were lost driving around the city. They arrived four hours late, during the second-last over. All our batsmen had to keep going in again and again."

Another story was passed forward, and Vladimir nodded.

"Once we had a foreigner playing. He used to tell the boys he was going skiing with Steve Waugh and Sourav Ganguly in the Tatras each weekend. They know who Ronaldo is. They don't know who Steve Waugh is. This guy, he wanted to restart a tournament after being bowled for zero. And he tried to stage a team walkout in Vienna when an lbw appeal was turned down. I said, 'No. What are you doing? Let's play the game.' He left 14 players to get home in two cars."

Such actions proved incompatible with the Slovak spirit. This foreign troublemaker was dismissed from the club without the chance to add to his tournament duck.

"This is the last sport with fair play," said Vladimir, "and I'm determined to keep it that way."

The next morning Anna took the day off work to show me around Hajske. The village was founded in the thirteenth century, during fighting with the Ottomans. The Hungarian-Slovak soldiers were camped on one side of the River Váh; the Ottomans stationed themselves opposite. The Ottomans had cows, while the Hungarian-Slovaks had little to eat. The Slovak captain got hold of a bull and kicked it till it mooed in the night. By the morning, every Ottoman cow had crossed the river to mate. The Ottomans were left hungry and defeated. For his brilliance, the Slovak captain was given the title Count the Thief. Centuries later, said Anna, another count in the village was bitten to death by fleas.

Anna took me to a shrine where miracles were said to have occurred. A lame man had famously thrown down his crutches on site. Next, we walked down a Roma street.

The Romas, sometimes called gypsies, were believed to have migrated to Europe from India in the eleventh century. Slovakia had faced a hammering in the press and from the EU over its modern-day treatment of Romas. One glance at this street revealed major problems. Families of 10 were living in collapsing brick huts that looked as though they'd been built by a man on crutches in the night.

I approached a group of tattooed smokers, including a Pat Butcher lookalike leaning idly on a red Lada.

"Watch out," whispered Anna, three steps behind. "They don't know you . . . They might throw a piece of scrap metal at you or something."

Anna walked up to ask if I could take some photos. The Romas nodded, and posed proudly. Anna said something else to them.

"I just asked why they aren't working," she told me. "They say they are not so poor that they have to work."

As we walked down a parallel street, where every house had a prize-winning rose garden, military music burst across the village. It came from tannoys fixed on telegraph poles.

"Are those from the communist days?"

"Yes," said Anna. "They announced meetings for the workers. Now the town hall uses them for other notices. They tell us if planes will be applying fertilisers on the fields that day, so we can put our bees inside. When it was Cricket Day, they announced the event for a whole week!"

"Why military music?"

"It means, 'Put your pot aside, come outside and listen.'"

"Do they play other music?"

"Sometimes traditional, sometimes '80s."

"Bon Jovi?"

"No. It might give the old ladies heart attacks."

When the record ended a lady began a long announcement. "She says there will be shoes, trousers and underwear for sale in the centre today," said Anna. "The market is coming. She will read out everything that is for sale."

The list was still droning on when Anna showed me the prospective new cricket ground. It was currently a wheat field behind Vladimir's gran's house. To finally free themselves from the football officials the cricketers would have to create their own terrain.

Continuing our tour, Anna announced, "This is where the count who was bitten to death by fleas lived. The communists bulldozed his mansion." We stared at the patch of grass.

"Because of the flea infestation?"

"No. Because it was a sign of wealth."

"That's awful."

"Yes. We lived two lives under communism: one in public and one in the house. If someone asked you something on the street, you had to answer differently. Vladimir's grandfather used to queue from four in the morning to two in the afternoon to get meat. Meat was on Saturdays, ice cream on Thursdays."

PJ O'Rourke, in *Holidays In Hell*, wrote, "To grasp the true meaning of socialism, imagine a world where everything is designed by the post office". I could see great parallels between this old system and modern-day Britain. Instead of queuing at the meat and ice cream shops, we did it on the phone to call centres.

Finally, Anna and I reached the much-advertised market. Tables had been set out by the roadside, with shoes and tracksuits spread across them and over a Lada's bonnet. I wasn't sure if the car was for sale too.

I asked some babushkas inspecting the goods if I could take their photo. Anna translated. "Yes," they replied. "But we are old, and we have herpes."

"This is terrible," said Anna, embarrassed. "Now you will think our village is so poor!"

"No, no," I assured her truthfully. "This is wonderful. I'd take it over Tesco any day."

*

When I was a whippersnapper I always wanted to play international cricket. I dreamed of steaming in as a tearaway for England and uprooting Brian Lara's off stump. It was a sad day at school when, alas, fully grown at five foot eight, I had to ditch fast bowling and switch to gentle leg spin. I realised I was never going to make it for England. Not deterred entirely, I lowered my sights, setting them on Scotland. It was even more pathetic the day I realised I wasn't going to cut the crust there either. Never in my youth in the Scottish hills, however, did I imagine I'd get my first international cap for Slovakia.

"All our games are internationals," said Vladimir as we drove to the football field in his red Škoda. "Tonight it's Slovakia A versus Slovakia B. You can be captain of the A-Team, my friend."

Captain. On debut. Of the A-Team. My cheeks flushed and my chest swelled. It was a shame my parents couldn't be here to see this.

The Slovaks arrived by rollerblade, bicycle and moped. The plastic pitch was again wheeled out to the centre circle. Once Vladimir had broken up a minor scuffle between kids, the players gathered for the toss. In my first coin-flip as an international captain, nerves spoiled the occasion. The coin landed down my shirt. When it popped out, it showed heads and I'd lost. As so few players spoke English, I couldn't work out which team was batting and which was bowling. I didn't even know who was in which team.

It appeared my A-Team had been inserted first. The B-Team medium-pacers showed little mercy in their tracksuits, exploiting centre-circle demons to the full. The ball kicked and spat past our openers' heads, and in the follow-up deliveries promptly flattened their stumps. The bails landed in the hands of the old-fashioned backstop.

Slovakia's bowling attack was to be feared. During the 2004 second Test of England versus West Indies, *The Guardian*'s live website commentary wrote that Slovakia's bowlers, in their victory over Poland, "were a lot tighter than the West Indies'".

In a recovery job Kevin Pietersen's mum would have been proud of, our middle order plundered the short, square boundaries. Each four was cheered by players and spectators as though this was a World Cup Final. Even the players' girlfriends had turned out to clap and do the scorebook.

At the end of an over I walked down the wicket to discuss tactics with my partner. "Don't be afraid to pick up your bat and smack it," I said. My partner stared back, not understanding a word. I realised I'd have to resign my captaincy forthwith. There was no way I'd be able to set fields in the second innings.

After Vladimir's tight mix of pace and spin, the B-Team used paper-scissors-stone to decide who'd bowl their final overs. By the end of our allotted 20, the As had accelerated to 97 for 5. Bearded truck driver Stalin, one of the four Juríček brothers, had unselfishly guided me to my first international 50. Tired from his 0 not out, he then had to leave to paint his room orange. A substitute was sought from the stands.

At the innings change, a storm began to whip across the field. Entrusted with the new ball by the second captain – a rarity for a leg-spinner – I suffered a haunting flashback of my first school match. Back then we played in starched white school shirts and cream cotton shorts. We wore knee-high red socks, held up by garters, with combs tucked into their rims. School rules dictated hair *always* had to be side-parted. As former England managers will testify, this is what made a good cricketer.

The wind in that first game caused my hair to fly all over the place. I lost my side parting and my radar. I bowled 13 wides in a single over. It was a feat that saw me go from the under-12s opening paceman to scorer for the rest of the season. As I looked at Chairman Lubos facing me now, bent over at a right angle, I had a horrible feeling my international career could meet the same fate.

I approached the wicket and released. Lubos's leg stump was sent cartwheeling backwards. The poor lad had been up since four that morning for work.

Their favoured forward defensive prods à la French cricket couldn't save the Bs' top three being fired out. And when they suffered two direct-hit run-outs from the boundary in two balls – the second from a lazily jogged single – it all looked to be over.

But Vladimir, relishing his captain's role, looted the vacant legside boundary with sweeps. He gained admirable support from the player selected for university without ever having scored a run. He chose this opportunity to register his personal best. He scored 2, and received the loudest cheer of the day.

In a desperate move we tried the same bowler from each end in succession. Even this illegal ploy couldn't stop a final stand of 40 and a loss by two wickets, with just one ball to spare.

As Vladimir was carried off the field for his winning 55, with 30 villagers cheering, he turned to say, "This was our greatest-ever game!"

I was changing alone in the Slovak pavilion after the match. Among the old balls and worn gloves on the table was a magazine clipping. I leaned over to study it, unable to understand a word. A spectator entered the hut.

"Good game," he said, raising his arms. "The best!"

"Thanks . . . Are you from the village?"

He shook his head. "I come from Bratislava, to see game."

I held up the article. "Could you tell me what this says, please?"

The spectator took the magazine clipping and his face adopted a grave expression.

"This is about old player," he said gruffly. "Not here any more. He tell magazine he was *professional* cricket player. He say he earn three million euros to play cricket in Scotland and Italy for season."

"Three million euros!" I screamed. "In *Italy and Scotland*! That'd make him the highest-paid player on the planet more than three times over!"

My translator shook his head. "This was very, very bad player. I think he was . . .", he looked from side to side, " . . . well, I have *heard* he was Mafia."

"Mafia!" I cried.

The spectator nodded. "I heard this from men in capital, Bratislava. This player, he is not from here. He no longer play."

"What happened?"

"We see him on television. The police, they handcuff him and take him in police van."

"That must have posed all sorts of selection problems for the weekend."

"Yes. I think he was . . . smuggling illegal people. He wanted to use team for this, but he no succeed. He is gone for long time."

I slapped my forehead. Of course! What better vehicle for trafficking illegal immigrants! You go to the government, who aren't going to have a clue, and present the forms requesting a wicketkeeper. Permission to enter granted! You're into the rest of Europe.

I shook slightly at these revelations. There was indeed a dark side to Eastern European cricket. I had no reason to doubt my translator. He was every bit as innocent as the rest of these cricket-smitten villagers. This Mafia rascal, and his hijacking plans, had no place in a club like this. I felt contempt for him and relief he was gone. I suspected, however, this wouldn't be the last shadowy find on my trip.

*

Leaving Hajske in the early morning, I was a tad misty-eyed. Anna and Vladimir had left me permanently indebted, and I doubted the elation following our game could ever be matched.

"You deserve a knighthood for your work, Vladimir," I said, shaking his hand before climbing into the Škoda.

"No. No awards." He smiled. "I just want people to hear our story. To know that we are here, and that we like cricket. It's good for the boys."

I set out east across the country on a taxing drive through heavy rain and fog. Twice I had to perform emergency stops at 50 miles per hour, when oncoming cars overtook without any gap to pull back into. Their drivers flashed their lights, making comedy of the situation.

I passed villages in need of paint jobs, immaculately kept churches and heavily polluting cement mills. In the town of Zwolen, I glimpsed the Gothic castle in which my Kiwi mate, Jim, who I'd played cricket with in Toronto, would shortly be getting married. If there was anywhere to stage a wedding it was Slovakia. You could buy 10 pints for a pound in the shops. Even fourteenth-century royal castles came at a bargain.

By the fourth hour I had got cramp in my legs and pulled into the Omega Restaurant. I locked my wheel and staggered weakly through the restaurant doors in search of lunch and an overdue pee. Inside, the smell suggested a boiled pig's face was floating in the soup du jour. The dining room had all the ambience of a Soviet gulag cafeteria, and at each table there huddled a squad of uniformed policemen. The menu was fixed on the wall with snap-on stickers. I stood for some minutes in the centre of the floor, struggling to translate. The gender-bent dinner ladies scowled at me from behind their trolley.

Get out of here now, I thought suddenly. Get out!

Was this a warning from great-uncle Ivor? I looked at the policemen, licking their greasy bowls, and then at the viscous goo bubbling under hot lights. No one would understand English here, let alone 'vegetariánská'. In a paranoid state I bolted from the room and raced back onto the road.

Further east, I reached familiar territory as shantytowns sprung up in hillside gullies and ragged Romas plodded back from factories.

I first came to this region on a road trip with my brother, though our visit had been far from intentional. We'd set off from Budapest for Bratislava, along with a Cardiff social worker who we'd picked up in our hostel. Rob was a Christopher Walken lookalike, except he had a lazy eye.

We reached the Hungarian–Slovak border in the Škoda and passed through the first barrier with ease. At the second barrier, the Slovak guards asked to inspect our car papers.

"They're in the glove compartment," I said to my brother, Doug, who rummaged around without success. I switched off the engine and popped the boot, but after a five-minute hunt I discovered the car papers weren't in there either. Every motorist behind began to honk.

We tore up every carpet and unravelled every ball of socks three times. The guards shook their heads and confiscated our passports. Coincidentally, all three of us shared the same surname, making this look even more suspicious. I feared we might soon be arrested.

"They were in here somewhere!" I screamed.

An hour went by. The guards signalled there was no way we were entering Slovakia. If we turned around and tried to re-enter Hungary, we wouldn't be allowed in there either. We were officially in no man's land, suspected of driving a stolen vehicle. Until the British Ministry of Transport vouched for us, we were trapped under a canopy the size of a petrol station forecourt.

I tore at my hair. Social worker Rob muttered unhelpfully, "I should've got the bus." The chief Slovak guard, his moustache twitching at every honk of a horn, waved us aside.

"It's bribe time, boys," I said.

"Okay," said the guard, leaning in at my window. "You came here *with* papers. You enter Slovakia with papers. You lose papers *in* Slovakia. You no mention my name."

I floored the accelerator and realised we were now trapped *in* Slovakia.

Rob, who claimed to have extensive knowledge of the region, took charge. After 50 minutes, he guided us up a wooded hillside in the dark.

"We park behind that tree," he said, "and we camp on this hill. At six o'clock tomorrow we'll throw everything in the car, we'll drive for one hour, then we'll stop in a lay-by. Then we'll repack the kit properly. I don't want any dicking around. Right, boys?" He sounded serious.

"Rob. We're in the middle of Slovakia, population: zero," I said. "What could happen?"

"This is what we're gonna do," he snapped.

I felt scared. I was with a man who looked like Christopher Walken, who I'd known for one evening, on an uninhabited Slovak hillside, unable to see how we'd leave the country without car papers.

It was quarter past five in the morning. "Get up!" screamed Rob outside our tent as though we were in the middle of a manhunt. "I can hear motorbikes across the valley!"

Doug and I dared not disobey Rob's orders. We threw our tent in the boot, and reversed the Škoda out from behind its tree. As we rattled down a stony lane, a headscarved old lady stepped out of her farmhouse, holding a cow.

"She saw the number plate!" yelled Rob. "'Er husband and 'er sons'll be after us on their motorbikes soon! Go, you idiots!"

We drove through the rain, not even stopping to repack in a lay-by as per Rob's instructions. All I could think about was reaching the British Embassy in Bratislava and sorting out my car papers.

"How far are we from Bratislava now?" I asked Rob, who had taken possession of the map.

"Hundreds of miles!" he replied, cheerfully. He had taken us completely the wrong way.

"What?" I said in disbelief.

"Look, we're in Slovakia . . . Let's chill for a few days. You don't want to go to Bratislava. It's 'orrible."

"*How* are we going to get out of the country?" I snapped.

"Worry about that later," said Rob, giggling. "Look, this is a national park. You'll like it. We'll hang up the tents and go for a hike."

We approached a meadow clearing surrounded by forest. There were four large concrete hotels around its edge, and a coach load of Slovak septuagenarians in the car park.

"This is where we're staying," announced Rob.

We checked into a hotel and began telephoning the DVLA in Swansea on Doug's mobile. There were no options on the automatic answer service for lost car papers in Eastern Europe. Round and round we went, pressing every button, at great expense. When we at last chanced upon a human operator, he said, "If you write to us in Swansea, you should get a response within 15 working days."

"We're in Slovakia! We can't get out of the country!" said Doug.

"Then you need to arrange a UK courier to bring out your papers."

"Can you fax a copy, please?" I asked.

"Okay," agreed the operator. "If you jot down all the details and fax us, we'll get onto it."

Rob, Doug and I sat down in our room to draft the fax. The wording had to be precise and effective. The headline needed to grab attention. We couldn't afford to have this tossed in a to-do tray.

"**Help! Urgent assistance required**," I marked at the top. "**We are currently trapped in . . .** "

"Where are we, guys?" I asked.

"The Hotel Relax," answered Doug.

"Well, good for you," I imagined them saying back in Swansea.

*

I strolled into the Hotel Relax alone now. It had since changed its name. Schoolkids ogled me as I wandered the corridors in search of reception. I entered the sauna by mistake.

At the front desk I was told there were no vacancies. I couldn't believe it. This was mid-week, out of holiday season, in an eastern Slovakian meadow, under pouring rain, and there were no rooms.

I tried the Hotel Trio behind. An old hag babbled at me, then slammed the door in my face. At the third hotel, a man rolled an olive-oil barrel across my path, then shouted at me to move my car. I made a sign for shelter with my hands. He shook his head.

"Right! Get the tent out!" I spat, trudging furiously across the drenched meadow. I opened my car boot and discovered my tent had been put away wet. It now looked like it had contracted tent syphilis.

I flattened some tall grass at the meadow's edge and spread out my groundsheet. As I pushed the first peg into the ground I heard an angry buzzing. Looking down at my foot, I saw what appeared to be a large piece of broken puff pastry. Out of it streamed hundreds of wasps.

"Fuck!" I shrieked, sprinting through the grass. Three wasps clung to my tee shirt and stung me on the back. "Aaaaagh!" I screamed. "WHAT ON EARTH AM I DOING HERE?"

When I stopped running I noticed there was one more hotel in the meadow I hadn't tried.

I was overlooking the former Hotel Relax, my car papers safely at my side, a tall glass of pivo in hand. In the adjacent dining room was a wedding party, and next to that was a kids' disco. I took a long draw from my pint, and thought about why I had returned to this place. Had I honestly just driven seven hours across Slovakia to see an old hotel with painful memories? Was it part of the healing process? Yes, yes, it probably was.

I had issues, I decided. Acknowledging this was the first step to recovery. My trip had lost focus; that was for sure. I was 300 kilometres away from the nearest cricket field, and though Tuesday night's innings had propelled me to the top of the Slovak averages, it had exposed technical flaws in my game. What I needed, more than anything now, was a coach in my passenger seat. I needed an Australian. But where in God's name would I find one out here?

I emptied my glass and walked into reception. A young man's voice at the computer said, "Mate, how the fuck are we gonna get outta here?"

Slovakia A versus Slovakia B
SK Hajske Stadium, Hajske, Slovakia
08.06.2005 (20-over match, 11-a-side)

Result: Slovakia B won by 2 wickets
Toss won by: Slovakia B
Man of the match: Vladimír Chudáčik

Slovakia A		R	B	4	6
Matušica K+	run out (Somorovský, Chudáčik)	10	26	1	0
Howarth	c Chudáčik b Somorovský	0	10	0	0
Bogády	b Machariáš	0	2	0	0
Bell (*)	not out	52	49	10	0
Juríček Ju*	c Petrovský b Machariáš	7	17	0	0
Juríček Jo	b Petrovský	1	19	0	0
Juríček T (Stalin)	not out	0	1	0	0
Karásik	dnb	–	–		
Matušica F	dnb	–	–		
Franta J	dnb	–	–		
Bennar L	dnb	–	–		
Extras (b7 lb2 w12 nb6)		27			
Total (5 wickets, 20 overs)		97			

FoW: 5–1 (Howarth, 1.5 ov), 6–2 (Bogády, 2.2 ov), 49–3 (Matušica K, 9.5 ov), 63–4 (Juríček Ju, 13.4 ov), 81–5 (Juríček Jo, 18.5 ov)

Bowling	O	M	R	W
Machariáš	4	0	13	2
Somorovský	4	1	10	1
Múčka	2	0	24	0
Chudáčik	4	0	24	1
Kišš T.	3	0	9	0
Petrovský.	3	0	13	0

Slovakia B		R	B	4	6
Petrovský	b Bell	0	1	0	0
Hambalek Ma+	b Bell	5	7	0	0
Lencéš	c Howarth b Bell	9	9	0	0
Chudáčik *	not out	55	55	0	0
Somorovský	b Juríček Ju	2	10	0	0
Kaduc	b Juríček Jo	2	8	0	0
Kišš T	run out (Matušica F)	1	4	0	0
Machariáš	run out (Juríček Ju)	0	0	0	0
Urban	b Juríček Jo	2	12	0	0
Karásek	not out	1	11	0	0
Múčka	dnb	–	–	–	–
Extras (b8 lb2 w9 nb2)		21			
Total (8 wickets, 19.5 overs)		98			

FoW: 0–1 (Petrovský, 0.1 ov), 10–2 (Lencéš, 2.1 ov), 14–3 (Hambalek Ma, 2.5 ov), 35–4 (Somorovský, 7.2 ov), 38–5 (Kaduc, 8.4 ov), 41–6 (Kišš T, 9.2 ov), 41–7 (Machariáš, 9.6 ov), 58–8 (Urban, 14.2 ov)

Bowling	O	M	R	W
Bell	4	0	14	3
Howarth	4	0	16	0
Juríček Ju	4	1	10	1
Juríček Jo	4	0	22	2
Karásik	4	0	24	0

7
THE WORST COACHES IN THE WORLD

In the shadow of Lenin, Budapest. From the left: Michael, Nick, Paul and Jay, the Aussie genetic engineer

Michael and Nick were thrown when I first mentioned Eastern European cricket. In true Aussie fashion, they reacted in the bar, spouting, "What the fuck?"

The Perth pair were wondering how to get from an eastern Slovak meadow to Belgrade, via Budapest, when I approached them in the hotel.

"Fancy a ride in a Škoda?" I asked.

"Oh, yeah!"

In return they would analyse my batting and ready me for that first century.

"Thank God you're able to take us in yer car," said Michael. "We reckoned we'd be gassed, robbed and raped on the train."

Michael was a Chinese-Irish Australian. Nick, in his own words, was a "Greek-Malaysian Australian from New Zealand". Both were disillusioned law undergrads, confident they'd soon be rolling in it. They had just completed an exchange semester at university in British Columbia.

"Did *Legally Blonde* help you with your marks?" I asked.

"Yeah, we took a field trip to Harvard and saw where it was filmed," said Nick, who once thought the Oktoberfest was in August.

The next morning, after scaling a hill and touring a magnificent thirteenth-century château, we left Slovakia for the grass plains of Hungary. Now with EU membership, there was no repeat of car-paper problems at the border.

Only two-thirds of the road had been tarmacked in northern Hungary, leaving a 12-inch drop onto our narrow strip. It meant we had to drive down the centre, at a 20-degree angle. A lorry thundered towards us, and I slipped back over to our unlaid strip. The lorry began to follow our path. We faced a choice of being crushed under it, or taking a headlong plunge into a trench. I braked, closed my eyes and readied myself for impact. The Škoda shook violently and, when I looked in the mirror, I saw the lorry had skidded into some traffic cones. I looked out of my window and saw we were hanging precariously over the edge of the ditch.

"These are the worst drivers in the world!" yelled Michael.

"Actually, it gets worse than this," I said, giving the wheel a full left lock.

Nick had every illegal download on his iPod, including his favourite New Zealand boy-band flops. I didn't fancy listening to those, so he popped on Alanis Morissette. As we sang along to

'Ironic', we overtook a Škoda full of nuns, and received a wave from a blonde in a gold bikini bending over beneath a beech tree.

"Caw, look at all these hitchhikers," said Nick about a string of prostitutes. "Why are they all staring at your car?"

"'Cos the steering wheel's on the wrong side," said Michael innocently.

We raced along empty EU-sponsored motorways and entered the art-nouveau capital, Budapest. Nick and Michael guided us between grimy-faced apartment blocks to a hostel near the banks of the Danube.

I couldn't say I was thrilled at a return to the backpacking circuit. I thought of sweaty pillows, creaking beds and 40 thieves fighting over a flooded bathroom each morning. When shown the facilities, the words 'fungal infection' and 'bedbugs' sprang to mind. Worse, there was the ever-present smell of dorm sex. Michael, Nick and I nodded our approval to the manager and checked in for three nights.

Regrettably, the Hungarian leg of my trip would be without official cricket. The game had been played here by Englishmen at least as far back as the 1890s. What followed is murky. One hundred years later, a new Budapest club was formed, which regularly toured Austria and Germany. When they played the British Embassy, the match was delayed until the diplomatic kitbag arrived from the airport. There was even one Hungarian cricketer who drove 300 kilometres from Miskolc each Sunday for practice, leaving his house at 5 a.m.

But the recent closure of the Sri Lankan Embassy spelled disaster for the Magyar Cricket Club. That and several key players had moved to Sunderland and New Jersey. There were no excuses, as far as I was concerned. Hungary was one giant valley floor. It was ideal for play, and yet Magyar CC had struggled throughout their existence to find a pitch.

Lack of organised cricket was not the only setback, I soon learned. Michael and Nick had some confessions about their so-called coaching expertise.

We were sitting at a restaurant eating 'naughty chicken, swimming in a cheese sauce', 'robber's meat on a kebab, gendarme-style', and a 'sensational meal with a vegetable filling'. (I wished more restaurants would sprinkle their menus with adjectives.)

"You see, we haven't really played much cricket," said Nick, with a chuckle, after my rundown on Hungary's history of the game.

"How much?" I asked.

Between them, Michael and Nick had one year's experience and two runs. Nick had scored both of them.

"That wouldn't even get you into Slovak university," I said, "'cos it wasn't at international level." Both runs had come in seventh grade – the very lowest in Australia.

"I don't know if it helps," said Michael, by way of consolation, "but I once let in 23 goals as keeper in a game of football."

"We can still help you," said Nick. "We can put you on a fitness programme, starting with beer."

"Yeah, and we'll have a little game before we head off," promised Michael.

Later that evening, as we returned to our hostel in the dark after a fitness session in a grubby pub, Michael said, "Have you noticed how every so often there's a horrendous smell on the street here?"

"Smells like sex," I said.

"Yeah, like our dorm back at the hostel."

A shadowy figure appeared among the bins at the end of our street. He began stumbling towards us. He was a fat, old man in a brown suit and tie. It must've been a bad day at the office. He held up his hand to stop us when he got close.

"Watch your wallet, Michael," I said.

"Sprechen Sie Deutsche?" slurred the drunk.

"Ein bisschen," I said.

The drunk took my right hand and placed $100 in it. Then he wrapped his arm around my waist.

"What the hell?" said Michael.

This was the strangest mugging I'd ever encountered. I'd read about models taking tourists to clubs where they'd be charged $74 a drink. Could this be a low-budget/bungled version?

The drunk attempted to lead me away, and I wrestled free.

"Du und . . . und . . . " he slurred, tapping me on the chest. He turned to Michael, looking him up and down, and then signalled he should come too.

"Stop!" I said, trying to hand back the money as he pushed me. "I don't understand!"

The drunk pointed at the money and then brushed my crotch. Now I understood.

I wasn't keen on a threesome, but there *was* $100 at stake. Surely there was some leeway for negotiation here? But what if the drunk had a gun? I thought.

"Come on! Let's get outta here!" said Michael in a panic, as the drunk made a reach for his chest too. We started to run.

"Stop! Stop!" shouted the drunk. "I am policeman!"

We rounded the corner and continued at high speed, stopping when we felt we were safe.

"Hello, hello," whispered a voice beside us. We turned to see three topless men and a dog in a raised plant bed. "Can you give us money?" said a scar-faced man.

"There's a guy back there who'll give you $100," I stopped myself from saying.

"Sorry, my friend," I said. "Good luck."

"Come on, let's go," urged Michael, clearly not used to confrontations like these in Perth.

"My friend," said the scar-faced man, jumping down from the plant bed. "He teach me a phrase. You want to hear?" Michael and I stopped. We nodded.

"May your skin break, may your mother go to fuckin' hell, and . . ." The man looked at his mates, who nodded encouragingly.

"Suck my dick," they finished in chorus.

There was definitely something in the atmosphere here. The whole city was charged with it. Michael and I hurried back to our hostel.

I'd been asleep for some hours when the door creaked open. I sat bolt upright in bed and watched a bald man and a woman creep inside. As I looked around the room, I couldn't place where I was. Panic gripped me. From the bodies in bunks, I seemed to be in some kind of refugee centre.

"Hey," I whispered to the couple who'd just entered. The bald man walked over.

"What *is* this place?" I demanded, grabbing his shirt.

"Huh?"

"Where, *where* are we? I was driving around . . . I had no map . . . and I . . . somehow ended up in this place. Where *are* we, man?"

The bald man looked down at me, puzzled. "I think you've had too much to drink," he answered in a Cockney accent.

"Thanks," I said. I shook his hand and slumped down on my pillow. While he walked away I digested what I'd said.

"Idiot," I told myself when everything became clear.

I lay awake in the dark for some time, wondering where Michael, Nick and I could get some net practice. Before I'd thought of an answer, an unpleasant noise filled the room. Beds began to squeak rhythmically.

"No!" I muttered. "God, no."

The metallic grinding hadn't been going long when I heard a girl whisper, "I want you to strangle me."

And then, in a hushed Cockney accent, I heard, "I'm gonna come."

I balked. Was anyone else hearing this?

"Wait, wait, wait!" commanded the girl.

But it was too late.

Deep silence followed. Even the snoring had stopped. I debated over what to do. This couple had to be stopped, or they could be at it all night.

"Goodnight," I announced to the dorm.

"Goodnight," bade five other voices.

Next morning, after winning the battle for the bathroom, Michael, Nick and I set off on a fitness campaign. We crossed the Danube into Buda and mounted the Castle District walls. Up there we inspected a hotel with a dentist in it and listened to cellists playing the *Star Wars* theme tune.

Leaving behind the eagle statues and views of the high-domed, Westminster-like parliament, we returned to flatter Pest. We walked five kilometres to the baroque Széchenyi Baths, whose spring waters were said to boost fertility in hippos at the zoo. In the open air, we soaked in steamy pools alongside hairy-chested old men. Some played chess in the pool, while others stuffed ice in their trunks.

I liked Budapest. It was a city of contrasts. It had been formed after a merger between the two sides, Buda and Pest, in 1873 and was now restoring itself after decades of neglect. It was one of the few cities where you could spot a Burger King with a

McDonald's sign on its roof. The city's one flaw remained the absence of cricket, but my coaches and I were soon to address this.

Diet was an important factor in my programme, my coaches judged, and I could no longer survive on vegetarian pizza twice a day, as I had been doing before my sensational meal with a vegetable filling. We threw my cricket bat in the Škoda and motored off to the biggest Tesco in the world.

"You can stock up on healthy nuts, tofu and soy milk," suggested Michael en route. I felt sick.

Budapest's Tesco really was the biggest in the universe. It stocked car tyres along with pet food and bird tables in its aisles. As I filled my basket with protein supplements, I felt contentment. This was off the tourist track. This was the Hungary I had come to see. We were living like Hungarians.

My checklist completed, I realised I had no forints to pay for my goods. I would have to visit an exchange bureau on the other side of checkout. I carried my basket to the exit gate and indicated to the security guard I'd like to leave and return shortly. He signalled I should put my basket on the floor, so I laid it down and walked out of the gate. The guard grabbed my forearm.

"Can I help?" I asked, turning back.

He snapped his fingers and pointed at my daysack. Fellow shoppers began gathering around to watch. I unzipped my bag and showed him its contents.

"As you can see, I have a half-empty deodorant roller – look, it has a pubic hair under the lid – and some five-year-old Boots sunscreen."

The guard nodded and I closed my bag. I tried to step away. He snapped his fingers again. I was to stay put. He began speaking rapidly into his walkie-talkie. My cheeks burned.

Ten horrible minutes passed while a crowd built. The guard continued to make calls into his walkie-talkie until a support crew arrived and began discussing how they'd deal with me.

"Sorry. I don't understand what's going on," I said. "Do you speak English, please?"

A second guard turned to me and glared. "Do you speak Hungarian? You are in Hungary now," he said darkly.

"Look, I'm just trying to change some money so I can buy tofu and nuts for my cricket diet. My basket's over there." I pointed to it. "What are you accusing me of?"

"Open your bag. Show us what you have taken," snarled the second guard.

Again, I showed the pubic hair under my deodorant lid. The guard sniffed at it.

"And what is this?" He pointed at the sunscreen. I handed it over. He read off the barcode into his walkie-talkie, and then came back with, "We do not stock this."

I was free to go. As I tried to leave, the second guard called again, "Wait!" He pointed at my sunglasses. "Are those yours?"

I showed him the paint damage on them caused by my Boots sunscreen.

"Next time, you show the man everything you take in, okay?" said the chief guard. I nodded and slunk off.

When I finally reached checkout, my misery was only com-pounded, as the cashier refused my Tesco Clubcard.

I found Michael and Nick sunbathing back at the car. Thanks to their law studies they could explain the trouble I might have faced.

"You're under local jurisdiction," said Nick. "There's nothing the British government could do." I knew these boys would go far and was confident they'd soon be rolling in it.

We left Tesco car park and attempted to reach Statue Park, three kilometres away. Michael was navigating. His skills matched those of his goalkeeping. After an hour, hopelessly lost among villas in the hills of Buda, he said, "Aw, look, guys, I can see the sea."

"Mediterranean, Black or Baltic?" I asked. You had to forgive the poor lad; he was from the most isolated city in the world, after all.

A mustachioed Algerian road worker was able to give us directions and we arrived at our destination within another hour.

Statue Park was an open-air cemetery for the bronze Lenins, Engelses and Marxes that once decorated the streets of Budapest. It stood beside pylons on dusty scrubland. Its entrance was a red-brick wall with a mounted statue of Lenin, whose shadow I now parked under.

We approached the kiosk. Soviet music was piping from an almost defunct radio. On the walls hung 'McLenin's' tee shirts with the slogan, 'The taste of communism'. Beside those, more tee shirts read, 'The Three Terrors: Stalin, Mao and Lenin: World Tour 1917–1979 . . . 1919 Belarus . . . 1924 Uzbekistan . . . 1975 Laos'. There were toy Trabants, Che Guevara socks and a CD entitled, 'Best of Communism 2'. I wondered if, at some point in the future, after the collapse of another tyrannous empire, there'd be parks full of plastic Ronald McDonalds and friends.

Our 42-statue tour over, it was time to set up cricket practice in the car park. Lenin was at cover point; a double iron gate served as stumps.

"Is it one hand, one bounce?" asked Michael and Nick, stopping me mid-run-up. They were the softest Australian coaches ever.

"Yes," I conceded.

Michael was bowled first ball.

"We'll make it a rule you can't be out first ball," I said.

"Was I out? Really?" said Michael. "I haven't got a clue about the rules."

We were soon joined by two more Australians – one, a genetic engineer, whose job it was to make mangoes flower earlier. He bowled useful spin. A coachful of Gaelic-speaking Arizonans then arrived and tried their hand after their tour. They took an instant liking to the game when I pointed out baseball was its bastard offspring.

"Really?" said one. "Man, we gotta start this cricket at home. I like how you can keep batting and batting."

I stood back to take in the scene. Here, under Lenin's gaze, interrupted occasionally by an ambulance, a portable loo and a Trabant driving across the pitch, was the magic of cricket. Sure, it wasn't pure or pretty, but it was drawing the most unlikely bunch together. Even builders on a nearby construction site had put down their tools and were engrossed in the action.

After some crisp, square cuts past Lenin for four, I felt ready to tackle more serious opposition, and believed my coaches had learned something too.

8

THE LOST TRIBE OF MEZICA

Ljubljana Fish Market

I left Budapest with four unpaid parking tickets and an Australian-Québecois called Paul. Raised in Alligator Creek, Paul was heading to China after an ugly break-up with his Montreal girlfriend of four years.

"I don't know anything about Slovenia," he said to me that morning over cornflakes in the hostel. "Fuck . . . is it cheap?"

"Yes."

"Ya still got room in yer car?"

Paul's cricket experience was limited to splattering deadly

cane-toads with a bat as a kid and some knock-arounds in his backyard. He wasn't much of a sportsman, he said. He was a musician and a computer analyst, who wrote tunes for video games.

We reached the Slovenian border and the guards demanded a search of the Škoda. I opened the boot to reveal piles of cricket equipment.

"Ah! Rugby!" said the guards in merriment. "But where are the horses?"

A grisly thought formed in my mind. Was Slovenian cricket a corrupt mix of imperial sports? Was coming to play here a dreadful mistake?

Paul and I began coaching the guards on the border. It amused them, but they still couldn't see how the horses fitted into all of it. Knowing how to grip a bat and play a forward defensive, they waved us on our way.

The drive through Slovenia brought torrential rain. At one point a lightning bolt struck a petrol station 20 feet from us.

"Aaagh! It's like driving through Sydney Harbour!" screamed Paul as rain began dripping onto our shoes. I pulled over.

The skies cleared and we continued past Chinese restaurants and neatly tended hop-fields. We began winding up an alpine valley, where tanned men worked the slopes with scythes.

The blurb I'd read on the Koroška regional website said, "There is a place where time not only stops, but runs backwards. Where worries go on leave. Where only ants know about the afternoon traffic jams near a decayed stump. Where fantasy and reality cooperate in a symbiosis, so that you can learn all about goblins and giants . . . Where primeval eroticism that drove the Prežih's Self-Sown into fatal relations, fights and decisions trickles through".

Where lead trickles into the water, I thought.

"So you've got a cricket match scheduled up here?" asked Paul, doubtingly.

"Yes, I hope so. My contact Borut said something about a game and a picnic this Saturday."

"You know these cricketers?"

"Not exactly. I had a look at Ljubljana CC's website. They've got photos of kids playing cricket here in flares in the '70s. Apparently they're still playing. But I don't have an address, so we have to track them down. How hard can it be?"

"So, you saw a photo of them as, what, 10-year-olds?"

"Yes."

"And how old is this Borut now?"

"About 40."

We entered the town of Mežica (population 3500) at seven o'clock. At two minutes past, we were out of it. There had been no sign of any cricketers; only a pub, a pizzeria, a church and two ski slopes.

"I wonder where they fit a cricket field in a V-shaped valley," said Paul.

I suggested we look for a place to camp before dark. We turned onto a mud track leading through woods and up a mountain. A kilometre on, just below the cloud line, we came to a plateau and parked beside a large white building with kids running around it. I got out and walked towards a group of adults.

"Hi. Do you speak English?" I asked.

A lady stepped forward, sheltering the children behind her. "Yes."

"We've come to play cricket. We're trying to find the Mežican cricketers. Do you know Borut?"

The lady thought for a moment. "No. But I know a man called Fonza. He plays cricket. Go back to town and ask for Fonza."

I returned to the car and we began descending the mountain. Halfway down the track we met a teenage boy and his Alsatian.

"Ask him if he knows Fonza," I said.

Paul wound down his window. "Fonza," he said. "Fonza."

The boy looked confused. "Umm . . . Fonza. Know him, yes, but have address, no." He pointed in the direction of town.

We thanked him and continued downhill. Next, we asked a teenage girl on the path. "Fonza," said Paul. The girl again pointed towards Mežica.

At the pizzeria, Paul and I gained more clues. Fonza ran a bike shop. He had recently moved to a town "many kilometres away".

"How does everyone know this guy?" I asked. "Does he cycle around in a clown suit all day?"

A jogger came past. I caught up with him. "Excuse me. Do you speak English?"

The jogger stopped.

"Yes, a little bit."

"We are looking for Fonza and Borut. Do you know them?" I asked. Paul and I took a step closer. The jogger looked scared. He took a step backwards. I realised how this might appear.

"You tell Fonza we're in town for a few days," I thought of saying heavily.

"We're here to play cricket," I explained, cheerfully.

The jogger's expression relaxed.

"We're trying to find Borut and Fonza."

"I know them!" said the jogger. "They are good friends of mine. I, also, once played cricket. But Borut," he shook his head, "he lives in the capital, Ljubljana now, and Fonza moved his bike shop eight kilometres away. I will call them now." He produced a mobile phone from his pocket.

The jogger turned to us after his conversation. "Fonza says you are a day early . . . "

I looked at Paul and shrugged. I'd never contacted this man in my life.

The jogger continued. "You will drive past the lead mine to the next village, Črna. There, you ask for a man, Dixi, in Črna Mountain Bike Hotel. You will stay with Dixi. Fonza will call Dixi to tell him you are coming. Tomorrow Fonza will come and find you."

*

Fonza was instantly recognisable next afternoon, skipping across a puddle in sandals and Lycra and glancing at the GB number plate. He had a shaved head and the build of an ice climber. He thrust out a hand as he reached us in the doorway of his bike shop.

"We've already found you a new player," I said, as Fonza unlocked the door.

"What?"

"We were just playing at one of the churches and some kids joined in. We taught them how to bowl. They've heard of you. Here, I've got one kid's number."

Fonza took the piece of paper and laughed. "Great," he said. "I already teach cricket in one school. We always look for more players."

Fonza rebooted his computer on the shop counter and opened the Ljubljana Cricket Club website.

"So, my friends. I am busy now," he said, "but I arrange for you to meet Andrej. This is him in 1974." He pointed to the smallest kid in the photos. "He will meet you at the pub in one half-hour. I will come after."

*

Andrej was seven when he began playing cricket, and it wasn't until 2004 that he saw his first game outside of Slovenia, in Bangalore. Now 38 and an engineer designing car seat interiors, he sat with Paul and me in the pub, recounting how he fell in love with the sport.

In 1974, under Tito's reign, Andrej's friend, Borut, went to stay with his pen pal in Birchington, Kent. Borut returned a fortnight later, clutching a bat, six stumps, a leather ball and a copy of *The MCC Laws of Cricket*. Within hours, Mežica's boys, aged seven to thirteen, were playing cricket and claiming spectacular catches on a farmer's meadow.

"We decided to stop playing football for the summer and start Borut's game," recalled Andrej, fondly. "At first we were sceptical, but then Borut told us we were the only cricketers in all of Yugoslavia! He said we were the 'national team'!"

"Who was the best player in those days?"

"At first Borut won every game, but then others caught up. We loved it. We played so late into the evenings we often got in trouble when we went home."

This was not merely backyard cricket. Borut insisted his friends follow every MCC Law. They flattened grass and stole chalk and sawdust to mark out every crease exactly as it was shown in the rule book. They had lbws and allowed no leniency for no balls or crooked bowling actions. Each bye, dot ball and how-out was recorded by the scorer, Fonza. Statistics had been kept to this day.

"In his next trip to England Borut bought some pads," continued Andrej. "We never wore these because it slowed us down."

"What did the wicketkeeper use?" I asked.

"Borut gave him his grandfather's gardening gloves."

The chat and beer soon got Andrej twitching to pick up a bat again. We emptied our glasses and drove uphill to his dad's house.

"We can hit a few balls here," said Andrej, stepping out of the car.

We walked around the back of the lodge and into Andrej's old study. There were 11 home-built PCs in the room, some of whose chipboards were no bigger than Highland Toffees. Andrej had built his first computer at 16, he said, and used it to power a model railway. By 1985, working for the government, he had developed wireless internet across Slovenia.

"You're like a Yugoslavian Bill Gates!" I said.

"It was nothing," he said bashfully.

Andrej crossed the room. "This is my radio," he announced proudly, flicking its switch to demonstrate crackling. "I call all over the world with it: Argentina, Gabon, New Caledonia . . ."

"Do you get cricket scores from it?"

Andrej chuckled. "No."

Andrej dug around in his files and handed me a sheet of paper. "This was one of my English essays from school. It is about cricket. It was such a big part of our lives."

The essay began: "The game of cricket was played in England more than 500 years ago. Although, at that time, it was not the game we now call cricket. Cricket is not played only in England, but also in Mežica . . ."

I read on about the formation of the team. Here was proof of a sociological phenomenon. "We had to train a lot," wrote Andrej, "because this game isn't easy at all. But after three or four weeks we became real 'professionals'."

When I had finished reading, Andrej, Paul and I walked outside out for a practice in the garden. There was a patch of grass, two metres by five, bordered by a steep mountain drop. Andrej took a tennis ball and bowled his loosener.

Although slightly off-balance and unorthodox, his action was legal and produced good tweak. Switching to the left hand for batting, he leg-glanced his first ball down the mountain.

"What's your favourite shot, Andrej?" I asked, after fetching the ball.

Andrej thought about it for a moment, then answered, "Four."

I wanted to hug him.

Tired from all the downhill fetching, we finished our practice and left to meet Fonza for dinner. "It will be my treat," insisted Andrej on the way.

We drove further up the mountain, past farmhouses, wood-sheds and cow fields. At the summit we overlooked the forested valley to Austria. Andrej said there were hobbits in the woods and tales of evil dwarfs in the mines. "They played tricks on the miners," he said, "so the miners left food out to appease them. One of the cricketers who became a miner told me."

"Did leaving out food work?" I asked.

"No, it caused a plague of mice."

Fonza and his pretty blonde girlfriend, Barbara, were waiting inside the restaurant when we arrived. We were the only diners. The waiter ushered us quickly into a small private room.

"I will translate the menu for you," said Andrej as we sat down. "Are you vegetarian?"

I nodded.

"Me too, since meeting my girlfriend," he said bashfully.

"Why are *you* vegetarian?" asked Fonza.

"It's cheap," I said.

"So is Whiskas!"

Andrej placed our orders and soon a waiter arrived bearing cold beers and four litres of wild mushroom soup. While we slurped away on our starter, the conversation steered quickly towards cricket.

The Mežican boys had played for 10 years until national service, girls and university broke them up. "As soon as ski season ended, cricket took over," said Andrej.

"Did you ever win against the other boys?" I asked.

"No. I lost every game, because I was the youngest and smallest. When I batted, they surrounded me. There was no mercy."

Fonza laughed. "Wait! You won once! He beat people twice his age!"

Andrej looked cheered, and returned the compliment. "Fonza has a diploma for winning first place in one tournament," he said.

"Yes, I still keep it on my wall!" said Fonza excitedly.

"He made it himself," quipped Barbara.

We moved onto our fourth bowl of soup. "Were there ever injuries in your games?" I asked.

"Yes!" exclaimed Fonza. "Tomac was hit in the balls!" There was much laughter.

"Ruudi was hit on the head while fielding," recalled Andrej. "He was knocked unconscious. We never told our parents." Andrej looked guilt-stricken.

"But you must ask Borut about all this," said Fonza. "He has all the records."

Happily, 1984 wasn't the end of Mežican cricket. Twenty years after the break-up, an article appeared in a Slovenian newspaper about the country's 'first cricket team', in Ljubljana.

"What happened?" I asked.

"Fonza got mad when he saw it," said Andrej. "We had been playing *long* before Ljubljana. So Borut went to meet them. They were so happy to hear from us! They gave us equipment and asked us to re-form the club. Last year we did, with cricket and a picnic. Nineteen of our original squad came with their families. It was like a band reunion!"

The soup had been taken away, unfinished, and we were eating traditional deep-fried dumplings, breadcrumbs and boiled potatoes.

"Has there ever been any match-fixing in Slovenia?" I asked.

Andrej, unflinching, answered, "Yes, Borut, he arranges this all the time . . ."

My God! Had he just accused the founder and modern-day President of Slovenian Cricket of throwing games?

"Do you mean he fixes *dates*?"

"Yes," said Andrej, unaware of any double meaning. I exhaled in relief.

Towards the end of dinner, stomachs and intestines close to exploding, Barbara asked Paul and me what our plans were for the week.

"On Sunday I've got a match for Ljubljana in Austria," I said. "And Paul and I are hoping to play cricket here on Saturday."

Fonza looked down at the tablecloth. "I have some bad news," he said tentatively. "A match this Saturday is . . . not sure. We do not have a proper ground, you see. We would need a friendly farmer to cut his meadow."

"Do you think we can find a friendly farmer?" I asked.

"I will see," said Fonza, "but it will be difficult."

"And what about the rest of your time?" asked Barbara.

I looked at Paul. "Maybe we could go into a school or something?"

"Good, then I will arrange this. I am school councillor. Call me in the morning."

The kids were munching crisps in the loft when we arrived. It was the last week before the holidays, so discipline was out. Barbara introduced us to the kind-faced Mr Ulci, the school's librarian and English teacher. He had been Borut, Fonza and Andrej's English teacher back in 1974.

"I remember Borut writing cricket diplomas in my class," said Mr Ulci, pronouncing every word slowly and precisely. "I asked him, 'How is it possible that tall Brumen in eighth grade plays against small Andrej Souvent in second grade?' Borut told me that David beats Goliath many times!" Mr Ulci gave a silent laugh.

Barbara addressed the restless 14-year-olds and then turned to Paul and me. "Okay. Now you go," she said, stepping aside and waving us to the front. I felt a cold trickle from my armpit.

Forty kids were staring at us. Paul and I were completely unprepared. The beers consumed yesterday evening at the restaurant had left our mouths dry and sticky.

"Umm . . . well." I cleared my throat. "Paul is from Australia, and I am from Scotland. Does anybody know where those two countries are?"

Silence. I could hear the clock ticking.

After 10 seconds, "Yes," came the mumbled answer, deadpan, followed by more silence.

All right then, I thought. "Which country sits below Scotland?" There were shrugs.

"Wait a second!" I cried. "You just told me you *know* where Scotland is!"

The kids realised they'd been tricked. They ran through the elaborate trap in their minds and smiled, albeit weakly.

"Does anyone know what Scottish people wear?" I asked.

After an eternity, one pupil called out, "A skirt."

"A *SKIRT*!" My voice reached new heights. "D'you wan' a figh', pal?"

The class giggled and Mr Ulci signalled his approval with a thumbs-up from the back.

"Do something in your Scottish accent again," urged Barbara from the wings.

"Shut yer puss or ah'll smash yer heed thrae ten breek walls," I said. The class, believing this meant something naughty, laughed and tried to mimic it.

I turned to Paul. This was gruelling. How we were going to keep it up for a whole class, I couldn't see. My trump card was a cricket speech. I didn't think it would win me many friends here.

Paul proved to be a natural English as a Foreign Language teacher. He began by demonstrating the length of the largest crocodile and then recalled a terrifying face-to-face encounter with a six-foot brown snake.

"Are there any dangerous animals in Slovenia?" he asked.

"Only English teachers," said Mr Ulci, prompting titters.

Paul moved onto a lesson in Mandarin, explaining how a harmless, everyday question, with just a slight alteration in pitch, can mean, "Can I kiss you?" He leaned over and tried to plant one on my lips.

"And you are here to play cricket?" prompted Mr Ulci, as startled as me by the kiss.

"Yes," I said. "Does anyone know what cricket is?"

More than half the kids raised their arms. Five of them played in school. But none of them knew of anywhere, other than Mežica, where cricket was played.

At this pleasing reaction I produced my bat and pads. The school's star player was volunteered to step forward and dress up for a demonstration.

Paul and I then put questions to the floor. Again, the silence was murderous. Eventually, after a poke in the ribs from Barbara, a girl squeaked, "Is Nessie the Loch Ness monster real?"

I had prepared for this one. Paul nodded at me, confirming this was my field.

"I think Nessie is a ghost," I said.

The pupils and Mr Ulci slapped their foreheads.

Paul and I were relieved men at the end of 50 minutes. Perhaps the class was too. If I'd been a smoker I'd have smoked two packs.

We walked in the sunshine to the pub. Andrej was waiting for us there. "How was it?" he asked.

"Well, the star player's forward defensive was a bit wonky," I said, "but Mr Ulci says 'hi'."

"Oh, good old Mr Ulci," said Andrej. "He loved our stories about cricket in school."

Andrej drove us to the famous '70s cricket ground. No longer a farmer's meadow, it was now chalky scrubland beside a six-storey block of flats and an agricultural shop.

We stood for five minutes where the wicket had been, the chime of a bicycle bell the only disturbance in the breeze. I pictured Borut, surrounded by his clergy, reading aloud passages from *The MCC Laws of Cricket*. I thought of the hours of meticulous pitch preparation before each game, and the desperate search for the ball among the grass while batsmen racked up singles.

"The farmer used to watch us playing from over there," said Andrej with some sadness.

"And when we hit the ball into the vegetable plot over there . . .", he pointed, " . . . we used to stop the game and steal tomatoes."

After another minute Andrej turned to me, looking puzzled. "Who else plays cricket in the world?"

"Australia does . . ." I began.

"Really?" he said, hands on hips. "Australia plays cricket." He shook his head and smiled. "That is surprising."

"Oh, they'd say the same about you."

*

Paul and I departed from Mežica when it became clear there was no friendly farmer willing to scythe his meadow. We drove over the gravel mountain tracks to Austria, carrying with us alarming rumours of cricket links to arms dealing, which would soon need to be addressed.

We reached Velden, a lakeshore holiday town where you could buy a curried schnitzel, see the World in Miniature and the Museum of Torture, then go dancing in the Swingers Club. Many cricketers had partied here in their whites over the years. Velden was the site of Central Europe's most exciting sixes tournament, scheduled for the following weekend.

In the morning Paul and I left our lakeside hostel for the match. The pitch was a 10-minute drive down empty back roads, beside a cornfield and a four-storey hotel.

"Everyone *must* be there by 9.45 a.m.," Ljubljana CC's fixture secretary had stressed to me on the phone, "otherwise we forfeit the game." The Austrian League was as strict a competition as I'd ever played in.

At 10.05 a.m. Paul and I were the only souls at the ground. "What d'ya reckon, Paul, d'you think there's another ground?"

"What did the Slovenes say about it?"

"They said it was in front of a hotel – like we have here – that there were 360° Alpine mountain views – which we can see. They mentioned a cornfield, a net, and that it was in Velden. God, look, there's even an artificial wicket. I just wonder if Velden has two grounds!"

We went into the hotel and I telephoned Slovenia.

"No, there's no problem," assured my friendly English contact back in the capital. "The players will be along shortly."

When we returned to the field Paul and I found two large men inspecting the wicket. "Fuck, couldn't be a better day for it," said one in an Aussie accent.

"Mate, looks like there's been a sacrificial ceremony with a chook," said the other. "Look at all the feathers."

Paul and I walked over and introduced ourselves. "We thought you might be playing at another ground," I said.

"Mate, you won't find another cricket pitch within a hundred clicks of here."

The opposition arrived. They were called Five Continents, but every player was from India. They wore India's World Cup strips with their names on the back.

More cars arrived on the field, spilling players and kit. "Come on, guys! Hurry up!" called Ljubljana's pony-tailed skipper Mark. "You not in yer whites yet?"

Aussie Mark was Slovenia's most prolific run-scorer. He'd struck a century against the Czech Republic, against whom he'd also taken 7 for 31. Like former Yugoslav President Tito, he lived in a mansion by Lake Bled. I approached him and offered a new ball.

"Cheers. By the way, yer mate's playing too." He pointed at Paul. "We're one short."

Paul looked like he'd been struck in the balls without a box, and yet found it strangely pleasurable.

"You're an Aussie. You play cricket, right?" said Mark.

"Err . . . in the backyard at Gran's. I've never faced a real ball."

"Well, that's more than most of our team. You're in."

Ljubljana CC was formed in 1997 by a group of expat translators. Their first game was against The Hague inside an athletics stadium, with a sandpit and a discus cage to negotiate. Even the Slovene president turned out to watch. Security wouldn't let him pad up, as they deemed it too dangerous.

Now Velden was effectively Ljubljana's home ground. The Slovenes paid around £20 to travel north for each game.

"It's 'cos of all the 'illegals'," muttered one Aussie player. "They can't get visas for Slovenia."

Captain Mark led us onto the pitch for fielding drills. "Last week was terrible, guys! Catches cost us the game. I don't wanna see *any* drops!" Due to its drops, Ljubljana was currently sitting last out of 13 in the league, faltering behind Pakistan, Sri Lanka and Lord's CCs.

Mark hit the first ball up. Slovenia's lacrosse captain bounded forward and dropped it.

"Fuck's sake! I can't make 'em any easier!" yelled Mark. Then I noticed the fielder's wrist was in plaster.

Five Continents' opening batsmen began walking out to the wicket – still in their India World Cup strips. We concluded our warm-up with three windmill twirls of the arms and readied ourselves for a 100-over battle.

Captain Mark called over from the cars by the boundary. "Could the new guys come over here?"

"Captain wants a blow-job," cracked a teammate, preparing to field in his underpants. Paul and I scurried across.

"Okay, guys. So we can all look like a team, take one of these each," said Mark, handing us Jaguar-sponsored club caps. "It'll cost ya 1500 Slovenian tolars each. Let's go."

Fixture secretary Brad was given the new ball for Ljubljana. A touring Kent team once described him in their newsletter as "a wild-looking man with a glass eye who bowled quick off the wrong foot like Mike Proctor".

"It's not glass," said Brad, as I tossed him the ball from mid-off. "It's lazy. I broke the nerve while playing football."

Brad used his injury compensation cheque not to go to India for the 1996 Cricket World Cup, as was his dream, but to come to Slovenia and join a girl he'd met six years before in a Peckham squat. He played his first game of cricket for Ljubljana. But he was no novice. Brad was a paceman who would have succeeded at the heights of grade cricket. Soon, he had the Austrian openers leaping about the crease, while his "HOWZATs?" echoed around the Alps.

At the start of the second over, the umpire's mobile phone rang in mid-delivery. "No ball!" called the umpire, stretching out his arm.

"Why?" asked the Aussie bowler.

"You didn't tell me what you were going to bowl." I'd never heard of such a rule.

"Next time I'll phone ya," replied the bowler, turning back to his mark.

When fag break came at 20 overs, Ljubljana CC was facing a gruelling chase in the afternoon heat. Five Continents' batsmen, despite swinging and missing three times an over, looked unmovable. They'd raced to over 100 for the loss of 2 wickets.

We collapsed under a large parasol at the edge of the field. "Fuck me!" everyone sighed.

While sunscreen was being reapplied and sweaty socks changed, my teammates revealed some frightening truths about Austrian cricket. Two players in another team, they said, were jailed for robbing, raping and murdering a prostitute.

"The one guy did it, then told on his mate, so they both went down for it," said Brad.

"Jesus Christ!" I exclaimed.

"Then there was that guy convicted of a bomb plot a few years back, remember that?" he continued. "Ironically, he was a member of the United Nations team."

These were clear breaches of the MCC's code of conduct.

"What about the run-out?" asked another player. It prompted "ooohs" and sickened expressions all round.

The previous season a batsman was run out by two metres. His umpiring teammate declared, "Not out." A massive brawl ensued on-field, before tempers settled and the game resumed. But when the teams came to shake hands at the end, one player produced a broken bat handle from behind his back and chopped off an opponent's thumb. It took a rescue helicopter and five hours' surgery to reattach it.

"The police were called. The case went to court. Both players were banned for life," said Brad. "The Austrian authorities are now reconsidering letting the victim play again, which is the least they can do."

The police had launched a crackdown on Austrian cricketers since these court cases, I was told, and many players now had to carry photo-IDs with them. The *Kronen Zeitung*, Austria's biggest-selling tabloid, even published a full-page colour cartoon of cricketers beating each other.

Back on-field, Ljubljana resumed in the worst possible manner, spilling two catches in succession. The first was a diving effort by our keeper. The second was a dolly at mid-off by me. The batsman drove it straight at me and I palmed it to the turf. My chin sank. Even the guy with a broken wrist was fielding better.

"Aaaagh! If I had a gun . . . " screamed captain Mark on the other side of the wicket.

I watched helplessly as the next four balls were slapped for 6, 6, 4 and 6.

But then the Slovenes showed how it was done, holding onto two swirling chances by the boundary. Five Continents suffered a mini-collapse, losing 3 wickets for 7 runs. Our spirits were lifted, and we eventually bundled them out for 245. It was a doable target, given our fearless Aussie line-up.

Captain Mark had forgiven me enough to let me open the batting with him in reply.

"Good luck, fellas," said Brad, as we walked to the wicket. "Don't come back as our newest duck-on-debut member."

Twenty of Ljubljana CC's squad had scored zero on debut. One player was out first ball of a game, first match of the season, in his first outing for the club. "That's in a category of its own," Brad said.

I took my guard and tried to get Julie Andrews's singing out of my head. I could see peasants scything on the hillsides. The Austro-Indian seamer raced in and unleashed a bananaball outswinger. It nicked the edge of my blade, and I turned to see the wicketkeeper claim the catch. But the ball flew between him and first slip, squandering my chance of joining Slovenia's most prestigious club.

The Austro-Indians bickered constantly throughout our innings, despite being on top. Every flick of the pad prompted them to run around in circles, celebrating. Added to their screeches was the din of an air-raid siren, followed by three fire engines racing along the boundary. "That's strange, we had a fire in that same spot last week," said Brad when he joined me at the wicket on 72 for 4.

On 38, my stumps were flattened by a brutal Amrit inswinger. Ljubljana was in some trouble at 78 for 8. Paul was fretting over how to stop his box slipping down his trouser leg when I crossed the boundary.

"You're up, mate," I said when I heard the clatter of more stumps.

Paul looked like he'd vomit as he marched out, but in the middle he seemed set for 100. He confidently punched his second ball past mid-off for 2. Alas, his partner was clean bowled next over, leaving him 98 short. We had lost our last 7 wickets for

9 runs and the game by a whopping 164. Five Continents huddled on-field for a ring-a-ring-o'-roses victory dance.

"Shit!" sighed Ljubljana's players, before packing up and crossing the Alps.

*

Two days later, I was sitting with fast bowler Brad in the office of his Ljubljana English school. *Dr Who* books and European Cricket Council DVDs were piled high on the desk. There was a poster of *Braveheart* on the wall.

"'Škoda' means 'what a pity', or 'damage', in Slovene," said Brad, leaning back in his chair and chuckling.

Raised in Canberra, Brad was one of the few people who could claim to have been tucked into bed by a drunken Australian prime minister. "My dad ran a hotel. I was five years old when Bob Hawke stumbled in to say goodnight."

Now 38 and a Slovene through marriage, he devoted much of his time to promoting Slovene cricket. He and his club colleagues were building an army of cricketers. They had coached more than 600 kids and, after much lobbying, secured cricket as part of Ljubljana's school curriculum.

"It's hard in a way," he said. "You're trying to push yourself out of the team."

Brad had seen some unusual things on the cricket field over the years, including a Czech player taking a piss at slip during a game. The Czech had then slept under the covers that night. But nothing was stranger, he believed, than what he'd witnessed in Milan.

"I saw this guy retire from batting because of sledging from his own team. He left the wicket and drove home."

Brad suggested a tour of Ljubljana's club website, which he updated in his spare hours. On the opening page we read a passage from *Cricket* by AG Steel and The Right Honourable Alfred Lyttelton:

> A cricketer should live a regular life and abstain at table from all things likely to interfere with his digestion and wind. Above all else, smoky rooms should be avoided. A small room, filled with ten or more men smoking as if their very existence depended on the amount of tobacco consumed, soon gets a trifle foggy, and the man who remains there for long will find next morning on wakening that his head feels much heavier than normal and his eyes are reddish and sore. A captain should never hesitate to speak to his team on these matters should he think a warning or rebuke necessary.

Brad and I laughed as we read on.

> The necessity of moderation in drink is happily a thing few cricketers need to be reminded of. There are many opinions as to what is the best drink for men when actually playing. By best we mean that which does least harm to the eye. In hot weather something must be drunk, the question is what? Our experience is that beer and stout are both too heady and heavy, gin and ginger beer are too sticky and sweet to the palate, ouzo is alright if playing in Corfu. In our opinion, shandy-gaff, sherry, or claret and soda are the most thirst-quenching, the lightest and the cleanest to the palate. In a long innings the heat and dust are apt to make the mouth very dry and parched and a clean drink is especially desirable.

AG Steel had been one of England's finest all-rounders. In 1884 he scored the first Test century at Lord's, against Australia. Teammate and co-author Alfred Lyttelton took 4 for 8 in a spell at the Oval Test, bowling underarm lobs with his wicketkeeping pads on.

"You'd wanna take their advice," said Brad. "Though you might get beaten up for drinking shandy-gaff."

Brad clicked on 'Player Profiles' and his grin widened.

Ljubljana CC, when it wasn't recruiting from the refugee centre an hour before play, was made up of superstars. One Slovene, a Jew called Kristian Killer, had appeared on the Religious Special of *Who Wants to Be a Millionaire?*

"He's the only player never to score a run, yet never to be dismissed," said Brad.

Borut, the father of Yugoslav cricket, had also featured on *Who Wants to Be a Millionaire?* – twice.

"The second time he phoned us up," said Brad. "'Didn't I do well?' he asked. 'Yes, Borut . . . You won five million.' 'No!' he said. 'But I mentioned cricket in the first five seconds!'"

Brad clicked on more player profiles. "You know the reality TV show *The Bachelor*? Our guy, Damir Alidžanovič, was Slovenia's bachelor. When the cameras turned up to film him in our match in Switzerland, someone smashed one of our fast bowlers in the face. The cameras filmed him with blood dripping down his chin. They asked, 'So, is cricket a dangerous sport?' The Swiss team had three dentists in their side, so they stitched him up."

"How did Damir do on *The Bachelor*?" I asked.

"He's still with the winning girl, though he hasn't played cricket since."

Another Slovene cricketer once supported James Brown in concert in Maribor.

"He bowled with his left arm and fielded with his right," said Brad. "He was a vegetarian for seven years, and broke it with a steak, which he sent back for being 'overcooked'. For the first dance with my wife at my wedding, he sang, 'Everybody's Got Something to Hide Except Me and My Tapeworm.'"

Brad opened more profiles. "Oh, look, there's David Gum – another duck-on-debut. He refused to bat with gloves."

Brad continued, "This was interesting. We had a poll whether Mladen Rudonja, a striker in the Slovene football team, would ever score. In over 50 appearances he never had. Ninety-nine per cent of voters said, 'No'; three per cent said, 'Yes'. He scored the next week against Romania to put Slovenia in the World Cup. He became Sports Personality of the Year. We made a public apology and awarded him life-long membership of the club."

Word of the Slovenes' superstar status had travelled far. Each day Brad received emails from Pakistani cricketers wanting to come and play professionally in Slovenia.

"We got an autograph request from a 14-year-old in Chicopee, Massachusetts, yesterday," he revealed proudly.

Brad clicked on the club record pages. "Let's see if there's something here. Statistics can be funny."

A kebab vendor had the astonishing career bowling statistics of 0.1 overs, 0 maidens, 0 wickets, 8 runs.

"How's that possible?" I asked.

"He bowled four wides in a row, then the batsman hit the first legal delivery for four to win the game. He never bowled again . . .

"Aw, this brought tears to our eyes," continued Brad. "This was the club's ninth wicket record and the highest score by a Slovenian. This guy, Urban Blaznik, was right-handed for seven years, then changed to left-handed. He scored 18 against Bulgaria, putting on 41 with Borut. To see two Slovenes do that on the cricket field made all our efforts worthwhile."

I left to return to my hostel and get ready for evening nets. As I walked past Ljubljana's yellow train station, clouds from a Tim Burton film gathered above, and wind began whipping grit into my face. Forked lightning flashed all around and I bolted.

Back in my hostel, I cowered on my bed. The building was a converted prison beside a methadone clinic (you never stray far from home). Behind was an artists' squatter commune. Lightning struck the roof, and in the same moment our cell door split from its frame and fell to the floor.

To calm my fears, I chatted with my cellmate. She was an Australian astrologer without a surname. She showed me her passport to prove it. She, too, had a ghost shadowing her, she said, but this one took possession of her body and altered her face.

Great-uncle Ivor'd better not get any ideas, I thought.

After the storm I left to meet more of Saturday's teammates. We gathered at a terraced restaurant inside a concealed cobbled courtyard. Service was slow. We'd been waiting an hour and a half for a menu.

"This is nothing," said one English teammate. "In Slovenia they practise Slo(w) food. A meal is spread over six hours."

I asked about the cricket club's difficulties breaking into Slovene culture. Alasdair, an English teacher from Essex who ran the club for many years, slapped his forehead.

"When we tried to import a cricket set," he said, "customs impounded it, claiming it 'threatened the integral industry of manufacturing in Slovenia'. We were allowed to re-export it to any EU country without charge. So we sent it to Austria, drove over the border, picked it up, dirtied it by the roadside, and drove it back to Slovenia."

It took the club four years to secure its second pitch, within the grounds of a psychiatric hospital. Licence to use the field came just three days before Slovenia began hosting the European Championships.

"A guy from the ECC had flown out to build the wicket," explained Alasdair. "We had to keep him distracted because we didn't have the ground."

After slide shows and briefings, a panel of doctors turned down the club's application for a second time.

"The only alternative was a field of molehills, not attended to in 20 years," said Alasdair. "Luxembourg and Finland were flying out! Bulgaria and Switzerland were on the train! We brought Ljubljana's deputy mayor to the ground on his motorbike. He phoned the prime minister and the minister of health. They wrote to the hospital, who loaned us the field for a week's trial."

Slovenia's cricketers were so afraid someone would steal their bed-sheet sightscreens in the night that they got a player to camp out in his car. At one in the morning, a stranger knocked on his window and held up a photograph. "This is the man I murdered," he said.

Three days into the tournament, Alasdair spotted a doctor watching from the boundary. "What do you think of it?" he asked.

"I think it's good," said the doctor.

"So why did you turn down our application twice?"

"We were worried about the horses."

Weaker men might have buckled under Slovene bureaucracy, or at the prospect of playing within the grounds of a mental hospital. Patients regularly wandered onto the pitch mid-over, saying, 'I'm Che Guevara!' The locals looked on from their flats, believing the men in whites to be inmates.

"I have to ask," I said, readying myself for a testing question. "I've heard rumours about links to . . . weapons trading. What's the story?"

The whole affair turned out to be harmless. Links to the cricket club were both distant and innocent. It had happened during the break-up of Yugoslavia, when the Slovene government believed Serbia would launch a chemical attack. The government ordered three million gas masks for a population of two million, "in case some didn't work". The war only lasted ten days and the gas masks weren't required. The government then decided they didn't have to pay for them.

"They're still sitting in a warehouse on the coast," said Alasdair. "There's a dispute over who owns them. The guy who ordered them was picked up by Interpol in Vienna, but the case was flung out of an Austrian court. He then left for better cricketing shores."

"That's awful!" I said. "Imagine fulfilling an order for three million cricket balls and not being paid for them."

That night, from the artists' commune behind my hostel, it sounded as though virginal sacrifices were taking place in the midst of a tam-tam rave. In Slovenia it was traditional for men to be crucified on their stag nights. I believed that, too, was taking place en masse.

I rose in the morning with barely two hours' sleep and prepared to meet more Mežican cricketers. The first was the team's overseas player, who happened to be a Scotsman called Angus with a brother called Douglas.

Angus was an Edinburgh puppeteer, film-maker and playwright. He arrived at my hostel by bicycle, wearing a brown leather waistcoat and a kid's bright orange schoolbag. As promised on the phone, he didn't sound very Scottish. He suggested we make our way to the old town. He pedalled while I walked alongside.

Ljubljana was laid-back in the morning sun. Hippies slept in trees, drunks on benches. A policeman leaned against a wall, attempting a crossword. He nodded as we passed.

Angus took me through the vibrantly coloured old town, pointing out the hilltop castle and the triple stone bridge over the Ljubljanica. It was rumoured Jason and the Argonauts sailed down this canal-like river after nicking the golden fleece.

Estonia wear whites to hide in the field – a former Soviet missile factory, Tallinn.

"Keep your eye on the ball."
National coach Page is hit
on the head in Prague.

The supporters go mad – Roma cricket fans, Hajske, Slovakia.

Slovakia A – Stalin back right.

Slovakia B – Vladimir front row, second from the right.

"Yes, but we are old and we have herpes." The babushkas of Hajske.

My first international fifty.

A Slovak feels the effect of plum brandy at the drinks break.

Ljubljana CC, Brad on the far right – in Velden, Austria.

Team Yugoslavia, circa 1974. Borut pictured centre, Fonza second from the left, Andrej second from the right.

Borut and me, Šmarna Gora, Slovenia.

Luke and Hudson in the Adriatic – Zadar, Croatia.

Winemaker Oliver and Scouser Tom at the dockside nets – Island of Vis, Croatia.

The Serbian Olympic Cricket Team – Milos front row, second from the right.

Bulgarian CC celebrate victory over the Medical Students, Sofia, Bulgaria – Saif third from the right.

Romanians discuss the first day at the Test, Transylvania.

"Take that, Mr Mubashir" – an inter-continental 6 from Europe to Asia.

A small weed problem on the Gomel pitch, Belarus.

From the bridge we descended the steps to the fish market, built into the bank. Instead of carp, 'krap' sat in the trays.

"I feel hungry," said Angus.

Over lunch in the next-door café, I asked Angus how he got into puppetry.

"I met a Slovene puppeteer in Edinburgh," he said, "then moved out to Ljubljana."

"You had nothing to do with puppetry before then?"

"I had only contempt for it."

Angus told me things about puppets I never knew. "It's a very dark art," he revealed. "It's not for children. You're manipulating figures. The puppet is a universal traveller. It can fly in many dimensions. It can fly in space."

I chewed my lettuce leaves while I thought about this. Angus looked over the river and told me about his tours. He'd taken puppet shows to Burkina Faso, Venezuela and Pakistan.

"The show in Burkina Faso was a front," he said. "It was the only way we could shoot a film without the bureaucracy. I wanted to film a gold mine where the workers were all on amphetamines."

Angus's film, *The Ring* – not the Japanese and Hollywood blockbusters – was a good film, about humanity and a circular journey, and it had scooped major awards. It took him to Bosnian death camps, after which he lost the ability to play piano.

"How did you meet Borut and get into cricket?"

"We needed a doctor for our trips. Borut was recommended. He taught me how to bowl using his medical bag for stumps. After that I joined the Mežicans. You know their slogan is 'Every Millimetre Counts'?"

Angus smiled. "Cricket saved me at a difficult time in my life. We have a lot of fun when we're playing. The Mežicans' practice ground has a stream running through it. It's on the border, which means hook shots land in Austria. Borut is friends with the border guard, so it's okay."

After a pause Angus added, "Are you meeting Borut? He's very keen to see you."

"I'm seeing him in 15 minutes."

Borut picked me up in his battered Peugeot on the Dragon Bridge. No longer was his hair long and blond like in his '70s photo, nor was he wearing a tight yellow tee shirt and flares. He had dark hair, a beard, glasses and an enormous grin. At the age of 44, he was now one of Slovenia's top cardiologists and had lost none of his passion for cricket. He knew every rule in the game, and was the first man in Slovenia to pass an umpiring test.

"When I met the Ljubljana players for the first time," he said, laughing as he drove, "there was two feet of snow on the ground. I asked if we could still play!"

Borut motored at lethal speeds towards Ljubljana's outskirts, swerving to avoid cyclists. He had arranged to hike up Šmarna Gora with his cousin Golob. As he recounted the history of Mežican cricket, I felt I was in the company of an extraordinary Yugoslavian.

"It started when I went to stay with my pen pal in Birchington," he began. "His dad, Mr Charles Nash, the coalman, was the single-wicket champion of the village. He taught me the rules. I knew my friends in Mežica would like cricket, so I bought all the equipment, and a friend gave me a copy of *The MCC Laws of Cricket*. When I got to Slovenian customs, the guards told me I would not succeed in developing a sport like this. Their words spurred me on!"

Borut punched the air triumphantly.

"We started single-wicket tournaments, naming them 'The Yugoslav Championships'. When somebody won, I told him he was the best cricket player in *all of Yugoslavia*! I gave him a cup. Unfortunately, it didn't have engravings."

"Did you ever play team games?" I asked.

"Only once. I *insisted* we play for the records. My team scored 119, the second team scored 14!"

Borut and I laughed.

Borut spent his evenings and English lessons throughout the '70s and early '80s crafting winners' certificates and scoresheets on his dad's typewriter. No one could accuse him of slacking on stats. He was the junior maths champion of the whole Koroška.

"Even today there are only a few spots in our records where the how-out, name-of-catcher, or number-of-balls-faced are missing."

We zipped out of Ljubljana and neared the tree-covered, twin-peaked Šmarna Gora. Borut parked on a grassy plot at the hill's foot. "This is where I will be building a house," he said. "Puppeteer Angus is designing it."

Borut's elder cousin Golob arrived with mountaineering poles, and we set off through the trees. Leaves crunched underfoot and damp patches rapidly formed on our tee shirts. Borut continued his story. Every one of the Mežicans batted left-handed, he said, because that was how he showed them back in '74.

"When something happened and we didn't know what it was," he said, "we all sat down in the meadow and looked at the MCC law book. My friends sometimes accused me of making rules up in my favour!"

The boys had many disasters to overcome in their decade of cricket. The farmer on whose meadow they played was killed when his tractor rolled down the hill.

"He used to watch all our games," recalled Borut fondly. "We were very sad, so we decided to play on in his honour. We renamed our tournament after him!"

Borut kept extending games later into the evenings. Sometimes the team celebrated afterwards by eating sausages and slugging cider with another farmer. They got beatings when they returned home.

"Once I managed to gather all the best players for a match," said Borut. "The batting order was arranged according to rankings from previous tournaments. It was to be the game of the decade ..."

Disastrously, the sole bat snapped mid-over. It looked like the end of cricket in Yugoslavia. But scorecards were kept, and Borut happened to have a friend over the border in Austria with a bat. He borrowed it, and the tournament resumed weeks later.

"Though I never returned the bat," confessed Borut, grinning cheekily.

"What happened when Ruudi was knocked unconscious?" I asked.

Borut stopped and stretched out his arms. "It was amazing! He was knocked on the head, but he still managed to hold onto the catch!"

In another setback for the Mežicans, the ball's seam came undone. But one boy's father, a sofa repairman, was able to sew it back together.

Borut, Golob and I continued clambering over tree roots, pausing every five minutes to regain our breath and locate the trail. My colleagues were relishing the workout. They were the fittest over-forties in all of Yugoslavia.

After half an hour we reached Šmarna Gora's plateau. "You see over there?" Borut pointed across the green plains to the Julian Alps. "That's Ljubljana's home ground."

We plopped down on a bench beside a walled church and a restaurant packed with pilgrims. Borut poured water from his flask and Golob left to explore the views. After we had downed three cups each, I asked Borut about his twin appearances on *Who Wants to Be a Millionaire?*

"The first time I got to the eighth question and lost a lot," he said sadly. "The second time I got to the fourteenth question and won five million!"

"What went wrong first time?"

"It was the presenter's fault! The question was about the hill in Laško. 'Was it Kum or Hum?' I said, 'Hum' five times. The presenter kept asking, 'Is it so? Is it so?' I thought he was trying to tell me, so I chose Kum. I lost 100,000 tolars!"

"How did you get to be on the show twice?"

"In Slovenia, we are such a small country you can go on again next season."

I asked if any other Slovene cricketers, apart from the Jewish Kristian Killer, had starred on *Who Wants to Be a Millionaire?*

"You met Fonza. His brother – a chimney sweep, and one of our original team – he was on it."

During our descent I asked Borut about Mežica's comeback match after a 20-year lay-off.

"It was strange wearing pads for the first time. We were badly beaten by Velden. They scored 206 for 5, then bowled us out for 25."

Borut grinned. "However, in our next game we beat Poland. We scored 75 for 1 in 6 overs, and bowled them out for 10!"

Poland seemed like nice people from their emails, but from the stories I was hearing – and I mean no disrespect by this – they sounded like a pushover.

Time was being whittled away on my trip. I was almost at the end of Slovenia without a run in the country. Next I had Croatia. Who knew what weaponry their bowling attack possessed? If every other innings on this tour failed, however,

I marked out the Poles – my final match in just over a month's time – as a safe bet for that 100.

Ljubljana CC versus Five Continents CC

Velden CC, Velden, Austria

19.06.2005 (50-over match, 11-a-side)

Result: Five Continents CC won by 164 runs

Toss won by: Five Continents CC

Umpire: Sony. Scorer: Parmjit

Weather conditions: Shining Super

Five Continents CC		R
S Kaul	c Eve b Halford	12
Parmjit Singh	lbw Furness	14
Satnam Singh	c Crawford b Archer	52
Vipin Sharma*	c Halford b Archer	38
Angrej Singh	c Halford b Donchi	5
N Sharma	c Donchi b Bell	38
S Chopra	b Eve	21
J Singh	c Eve b Oman	18
Amritpal	c Furness b Bell	9
A Lamba	st Crawford b Bell	4
Vikram Singh	not out	0
Extras	(b1 lb6 w24 nb3)	34
Total	**(all out, 43.4 overs)**	**245**

FoW: 21–1, 71–2, 132–3, 139–4, 139–5, 200–6, 210–7, 224–8, 241–9, 245–10

Bowling	O	M	R	W
Eve	7	1	40	1
Halford	10	0	52	1
Oman	6	0	27	1
Furness	7	0	49	1
Archer	7	0	29	2
Donchi	4	1	25	1
Bell	4.4	0	25	3

Ljubljana CC		R
Angus Bell	b Amrit	38
Mark Oman*	b Vipin	4
Rob Crawford+	lbw Amrit	0
Tom Furness	c Chopra b Amrit	10
Darren Halford	b Angrej	1
Brad Eve	c Chopra b Vipin	1
Steve Fish	b Amrit	0
David Archer	b Angrej	0
Ian Donchi	b Angrej	0
Jason Abbot	lbw Vipin	0
Paul Theriault	not out	2
Extras	(b1 lb3 w19 nb2)	25
Total	**(all out, 22.4 overs)**	**81**

FoW: 15–1, 20–2, 51–3, 72–4, 75–5, 75–6, 77–7, 78–8, 78–9, 81–10

Bowling	O	M	R	W
Amrit	10	0	42	4
Vipin	9	3	19	3
Angrej	3.4	0	19	3

SLOBODNA DALMACIJA

Split ● petak 1. srpnja 2005. ● cijena 6 kn

ZADNJA STRANA

ANGUS BELL POSLUŠAO SAVJET KANADSKOG VIDOVNJAKA I DOPUTOVAO U HRVATSKU

Škotski publicist piše o viškim kriketašima

SPLIT – Kanadski vidovnjak poslao je mladog škotskog spisatelja između ostaloga u Hrvatsku kako bi kompletirao svoju knjigu o kriketu. Dvadeset četverogodišnji **Angus Bell** iz mjesta Coulters na jugu Škotske u tolu je zemlju doputovao prije svega zbog viških kriketaša koji mu se savršeno uklapaju u ideju o širenju ovoga sporta u zajednice gdje to se ne najmanje očekivalo...

Vidovnjak po imenu Marley Monti u Montrealu mi je kazao kako se bih trebao ostati živjeti u Kanadi gdje negdje dovršim posao koji uključuje puno putovanja i pisanja. Prije toga nisam vjerovao u vidovnjake, no vjerujem ni danas, ali neke čudne stvari mi su se počele događati otkako sam odlučio poslušati Marleya Montija – kazao nam je Angus Bell na propu-

"Preko interneta sam dogovo- ro stanovljenje kriket kluba "Sir William Houte" na Visu i odlučio ih staviti u knjigu", kaže Angus Bell

tovanju kroz Split. Odlučio je, veli, smislili način kako poslušati savjet vidovnjaka, a ispri saidadžit to na svojim planovima. Kao spisatelj i zaljubljenik u kriket odlučio je napisati popistujasn knjigu o kriketu u zemljama koje njegvo nemaju tradiciju ovoga sporta. Obišao je stoga već Estoniju, Njemaćku, Mađarsku, Sloveniju, Slovačku,

atomsljenje kriket kluba "Sir William Houte" na Visu i odlučio ih staviti u knjigu. Odigrat ću s njohtu s njimu partiju i odlujeli im nešto opre- me kao znak dobre volje – pojasnio je Angus Bell. Dodao je kako mu se je den od čudnih stvari koje mu je vidov- njak Marley Monti predskšao dogodila na sa početke puta u Estoniji.

Kanadski vidovnjak Škotu je naja- vio da će mu ključnu figuru na putu biti izvjesni Jason.

– Čim sam došao na prvo odredište puta koji sam sam namislio, čovjek koji me dočekao u lokalnom estonskog kri- ket klubu zvao se – Jason! Nisam mo- gao vjerovati, jer vidovnjak uopće nije spominjao kriket i ja ni sam u to vrije- me nisam planirao knjigu o kriketu. A onda, Jason uopće nije estonsko ime – i dalje su čudi Angus Bell. U Hrvatskoj mu se još nšto čudno nije dogodilo, nšm što kaže da je odlučeljen čudnova- tu prvlačnošću logičkom naše obale...

Po okončanju putovanja "kriketa- skim bespučima", Angus Bell kaže ka- ko ga uikakav vidovnjak neće više odgo- voriti od toga da na nastani u Montrea- le, jer ga tamo čeka djevojka.

Ivo ŠČEPANOVIĆ

The back page of the *Slobodna Dalmacija*, Croatia, July 1, 2005

I was standing in the nets, preparing for my first ball in Croatia. I rummaged around in my shorts, ensuring my box was in place, and performed a ritual dance to get the blood racing. It was imperative I used this session to iron out Velden's flaws. Tour temperatures were rising, and I would have to learn to cope with the increased levels of sweat if I was to succeed. Here was the perfect opportunity: a flat track on a still day and some medium-pace net filler. I could play myself in for two overs, and then cut loose. As the bowlers tired and resorted to spin, maybe I'd even bring out my reverse sweep.

The bowler ran in off five paces and sent a ball spearing into my kidney. I doubled over and sucked in breath.

"Welcome, Angus!" said Mick – 'The Tiger' – jokingly in the background, like a true Australian. I rubbed my wound until it turned purple.

Zagreb's nets were angled at 15°, making me look like a tall man and an easy target for a bowler. Beyond the twin cages lay the circular ground, dotted with molehills, and surrounded by trees and apartment blocks. In the centre sat an artificial wicket, scorched by teenage campfires. A gas pipe ran under it and poked out at cover point. I wondered how Croatia got facilities like these, when top clubs in Scotland couldn't manage.

"We got the pitch from Austria," said Mick, in his red shorts and blue singlet, sitting down for a fag. "It took six of us to carry it. We stuck it through the car window. The PE Faculty donated the field, and the club's aristocratic sponsor bought us a lawn-mower and flattened the soil."

Mick, like the majority of Zagreb's cricketers, was a third-generation Croat who grew up in Australia.

"We spoke Croatian at home, attended Croatian church, played for Croatian football teams and learnt folkloric dancing," explained his elder brother Ivan.

Most of the players moved to Croatia with the collapse of communism. Many came to fight in the Balkan War.

Mick explained he arrived as a volunteer, aged 17, without prior military training. He became a section commander in the Tigrovi Infantry – hence the nickname 'The Tiger' – with 30 soldiers under him. Now, like many ex-servicemen, he faced the tough task of finding alternative work.

"None of us played a cricket match until coming to Croatia," said Mick. "One of the guys heard about cricket in Ljubljana in

1998, so we decided to form a rival club. At first we bowled six or seven wides an over."

Now, as my kidney would testify, Zagreb's pace attack was one of Central and Eastern Europe's fiercest and finest.

Together with a second set of brothers, who flew from New Zealand for every match, Ivan and Mick had helped to form a national team. Croatia stormed the previous year's European Championships 5–0.

"Our next tournament's in Belgium in August," said Ivan. "We've gotta raise 10,000 euros for it. The Vujnovic brothers – our captain and vice-captain – are coordinating the team and fund-raising from Auckland."

Zagreb CC hadn't experienced the same success as the national team. "We lost every game in the Austrian league for two years," said Mick, taking a long draw on his cigarette. "Sometimes we'd drive all the way to Vienna and the other team wouldn't be there. Eventually we pulled out."

Austria proved an expensive playground for Croatia's cricketers. Besides the £27 it cost each player every game, they faced a whopping 800 Deutschmark fine after beating Slovenia there in 2000.

"We went to Hooters after winning on the tournament's last ball," said Mick, grinning. "We were on our way back at four in the morning – very vocal, you know. There were some arguments with police, who called for reinforcements. Our reserve wicketkeeper and his brother were arrested and charged. We were all emptying our pockets on the street."

Mick laughed. "But it was great beating Slovenia."

The only other crisis to hit Croatian cricket was over the translation of the MCC laws. 'Bowl' was translated as 'throw', which meant they were short of a verb. No one was sure whether 'cricket' as an adjective should take the same ending as tennis, 'cricketski', or as football, 'criketni'. The debate went all the way up to senior university linguists.

"I hope we've helped you out a little bit," said Ivan as we finished nets and said our goodbyes.

I felt Ivan and Mick's passion for cricket and competitive Aussie streak had better prepared me to continue my trip.

"At least you'll know now to get out of the way of a ball directed at your kidneys!" laughed Mick.

That night I ran around the Zagreb hostel looking for passengers. Within minutes of knocking on dormitory and toilet-cubicle doors, I had backpackers tearing up train tickets. Welsh-Italian Luke from Tonypandy and Boston-born Hudson would join me.

We set off southwards next morning and I pumped my passengers for information. Luke was 19, worked in his family's café and had two cousins called Mario and Luigi. He would be returning shortly to study music technology at university in the mining valleys. Asked to describe himself, he said, "Well, people often say I look like Sylvester Stallone in *Rocky*, except I have a lazy eye."

Hudson explained he once drove four hours for a burger, but when he got to the joint it was closed. He'd started backpacking at the age of 15 down under. Since then he'd been subjected daily, like many US backpackers, to criticism over the US administration's foreign policy.

"The latest was yesterday," he said. "This guy shouted at me in the street in Zagreb. He said, 'FUCK YOU, GEORGE BUSH!' and stuck up his finger. The ironic thing is he was wearing a Florida Flames shirt."

I was happy to be travelling with this unlikely pair, although one of them was a criminal. Hudson, three months short of his twenty-first birthday, had been arrested and charged on suspicion of drinking *a* beer.

"It was at a house party. The cops came and said I was guilty by association. I decided to fight it. I was summoned to court. I said, 'This is ridiculous. I'm gonna change the system.'"

The case went to trial.

"It dragged on for a year. I had to make five court appearances. I had to fly home from backpacking in Europe. There was a 12-person jury – all old people. I tried to pick surfer dudes, who'd take my side, but they were all denied.

"One guy kept nodding off during proceedings. I asked my lawyer to declare a mistrial, but it wouldn't have worked. The judge had his head in his hands the whole time. The case took so long because we had to get two policemen to show up and testify, at a cost of $300 a day."

"How did they testify?"

"I was surprised. I thought they'd lie on cross-examination, but they kinda took my side. One said he'd smelled alcohol on some people, but not particularly on me."

Hudson went out for lunch while the jury deliberated. The trial ended when a jury member stood up and said, "We, the jury, find the defendant Hudson Turbity guilty of being a minor in possession of alcohol". The case cost the courts $5,000.

"The judge sentenced me with a $50 fine."

If his trial had been in Croatia, it would have taken significantly longer. Croatia has a backlog of one million cases for a population of four and a half million.

Our drive towards the Dalmatian coast gave us use of the virgin A1 motorway, opened that morning. Police cars and motorbikes were stationed every three kilometres, urging cars to accelerate with a wave of their walkie-talkie aerials. At the tollbooths staff tore up our tickets without charge.

I asked Luke about life in Tonypandy.

"Tell him the story about Uncle Gino," prompted Hudson.

Luke's Uncle Gino was the only man ever to try and pick a fight with Henry Cooper – the first boxer to knock down Muhammad Ali.

"One night he was escaping from the police," said Luke. "He drove through his closed garage door, switched off the lights, and got away with it.

"Uncle Gino's a pigeon-racer," continued Luke. "He was on holiday in Venice and saw a pigeon on a bench. He grabbed it and smuggled it onto the plane for the flight back. When he was on board, the bird started cooing. The stewardess and passengers looked over. So my uncle started making cooing noises himself. It worked and he got it home."

"Was the pigeon a success?" I asked.

"No. It had some disease. Within a week all his pigeons were dead apart from that one."

By late afternoon we had crossed the Velebit Ranges and reached Zadar on the shimmering Adriatic. The city had been built by the Romans, the Venetians, the Hapsburgs, then nearly destroyed by Serb rockets in 1991. Shrapnel marks were still visible in the outskirts. Weather-beaten women sat on deckchairs, touting single rooms in their homes. Men jogged past wearing Speedos. We rounded the bastille peninsula and parked outside the youth hostel.

We entered reception.

"Do you know a guy called Hansel who used to work here?" I asked at the desk.

The receptionist shook his head.

"His girlfriend's name was Gretel," I continued, "and he speaks six languages."

Hudson and Luke sniggered.

"Ah, yes!" cried the receptionist. "Ivica and Marica – the Croatian Hansel and Gretel. Yes! He will be here later. How do you know him?"

"My brother and I stayed here three years ago," I said. "Hansel offered to show us the front line, but we ran out of time at the beach. I've come back to say hello and take up his offer."

"You came back for that? Yes, now you mention it I remember him saying he was swimming with some foreigners a while ago. But he had a white car, yes?"

This I wasn't sure about. I thought we'd established it was Hansel. Now doubt was cast. Could there be two Hansels working at this hostel, both of whom spoke six languages and had girlfriends called Gretel, but only one of whom drove a white car?

"He used to leap off rocks into the sea," I said. "In Speedos."

"Yes, this is the one!" said the receptionist, nodding triumphantly. "He is on a bus from Rijeka right now with Gretel! He is late for work. He will be here at six."

Hudson, Luke and I checked in and shed our clothes. We set out for the pebbly beach, passing a house covered in crude slogans. It belonged to a carpenter claiming the Guinness World Record for the most calluses.

"Man, this place is great," said Hudson, jumping into the sea. "I can't believe there are no tourists. I'm gonna learn Croatian and buy five houses here. And you say they play cricket? This I gotta see."

"There's no cricket in Zadar," I said, apologetically. "It's further down the coast."

At six o'clock we returned to the hostel to find Ivica (Hansel).

"How is Gretel?" I asked.

"Great. Everything is great," he said, smiling. "Though I am in trouble for being late for work. So, you have come back to see the front line? I will take you tomorrow, but now I must work."

*

Ivica upheld his three-year promise next morning. We drove out of town, past fields of parched grass and a giant Spar supermarket.

"How come Spar's just a corner shop in Wales and here they get a whole hypermarket?" asked Luke.

Ivica's stories of Zadar and the war were poles apart from our cosy lives in the West. His hostel, like every hotel in the city, was filled with refugees during the conflicts.

"On the front line south of Zagreb," said Ivica, "Croat soldiers were being shelled every day, but no one could understand where the firing was coming from. Then one day a soldier noticed an old farmer in no man's land. The farmer was bending down to feed his pig. Each time he bent down, he was secretly loading a cannon."

Ivica signalled I should turn, and we pulled onto an empty country lane. Across the fields on our right stood Zadar's city walls, encompassed by the Adriatic; beyond the valley on our left rose the green Velebit Ranges.

"Whoa! How much would it cost to build here?" asked Hudson.

"Not very much," said Ivica sadly. "The whole area is abandoned."

Soon, the houses on either side of the road became empty, fractured shells. Scrap metal and concrete poked from the tall grass. Occasionally we saw a sign with a skull and crossbones. Fifty yards parallel to us, a headscarved peasant was leading a herd of scrawny sheep.

"She must know a safe route," said Ivica. "We should be okay if we stick to asphalt."

The damage worsened with each village. We passed an abandoned school, pockmarked with bullets, its doors blown off and its roof collapsing.

Finally, the asphalt gave way to mud and gravel.

"Stop!" ordered Ivica, unnecessarily. This was one road I wasn't taking my Škoda down. But there was nowhere to turn.

"Crap," said Hudson.

I reversed a kilometre before making a tentative 14-point turn.

Hudson, Luke and I left Zadar that afternoon and continued down the coast, passing some of the 1185 submerged mountain-top islands. By evening we had entered Split, Croatia's second largest city and home to the country's strongest baseball and bobsleigh teams.

On my first visit to Split, three years earlier, I arrived with my brother long after midnight. It wasn't the ideal time for finding accommodation. We parked the Škoda in a lightless enclosure outside the high Byzantine walls, and slept in the front seats. In the morning we awoke to discover a sea mine, an anti-aircraft gun and a shell cannon 12 feet in front of the windscreen. Worse, when I stepped out, I found 60 used condoms within a closer proximity.

There was no possibility of Hudson, Luke and I doing the same thing this time. Large cricket boxes filled the back seats, and the weapons enclosure, I noted as we drove past, was now a construction site. As Luke and Hudson would be kipping on a ferry floor the next night, bound for Italy, we trawled the ghetto suburbs in search of a cheap hotel, and crashed out, dreaming of war.

A cheeky-looking man with a receding hairline was waiting as I descended the hotel steps next morning. Ivo was a journalist, tipped off by the British Embassy. He was the famous hack who broke all those stories like: 'Sex-Crazed Donkey Banished to

Remote Island for Having Sex up to Sixteen Times a Day'; 'The Russian Dog That Talks'; and – my personal favourite – 'Dog Shoots Man'.

He stretched out a hand. "Welcome to Split. My car's just around the corner. I'll take you for coffee."

Ivo was no name-dropper, I should point out, but he had interviewed folk like Gerry Adams, U2 and the cast of *Baywatch*. He had featured David Copperfield and the Three Tenors, separately. Recently he'd interviewed John McEnroe and John Malkovich, while years before he'd spoken to Daryl Hannah, Naomi Campbell and Sam Fox.

And now me. I felt hopelessly out of my depth.

"You ever met the Dalai Lama?" I asked, as he sped through Split's suburbs.

"Three years ago. Here, actually."

"Yeah, I saw him too," I said. "I was disappointed. I wanted him to walk on blades, break sticks over his head and fly. He just talked about nuclear weapons being bad, which I'd figured out myself."

Ivo scrunched his forehead, then nodded, giving me the benefit of the doubt. He stopped his car to honk at a friend passing on the street. The driver behind was happy to wait for this, because he too knew Ivo.

"I was almost killed in my interview yesterday," said Ivo merrily, as we abandoned his car at the edge of the old town. "I arranged to meet this guy in a pizzeria. He turned up and said we *must* go elsewhere! I said, 'Hey! We're here now. Relax. Let's do it here.' He said no, we have to go! So we left. Ten minutes later the pizzeria blew up . . . Everyone thought it was terrorism. Customers were running around, screaming, with blood on their heads."

"Was it terrorism?"

"No. It was a gas leak."

We rounded the corner and came across the scene. Blood was spattered on the polished marble streets. The restaurant door frames were splayed and charred.

"No one was badly injured," added Ivo.

We picked our way along the palm-studded harbour, then through narrow alleys and cavernous, barrel-vaulted cellars. We reached Emperor Diocletian's retirement palace, decorated with pilfered Egyptian sphinxes and pillars.

Ivo and I padded across courtyards, under washing strung between Roman pillars. At every café NBA basketballers, footballers, actors, presidents, famous writers and musicians turned to wave to Ivo.

"Why are all these celebrities here?"

Ivo shrugged. "This is Split."

The Splits were a tall race, which explained their success at basketball and why urinals were mounted so high up on the walls. I had to balance on tiptoe to relieve myself when we stopped at a café.

Over coffee in the sunshine, while swallows dipped overhead, I asked Ivo about his journalistic adventures.

He'd covered eight Eurovision Song Contests, Miss World in India and the 1998 Oscars. In South Africa he was roughed up by Whitney Houston's bodyguards.

"I was arrested in Kosovo during the war," said Ivo coolly. "The Serb police took me to a cemetery and opened some graves."

"Were you scared?"

"No, they were just messing with me."

Ivo scratched his forehead. "The only time I was slightly scared was in Albania. I got trapped there for a month after the first democratic elections. I came in on a trading ship. When I tried to go back, customs told me, 'You never entered, you can't leave'. I had to get an apartment."

"How did you get out?"

"I was smuggled out on a ship of sick refugees sailing for Italy."

Ivo was like a real-life Tintin. "What about these crazy articles you write?" I asked.

"People phone me every day with this stuff. Just recently a car salesman set fire to his boss for not paying him. Then there was the man from Rijeka who came up with the ultimate fair-play tennis invention – one side of the court is clay, the other grass."

Over the next espresso, Ivo recounted his story about the world's luckiest man, from northern Croatia. "He survived a train crash, three major car accidents and a plane crash. He said he was trying to seduce the stewardess at the time, and they were the only survivors.

"He was born two hours out to sea. His father cut his umbilical cord with a knife and dipped him in the water. The hospital said it was a miracle he was alive. Now he's living in an old people's home. He's just won a million euros on the lottery."

"Have you ever done any . . . " I paused for effect, "*psychic* stories?"

Ivo pouted his lips. "Yes. There was a Bulgarian psychic in Split who said she could diagnose any illness at a glance. I teased her about the football scores."

I drew enough comfort from this to spill my psychic story. Ivo looked troubled at first, but soon came round when he saw the evidence.

"And you came to play cricket in Croatia because of this?"

"Yes. Did you know there was cricket in Croatia?"

Ivo nodded. "I have played it myself."

*

I left all that I couldn't carry in Ivo's garage and abandoned the Škoda outside my hotel. My next action would take place off the mainland.

The ferry across the Adriatic took two and a half hours, during which time an old man paraded the deck in lime-green Y-fronts, resting his hands on the backs of others' chairs. To my relief, he didn't reach my seat before the ferry entered Vis Island's horseshoe bay.

Terraced vineyards scrabbled up the hillsides and a peninsula jutted out with a Franciscan monastery on it. The tiny town of Vis looked more suited to lobster fishing, or even skiing, than cricket.

The ferry docked and I stepped off, carrying my rucksack, my bat and a large box of cricket equipment. After a quick call on a payphone at the port, my host arrived in a thunderous blue van.

"Hello, hello, Angus!" said Oliver, racing around from the driver's side in his sandals and shorts, smiling through his goatee. "Angus Young, AC/DC!"

I shook my head.

Oliver was a famous winemaker and the man responsible for starting the island's cricket team. "We don't have terrorists, but this is a terrorist van," he said. "Excuse the tomatoes."

Oliver slid open his van door and rearranged the boxes of veg, beer crates and olive-oil barrels. "Delivery for my restaurant," he explained. "I've just got to drop my son off."

There was little need for seat belts, said Oliver, as we swung around the narrow hillside bends, because there was never any traffic on the island. "The only thing you have to watch for is hedgehogs."

After depositing his young son, we crossed the hill, dropped into a valley and arrived at Oliver's isolated family restaurant. Wooden shutters covered the farmhouse windows and grapevines crept over the dining terrace. Oliver led me past two guests and sat me at a picnic table. He took out a match and lit his outdoor oven.

"I started a cricket club; I didn't know how to play cricket. I started a restaurant; I didn't know how to cook," he said between blowing onto the coals.

Oliver jogged to the fridge and swiftly returned, uncorking one of his finest dry whites. While we took large swigs, he recounted the history of cricket on the island.

The Sir William Hoste Kriket Klub formed in 2003, but it was not the earliest example of the game here. Cricket was introduced to Vis two centuries before, during the Napoleonic Wars, to stop British sailors raping and pillaging.

"I found a letter in Tom Pocock's book, *Remember Nelson*," said Oliver, "from Sir William Hoste – the naval captain in charge here. I'll show you."

Oliver led me from the picnic table to a low-beamed, musty cellar in the farmhouse. Above an ancient wine barrel hung a framed print of Sir William Hoste. "His family in England sent it to me when they heard about our team. Here, look at the book."

Oliver located the letter. "We have established a cricket club at this wretched place," Sir William Hoste wrote to his mum, "and when we do get anchored for a few hours, it passes away an hour very well. Teddy is the head of the party."

"Funny, eh?" said Oliver. "He made his brother Ned captain. I thought it would be good for tourism if I did the same. Start a cricket team, I mean. You can play all year round here."

Cricket's resurrection on the island was not complete without another catalyst. A *Playboy* article sparked the revival.

Oliver passed me the now-famous copy. It contained a three-page travel feature on his restaurant and hotel.

"This issue had particularly great girls," joked my host. "Rebecca from England in the centrefold . . . You'll see I mentioned restarting a cricket club. Rob, the co-founder of Zagreb CC, came across a copy and called to say he would help. You'll meet him tomorrow."

We returned to the warm evening air and began chopping carrots for Oliver's monkfish special. He refilled the wine glasses and talked about the make-up of his team.

"We have three winemakers, four high-school kids, a dentist, a diver, a PE teacher, a translator and a fisherman. There's also a man who moved here from Liverpool when he heard about the cricket. He's our only spinner . . . Mostly, we have woodchoppers – I mean our style of batting."

"Who do you play against?"

"A team of air traffic controllers in Split. We played them a few weeks ago. It's big rivalry."

Of all things, the air traffic controllers discussed cricket between landing and take-off.

Oliver had never seen a bat until the ICC sent out a coach, even though his club had been running for several months.

"I told my friends, 'Come on! The coach is coming. Don't embarrass me!' Fifteen of us gathered in the school gym. We played like kids of 10."

The islanders' first proper game was in a handball court against the Saumur Strays. The Strays are a team from the Loire Valley in France, run by another winemaker and chaired by Sir Mick Jagger. They are famous for playing in obscure locations. On this occasion they left their vineyards and rode the train overnight to be the first cricket team touring Vis.

"No one wanted to face the first ball on the island for 200 years," said Oliver. "They were too jittery. So I grabbed a bat and marched out. I was clean bowled first ball."

Vis were dismissed for 15 and the Strays easily knocked up 16 for 1. The local paper, in its innocence, reported that Vis came tantalisingly close, losing by just one point. The game was the first item on the national news that evening, and soon Croatia's most famous rap band, The Beat Fleet, began singing about the island's cricketers. They revered them in the same light as the mainland's bobsledders.

Oliver said, "The players had never played a football game before, but now they had played cricket. 'It's better than football,' say the kids. Now we have 50 of them."

"*No one* plays football?"

"There's no ground. The only other competitive sports are Italian lawn bowls and chess. In the past the islanders played donkey polo, but you won't see many donkeys now."

In the morning, still bouncing off Oliver's apartment walls from a night on his fortified wine, I adjusted my pace to island life. Like every resident in view, I donned flip-flops and padded around the harbour front, resting occasionally in palm-thatched cafés.

Dogs slept on doorsteps and gangs of schoolkids played at shooting each other with laser-sighted BB machine-guns. Doors were left unlocked and keys remained in car ignitions. At the garage, waves lapped beside the petrol pumps. Every 10 minutes a solitary three-wheeler van, or state Zastava, puttered past.

I walked over to the palm-rimmed peninsula with its monastery, still run by monks. The peninsula was the island's original cricket pitch. Oliver's dream was to reclaim it, but it was currently protected ground. The remains of a Greek theatre were said to lie beneath.

As the shops closed between noon and five, I plodded over to collect some beers for the empty beach. While I stood in the newsagent's, something on the stands caught my eye. On the back page of the *Slobodna Dalmacija* was my photo. I was playing a backward defensive stroke and wearing my backpack. The headline read, 'Škotski publicist piše o viškim kriketašima. ANGUS BELL POSLUŠAO SAVJET KANADSKOG VIDOVN-JAKA I DOPUTOVAO U HRVATSKU'.

What the hell does that mean? I bought a copy. Ivo's name was on the byline. He had done well. I hoped that with the backing of the Balkan press my route to book publication would be easier.

I telephoned Zagreb CC's co-founder Rob from the port's payphone. Rob was a translator and media analyst. Perhaps he could shed light on this newspaper article. "Where are you?" I asked.

"I'm waving at ya right now," replied Rob in a heavy Australian accent.

I turned and saw a tanned, stocky figure in a red MCC polo shirt. He was waving from 20 yards away, a mobile phone pressed against one ear.

"Rob, is that you?" I said into the mouthpiece.

"Yeah, mate," Rob replied, and the figure continued to wave. I hung up and approached to shake hands.

"We've just been reading about you in the paper," chuckled Rob. "You're a celebrity! They announced your arrival on the island radio this morning. And my landlady phoned me yesterday saying she saw someone coming off the ferry with a cricket bat."

There was nowhere to hide on Vis.

I followed Rob back to his table in the pub. The only spinner, Tom from Liverpool, was there as well. The waitress whispered across, and Rob nodded. "She just asked, 'Is that him?'" said Rob.

Rob produced his copy of the paper. "What does the headline say?" I asked.

"It says, 'Angus Bell listened to the advice of Canadian fortune-teller – or *psychic* –" Rob frowned, "and arrived in Croatia. Scottish publicist – or writer – writes about cricketers on island Vis'. What is this business with a fortune-teller, anyway?"

"He told me I was going to write a book and that it'd soon be my job to travel," I said.

"And what are the chances of this book *actually* getting published?"

"Well, the psychic said it would happen."

"Oh, *the psychic* said it would happen!" Rob threw up his arms and shook his head. He ordered a round of beer.

"There's been a few writers come to Vis," said Liverpudlian spinner Tom. "Evelyn Waugh came here and said Tito looked like a lesbian dressed as a man. Tito wasn't happy."

"And Bill Bryson was here too," I said.

Rob put down his pint and leaned forward in his chair. "I tried to write to Bill Bryson about that! He said he came here as a teenager, backpacking! I tried to write to him and get my money back. Vis was a closed military island till 1989! Bryson was talking about meeting Swedish girls and going to casinos. He and his mate couldn't find the girls for the rest of the week 'cos they were staying in another hotel. There's not even two hotels here now! I figured if he made that up, what about the rest of the book? If it'd been Brač or Hvar, fair enough – not Vis."

As the rounds flowed, I asked Rob if there were any unusual Croatian cricket stories.

"When London Welsh came to Zagreb on their rugby tour," he said, "they stopped off to play a game of cricket. The next day they came to me, full of pride, announcing, 'We christened your wicket in the night!' They had a bloody orgy on there! I told them, 'I'm not happy about that! I built that pitch!' They could've done it anywhere!"

After a pause I asked, "Is it true some Croatian cricketers fought in the war?"

"Half the bloody team!"

"No one wanted to talk about it," I said.

"Nah, they wouldn't."

"Did you fight in the war?"

"Yeah."

"Can I ask where?"

Rob looked tense. "It's not important."

I decided to drop the subject.

"Has Croatia ever played Serbia at cricket?"

Rob wafted his arms again and spoke animatedly. "Oh, the ECC had some idea about that a few years ago. They thought cricket was this great thing that would build bridges. They wanted to arrange a friendly match in Zagreb. I said, 'No way! We've just been fighting a war against them!'

"You can quote me on this. I told them, 'If Croatia *ever* hosts a Serbian team, I will resign!' Either we'd win the game, or it'd never finish."

He added, "I told the ECC, 'I'm not gonna spend money on police protection. I don't want the Serbian flag flown in Croatia!' I would put an end to an entire tournament rather than host them. It's like Palestine playing in bloody Israel! But that's just my opinion. When you go to Serbia, ask them what they think about coming to Croatia to play cricket."

After all the talk and another round of pints, we agreed it was time for nets. We left the pub and walked uphill to meet rival winemaker Antonio.

Antonio was a product of Vis cricket. He played with the Aussie and Kiwi Croats in the national team and was guardian of

Vis's equipment. We found him in his cellars inside the old military-base tunnels. It looked like a Bond villain's lair, filled with oak barrels and stainless steel wine tanks.

Antonio greeted us and sat us down at a long oak table. He uncorked a vintage rosé and pointed at a chest of drawers in the corner. It was the Croatian cricket trophy cabinet. On top stood a bat and a helmet; between the empty wine bottles sat a jar containing an apple in methylated spirits. It had been bitten into by the Kiwi-Croatian captain, explained Antonio.

Two bottles drained, Antonio scooped up his pads and drove us round the bay in his truck to nets. Oliver was called, and joined us on a rare break from his restaurant.

Vis's net was a rusted dockside cage, sandwiched between a warehouse and the Adriatic. Fishermen repaired boats at mid-on. Pallets, tools and rusty pipes cluttered the cage's interior. Rob laid a green carpet on the concrete and pinned it down with rocks.

The islanders were gifted athletes. As they were used to higher alcohol percentages in their wine, their bowling actions remained smooth and pacy even after the afternoon's refreshments. I couldn't compete. Half my deliveries flew 10 feet over the cage and landed in a giant cactus at backstop. "Don't worry. The snakes and scorpions aren't poisonous here," Oliver assured me as I poked underneath for the ball.

The other half of my deliveries were confidently driven past the fishermen, into the Adriatic.

"Now there's something you don't see every day in Scottish cricket," said Oliver. "Did you know a cricket ball floats?"

*

Before the departure of the ferry on my final morning, Oliver promised to show me the cricket ground. "We're looking for another one," he said. "Maybe we'll build in my fields. But there's debate over where it should go; whether it should be closer to one person's place or another's."

"You need a solution like Canberra," I said. "When the Aussies couldn't choose between Sydney and Melbourne for their capital, they built Canberra."

Oliver, who was born in Australia, appreciated this and started his terrorist van.

The Vis ground lay in a steep-sided valley, within an abandoned military base. The barrack building/pavilion walls were graffitied and every window was broken.

Oliver led me onto the field. "It's too small, as you can see. And we're all too busy with work at the moment to play, so we haven't cut it. You should come back in winter when we've less work and we'll play a proper game. We play cricket all the time then."

The wicket was a concrete helicopter landing pad with head-high fennel plants poking through its cracks. "It's still the official landing pad on the island for emergencies," said Oliver. "It's great if there are injuries in a game."

Beside the ground, over the high boundary ridge, was an ex-minefield. Oliver assured me it had been cleared, initially by letting 50 goats loose on it. But if a six was hit in that direction, no one went to fetch it.

"D'you think you'll ever get the peninsula as a ground?" I asked.

"Who knows? It would be perfect. As people sail in, they see cricket."

After a pause Oliver added, "We do have another cricket ground . . . But it's in south-west England. An oil trader who holidays here every year bought an estate with a cricket field. He said, 'I've got a ground, but no team. You've got a team, but no ground. Come and play.'"

Oliver and I laughed, then climbed back into his van and thundered along the roads to the port.

*

Back on the mainland, four days till my next cricket game, I found the drive to Dubrovnik a lonely and dangerous one. The single-lane road hugged the sheer cliff-line and Polish motorists overtook on every bend. All four windows were opened fully, yet the Škoda was like a solar-powered sauna. I thought about steering into the Adriatic, or checking into one of the many nudist camps and shedding my shorts.

Croatia's southern tip was cut off by 23 kilometres of Bosnian coastline. There were no checks at this border, but still Croatia planned to build a bridge bypassing the slim section. It would cost 250–300 million euros. I thought it strange that these countries, after years of blowing each other up for independence, were now set on joining the EU and eventually scrapping border controls.

As I wound south, I thought about how I could find a passenger. It was a pressing concern. I would shortly be entering territory into which I'd never taken my car; more dangerous territory, with crumblier road surfaces and Cyrillic (кириллический – that's Cyrillic in Cyrillic) road signs. I required a Russian map-reader who could change a tyre; a man with contacts to appease Mafia and corrupt policemen.

Last time on this Dalmatian trail my brother and I carried two passengers. The first was Dylan, a Harvard graduate who earned $200,000 a year and lived in a Santa Cruz warehouse with

10 hippies. He was on his way to Mount Olympus when we offered him a ride. His plan was to meditate on its summit until he believed in Greek gods. He looked like Adam Sandler, except for a lazy eye.

The second hitchhiker was San Diego Scott. After dabbling unsuccessfully in the film industry, he was urgently looking for a wife. Most of his research so far had been on Brač Island hookers.

"I figure if I don't get lucky in Croatia, I'm gonna bleach my hair and head to the love parade in Berlin," he vowed, lowering his voice to the very pits at the end of each sentence.

San Diego Scott was the sweatiest man I'd ever met. Even when eating ice cream in the shade, his nose dripped. "I'm gonna make you guys a spicy goulash when we get to Dubrovnik," he promised in return for the lift. I had visions of the oven heat and spice causing him to sweat into the dish.

The four of us found a letting agent when we reached Dubrovnik. Our agent was a leathery-faced old man with teeth like a mouthful of tic tacs. He promised us a prime apartment overlooking the beach. "All the lovely ladies, they will want hot, hot sex with you in this apartment," he said. He knew how to sell it. "Come. I show you landlord. He happy for you to bring ladies back and make sex *all* night."

The agent led us down some steps to the landlord's villa. The landlord looked like a pale Jabba the Hutt and was standing on his porch, watering plants. He was naked but for enormous white Y-fronts. I'd never seen a woman with breasts as large. Either spray from his watering can or sweat from his butt cheeks had caused his Y-fronts to turn see-through. He lumbered across and shook our hands.

"Hot sex!" said our agent, arms outstretched, smiling. The landlord let out an asthmatic cackle and the deal was sealed.

*

As I entered Dubrovnik now, passing the majestic old walls and skirting back round to the residential Lapad peninsula, I spotted my former letting agent on the street. There he was, miraculously, the same but for a new set of teeth. Business was going well.

"Heeeey!" I said, stepping out of the car.

He looked baffled.

"We met three years ago! Me, my brother and a guy who looked like Adam Sandler. You promised us hot, hot sex!"

"Ah, I recognise car!" said the agent, nodding vigorously. "You want room again?"

"Please – but no sex."

The agent made some phone calls and my new landlady arrived by car. I followed her to her home in the Škoda. She got me to reverse the last 500 metres, the wrong way down a busy one-way street.

"You nice . . . boy," she said, clapping my cheek as we walked up her garden path. She opened her front door to reveal an entire stairwell of religious icons.

"I pray for you," she said, running a hand through my hair.

When I'd said no sex, the agent had sent me to a nun.

I felt reborn after a shower and set off on a bus to the old town. From there I caught a ferry out to tiny Lokrum island. As the boat puttered out past the walls, I took in the full view of fortress Dubrovnik. The new red roof tiles within it told a story.

I was surveying the hill behind the city when a young man leaned over. "I was 10 when my aunt phoned and said the Serb army was coming," he said. "That night the Serb army marched to the top of the hill." He pointed to the right-hand peak. "They started shelling our city."

"Where was the Croatian army?"

"They went to the other side of the hill and fired at the Serbs. It was a three-way battle."

"Did you leave?"

"There was nowhere we could go. I had to run to school under gunfire every day. It went on for nine months."

Dubrovnik had been given the Team America treatment by the Serb army in 1991 and 1992. It was a miracle the city had been restored to its previous splendour.

When the boat docked on the island, I set off down a pathway among pine trees, keeping ahead of the other tourists.

Soon the path opened out onto a craggy beach. I removed my top and was getting ready for a dip when I spotted something strange 30 yards away. On a large grey rock, two naked old men were snogging. A short distance from them, a second couple were buggering in public view.

"What the . . . ?"

I turned to see the boat tourists nearing on the path. Some were stripping off and applying sunscreen. This had all the makings of another orgy.

I looked to the trees and ran into them. I chanced upon a trail of used hankies and torn condom packets.

"In the name of God!" I cried. There hadn't been a single mention of this in the guidebook.

I raced through the pines and returned in haste to the dock, where I waited for my boat back to the mainland.

That evening I went for another cheap pizza vegetariana. My liver was now hurting from more than a month on this diet. Avoiding the tourist haunts, I inadvertently crashed an

11-year-old girl's birthday party. Balloons floated in the corner and banners on the wall read, 'The Party Is Here!'

I sat like an outcast, looking on enviously. It was the loneliest I'd been all trip. I'd covered 3000 miles, through nine countries, and had another 5000 miles to go. I'd cut grass in the Czech Republic, discussed herpes with Slovak babushkas, and survived a shoplifting scare in Tesco. And there was no one but a ghost to share it with. Poor Candy was six time zones away. A dad noticed me looking glum and brought me over a slice of cake.

"It's more fun," he said.

I felt cheered after some sugar, and then confused when the group sang 'Happy Birthday' in English.

The party ended and I walked in the warm, still evening to the old city walls. A gang of scooter riders had gathered to watch a Hare Krishna concert at the gate. The Hare Krishnas were stuck on their two lyrics. "Hare, Hare Krishna. Hare, Hare Krishna. Hare, Hare . . . " they sang.

Maybe I should join them, I thought. As I reached the front of the crowd, the Hares stood up and set off on a musical lap of the walls.

I walked through the Pile Gate onto the polished marble promenade. Throngs of middle-aged British honeymooners were canoodling by the fountain and under monastery doorways. I could take no more and sought refuge in an Irish pub.

I sat with a pint of Guinness, surrounded by five silent, cuddling couples. I resigned myself to the fact that I'd be moving on without a passenger.

I started to drink quickly and turned to watch the TV. It flicked onto Somerset versus Warwickshire at Twenty20.

Out of the toilet door stumbled the pub drunk. He staggered over. "Blah, blah, hoy's de ferm?" he asked in Dublin-speak, placing a hand on my shoulder.

"What?"

"De ferm?"

"I'm sorry. What?"

"De *FERM*! Jesus!"

I stood up to move tables.

"Oh, you mean the *farm*?" I said. "It's great."

The drunk slumped down in my place and faced the TV. He tipped his Guinness towards the screen. "I wouldn't miss de cricket fer de world," he slurred.

I stopped and sat down again. Something about that last bit made me feel great. All was well with the world when a Dubliner could come to Dubrovnik safe in the knowledge he can catch the cricket. We were mates now, albeit ones who struggled to understand each other.

"Erm, by any chance are you looking for a lift?" I asked.

10

ON THE TRAIL OF TORVILL AND DEAN

The plan was to drive north through Montenegro, a region that vanished off my map and guidebook, and into Serbia. In the absence of youth hostels, I would have to camp in mountainous villages, or knock on farm doors at midnight. But Ivo's warnings had rattled me. The people of northern Montenegro were called Rolling Stones, because so many of them drove off cliffs. The road surfaces were single-lane tracks over perilous mountains. Trucks took up 80 per cent of the road, and you could bury a dead dog in the potholes. It was also the world's capital for stealing cars.

Ivo had gone to Montenegro to report on a man who had married and divorced three sisters. He said 14 people had surrounded his car, and the man who had married three sisters pulled a gun. He offered to shoot two men for Ivo.

"It'll take you at least two days to cross," Ivo told me. "As soon as you stop people will take everything and maybe shoot you, then drop you in a ditch."

I decided, therefore, to make only a day trip to Montenegro and take my chances driving through Bosnia again.

There was plenty of potential for cricket fields, I saw as I entered Montenegro. But the patchy football fields, on which goats grazed, soon gave way to folded limestone mountains and sea. Sandwiched between these were smudged buildings and the occasional boat broken down on the hard shoulder. I followed a juice and egg lorry past a fortress and then a string of second-hand tyre shops. The road surface meant they were doing a busy trade.

I reached the magnificent Bay of Kotor, one of the deepest fjords in Europe. It looked like Glencoe with swimming, and for three euros a car ferry whisked me to the far bank. Montenegro was using the euro – not by invitation, but because they liked it more than their own currency.

On the far side, I first-geared through medieval fishing villages. Every house had a harbour instead of a garage. At one point a bus met me head on, blocking the narrow track. I supposed it could go into the water, but the driver found an alternative route, tearing into the side of a parked Mercedes. The driver continued on without worry, although a section of his bus was left at the scene. Already I'd witnessed some of the dangers Ivo had talked about and this was merely Montenegro's holiday region. At Kotor's citadel I turned around and headed back to Dubrovnik.

There were 11 emails in my inbox when I returned, many of them titled, 'Psychic Cricket'. Ivo's story had travelled further than the Balkans. CBC Radio in Canada wanted an interview, as did CapeTalk in South Africa and BBC London. This was out of control. My heart fluttered. I pencilled down the details and went to phone one radio station from the post office.

Back at the landlady's villa, my prayers had been answered.

"I put boy in your room," she said, pinching my cheeks again. "Maybe, *maybe* he go with you. Ask him. Ask him quick!"

I opened my bedroom door. A curly-haired bloke with a chin stud hastily stubbed out a cigarette. "Hello!" he said.

Ian was an English-Guatemalan-Lebanese, raised in Chile then sent to English boarding school. "The only thing it taught me was how to hate," he said.

He was an atheist and an anarchist, who, until this trip, had been teaching religious education at a private school in Korea. Before that he had worked for the *Muslim Times*, despite not being a Muslim.

Now Ian was heading to Serbia to meet his ex-girlfriend's family. "The thing is, we only just broke up," he said. "The family doesn't know. It would be a great insult if I didn't visit, so I have to pretend that we're still together. They're going to sacrifice a pig on my arrival!"

Ian shuddered, lit another cigarette and puffed away nervously. "So, what about you?"

"I'm on my way by car to Serbia, via Bosnia, to play a cricket match."

"What?" Ian collapsed on his bed, choking with laughter. "A cricket match? What on earth gave you that idea?"

It was difficult to gauge how he'd take this, but better he hear it from me than on the radio. I explained that my dead ancestor, channelling through a Montreal medium, told me it was my destiny.

Ian coughed violently. When he had regained his composure and saw I was serious, he said, "I believe that shit. My auntie uses Reiki on her dishwasher when it breaks down. She swears by it."

Ian turned to me. "Look, I'm not being funny, but my plan is pretty similar. Could you give me a lift and I'll split fuel?"

With that I had my next passenger.

"So what are you up to this evening? Going to the pub, or having a quiet one?" Ian asked.

"Well, a funny thing happened today. I just got some emails about doing radio interviews on the trip. One station is supposed to call here in a few minutes."

"WHAT? They're phoning here? Who is it?"

"BBC London."

"WHAT? Have you told the landlady? She hardly speaks English. Does she realise how important this is?"

"I mentioned something to her earlier. I don't think she understood, though. I'd better tell her again, huh?"

I walked into the kitchen. The landlady looked at me, beaming. "So, you find . . . friend, yes?"

"Yes."

"You are . . . in love, yes?"

"Yes. Umm, remember I phoned you this afternoon from the post office?" Already she looked confused. "An important phone call is going to come through here in about five minutes. Is that okay?"

She returned a blank stare. I explained again and then the phone rang. My eyes popped. I signalled it might be for me.

The landlady answered. "Hallo? Hallo?"

Oh God, oh God, I thought. Please don't be live on air. I waved at her and said, "It might be for me."

When she realised she couldn't understand the person on the other end, she led me upstairs to the second line.

"Hi, Andrew," I said. "Sorry about that."

"Oh hi, Angus. It's Dave, actually. I was just speaking to a strange lady."

"Yeah, it's my Dubrovnik landlady."

"Okay, I'm gonna put you through to Phil's show. You'll be able to hear what's going on. Just wait till he speaks to you, okay? It should be a few minutes."

My artery walls began to pound. Ian sat on the staircase among the Jesus statues. In one ear I could hear him giggling; in the other, a live report from a rain-abandoned Twenty20 match.

A lightning bolt came crashing down at the end of the landlady's garden. There followed a thundershower of biblical proportions, which drum-rolled off the window beside me. I feared any second the phone line would be struck by a second lightning bolt, killing me on air. Then I heard a click. This was my moment.

"Hallo?" said a voice.

I balked. It was the landlady downstairs on the other line. I was rooted to the chair. I couldn't speak. Sweat was streaming into my eyes.

"Hallo?"

"PUT THE FUCKING PHONE DOWN!" I wanted to scream. I could hear her breathing heavily over the other interview.

Ian twigged what was happening and ran to grab her.

"Do you believe in psychics?" said Phil suddenly, back in London. "Well, one man does. In fact a psychic changed Angus Bell's life. On the advice of one, he went off around Eastern Europe, playing cricket for a book. He's on the line now. Where are you, Angus?"

"I'm calling from Dubrovnik, where we're in the middle of a thundershower ourselves."

"Great. So what's the story with this psychic, then?"

Phil listened, adding the occasional "ah-hum", "yes" and "*okay*!", though he never sounded convinced. In fact he sounded like I was fucked in the head. I decided to stop my Canadian accent and steer the conversation quickly back to cricket.

"So then 'cricket and Ukraine' popped into my head. I did a Google search and found a website about a cricket league at the Odessa State Medical University. I thought, if they have cricket there, they must have cricket across Central and Eastern Europe. I knew I had to play them all. What better way to boost my batting average?"

"Really, and why do you think 'cricket and Ukraine' popped into your head? That's strange."

God, Phil, please stop bringing this back to the psychic, I thought. "Well, the psychic, he had an explanation for this. He said I have the infant ghost of my great-uncle following me around, putting ideas in my head. The psychic said this ghost was living his life through me."

"Right, and who are these cricketers? Expats?"

"No, Phil. I've found entire teams of Slovak gardeners – nearly all left-handed because of ice hockey; a team in the Slovenian Alps, who began playing on a farmer's meadow in the '70s. I've just met a team of winemakers on a Croatian island, who play against air traffic controllers from the mainland . . ."

I went on, mentioning the alleged fingerless Tamil Tigers in Prague, the Austrian bomb plotter, and that Eastern European cricket was being used as a vehicle to traffic illegal immigrants.

"Wow! How are you getting these stories out of the players?"

"It's quite simple, Phil. I take them down to the pub over the course of four days and ply them with alcohol."

I was buzzing when the interview finished. The landlady was forgiven for her heavy breathing. She could clap my cheek any time she wished now. Ian no longer doubted my story, either. We polished off three bottles of Vis wine in the bedroom, and collapsed asleep. Tomorrow we'd begin our road trip through Bosnia.

That night I was plagued by cricket nightmares. The game so dominated my thoughts now that they were a common occurrence.

My cricket nightmares began at school, when I dreamt Mike Atherton was eaten by a shark at the start of the Australian Ashes. I was upset till lunchtime, when I realised it wasn't true and therefore England might not lose the series.

I sat bolt upright in the darkness. "Where's the team?" I cried.

Ian woke. "The team's not here," he said. "You're in an old lady's house in Dubrovnik. It's three in the morning."

"What? Where am I batting?"

"God, this guy's obsessed."

In the morning Ian and I drove out of Dubrovnik and up the back roads to the border. Croatia's guards were tucking into lunch inside their hut when we arrived. A biker in front got bored waiting and lifted the barrier himself. One guard ran out with a napkin tied around his neck. He checked our passports and let us through to no man's land.

At the Bosnian checkpoint the second guard stepped in front of the Škoda.

"Whoa! Don't hit him!" said Ian hysterically, as I clipped the officer. The officer returned a menacing glare and waved us through. Ian uncovered his face.

Three years before, driving into Bosnia had been like entering an Orwellian nightmare. I remembered grimy apartment blocks, every inch pockmarked by shrapnel, looking as though they'd topple at a sneeze. Power lines were cut, exploded cars sat on the roadside and people waited idly in towns without work. Some had used plastic sacks and rusted iron to piece their homes back together, while others had seen their entire villages abandoned. Even today, several hundred thousand landmines remained embedded; no one was sure where.

Ten years on from its gruesome three-way civil war, Bosnia appeared to be restoring itself. The Škoda meandered through the mountains, overlooking broad valleys and large-scale vineyards. In the rebuilt towns, 'NATO Fuck Of' was the graffiti message.

Ian and I crawled over the mountains and arrived in busy Medjugorje. Road signs at the edge of town, I noted, welcomed tanks but not guns.

It was in Medjugorje, on June 24, 1981, that six teenagers claimed to have spoken with the Virgin Mary. Overnight, this anonymous village became Bosnia's tourism hot spot. It threw up Irish pubs, crystal and gold shops and 'Paddy's' travel agency.

The town had just celebrated the twenty-fourth anniversary of the supposed first sighting. The original witnesses said that the Virgin would be reappearing on the big day. French neurologists, hired by the Vatican, no less, arrived to test the claims.

The witnesses' heads were bound with electrodes and torches were shone in their eyes. The neurologists sounded 85 decibels in their ears, yet still there was no reaction. At the moment the Virgin Mary was supposed to reappear, the witnesses' brainwaves indicated they were asleep. Not even the Vatican's crack team could explain what had happened.

Ian and I abandoned the car and traipsed towards the modern twin-towered church. We peered through the window of the Gloria souvenir shop and into Santa Maria next door. Postcards of Jean-Paul II were up for sale, along with paint-your-own plastic idols, books in 17 languages and papal robes for $235. Throughout town, Christians sat weeping on benches, holding hands and singing, "Kum ba ya, m'Lord!"

"Let's read out *An Eye for an Eye*," announced the bearded leader of one Southern Bible study group.

A Bosnian guide walked past us, explaining to her 30-strong brigade, "The Virgin Mary was seen hoovering up there on Apparition Hill."

Other pilgrims set off to climb Mount Krizevac on their knees. They brought back stories of cripples walking again. I had doubts my one-legged, wheel-chair-bound father would experience the same success.

Ian and I stopped for Irish scones at a pub, priced at one euro apiece.

"Christ, this place is horrible," said Ian.

"I agree. It's hell. Let's go to Sarajevo."

We left, passing giant turd-like haystacks in the fields, half-finished houses on the outskirts of towns and newly roofed mosques. Kids stood by the roadside, trying to sell plum brandy in old Coke bottles.

By evening we had reached Sarajevo's tower-block suburbs. No longer did it look like New York a day after the World Trade Center attacks. New skyscrapers had sprung up along Sniper's Alley, and those that had lain folded over on themselves for a decade had finally been bulldozed. Sarajevo had been transformed into a modern European capital.

There was to be no cricket action on this leg, which disappointed Ian, whose highest score was 1. I'd heard from Croatian diplomats who played here after the four-year siege. They had to clear shrapnel and spent shells from the stadium's outfield. But now, seemingly without any cricket in the country, Sarajevo's sporting pinnacle would remain Torvill and Dean's 1984 Olympic victory.

Ian and I circled the old town's crazy one-way streets while darkness descended. The Turks had not reckoned on the motor car when they built their market, and the communist planners were unsympathetic to foreign drivers. We flew past the assassination site of Archduke Ferdinand four times and pulled into the pedestrian mall.

"Aaagh! What are we doing here?" screamed Ian, as hundreds of shoppers brushed the sides of the Škoda.

"Look! There's a police car. Go!" Ian sank lower in his seat.

I wound down the window to ask directions. Though no one spoke English, and we spoke no Serbo-Croat, we understood we weren't allowed to drive in the mall.

I cruised past the police car and turned down a side street, hoping to squeeze past café tables to the road. But another policeman stepped in front. He approached my door.

"Bloody hell!" squealed Ian, covering his face with both hands.

"Relax," I said. I wound down the window.

"Documenti," demanded the policeman. I handed over car papers and passports. The policeman walked to the front of the car to note the number plate.

A knock on the passenger window startled us. A fat, mustachioed Turk was standing there.

"Oh God. We're gonna get mugged!" I shrieked. "This is a set-up! Don't open your window."

The Turk hammered again, harder. Ian lowered his window an inch. "Get the fuck out of here!" screamed the Turk.

"What?" said Ian.

"Get the fuck out of here! You can't drive in the mall! This prick, he's gonna charge you! Go!"

"He has our passports," I said.

"What's he gonna do? He can't do shit!"

"He's blocking our way for a start."

The Turk walked over to the policeman. After an animated discussion, they approached my window in unison. "He wants ten euros," said the Turk. "This is the fine. I say you just drive! What's he gonna do?"

"Tell him we have no euros," I said.

There was more dialogue between the two.

"This prick says there's a cash machine around the corner," said the Turk.

I wasn't sure about Ian, but I didn't fancy leaving my car and going to a cash machine down a dark Sarajevo alley with these two figures.

"I have a few US dollars," I said, digging around on the floor.

"Don't show your wallet, or he'll take everything," said the Turk.

I passed a $10 note through the window. The Turk handed it to the policeman. He looked at it for 10 seconds, then passed it back to the Turk, who returned it to me.

"He says go. Here are your papers and passports."

The Turk leaned in my window and clapped me affectionately on the cheek. "Make sure you take everything out of this car tonight, or it won't be there tomorrow. And you'd better be quick, it's getting dark! Goodbye."

We slipped past the café tables, back onto the road and drove up onto a pavement. Ian and I got out to investigate an accommodation information sign over a doorway.

"We're looking for a youth hostel," I said at the desk inside. Two men in leather jackets shook their heads.

"Do you know *of* a youth hostel?" I asked.

Again they shook their heads.

"Do you know of *anywhere* to stay?"

After some beard-scratching, one man answered, "This will be difficult ... and expensive."

"Well, how much?"

They shook their heads again to indicate that it was too much.

"We do not know anywhere," said one at last.

What kind of information agency was this? Ian and I stormed outside, and spotted another agency up the street.

"What kind of accommodation are you looking for?" asked a tubby man in a pink shirt.

"One with a bed," I suggested. Ian gave me a look.

"I see," said the agent. "I always ask. Sometimes I get people in here on what they call ... " he made inverted commas with his sausage fingers, "*do-Europe-on-a-dollar-a-day*. They ask me for construction sites, or bridges to sleep under. Sometimes they ask for a stable with straw. We also get Swedish people sleeping in converted pizza vans."

The agent became distracted by something on his desk.

"Do you know Mikki?" I asked.

"Yes," said the agent, looking up again. "How do you know him?"

"I stayed in his hostel three years ago."

"His hostel has been demolished," replied the agent. "They are building something new. It will be bigger, more expensive ... But Mikki, he was unprofessional."

"Oh?"

"He jumped into bed with his clients. I would never do this, because I am a professional. For example, last week I had 26 Swedish girls on their *so-called*," he did that thing with his fingers again, "Pink Caravan ... I did not sleep with any of them, because I am a professional."

"So it's not because you're a fat, balding bastard?" I held back from saying.

"Okay," he said, after a moment. "I will put you in a good hostel. I will call my friend and he will come down the hill and take you shortly."

"Is he a professional?" I asked.

"Yes. He is a professional too."

His friend arrived, looking like a spectacled substitute teacher. He drove ahead of us uphill and gave us the rundown of the rules at reception.

"If you cause me trouble, there will be problems," he warned heavily. "If you break something, you will pay for it. Do you understand?"

Ian and I nodded. This was a strange hostel. Use of the kitchen cost an extra 10 euros per person. We could get a return taxi to town and enjoy a boozy three-course restaurant meal for less.

"There is a lock-in between 11 a.m. and 4 p.m.," continued the manager. "If you are inside the building, you won't get out. We have bars on the windows."

"Will my car be safe in the courtyard?" I asked.

"If anyone gets in here, he will not get out alive," promised the manager. "I am on duty 24 hours a day."

"Except between eleven and four," Ian pointed out. The manager returned a glare.

"What kind of trouble have you had in the past here?" I asked.

"Big trouble. Once we had two Turkish men. They were the first and last."

"Why?"

"They caused me problems. My boss, he tried to lock them in the room. They tried to get out. Now we don't allow *any* Turks, Africans or Asians."

"That's just racist," said Ian sternly.

"No. It's true," said the manager. "These people, they cause problems. It's a fact. Once, we had two men come in. I do not like this also. They caused problems. They slept in one bed. I will not allow this again."

He leaned forward, his eyebrows arched. "I hope *you two* will not cause me problems."

We shook our heads.

"Good," said the manager, and left us to ourselves.

Between soup and pasta in the To Be Or Not To Be restaurant in the old Turkish market, I asked Ian why he always panicked at borders and around policemen. I thought he was going to confess to smuggling drugs in my Škoda, but his crime turned out to be less serious. He had been arrested and charged for screaming the word 'Fuck!'

"I was at a London riot," he explained after a large sip of beer. "A policeman was telling me to climb down from a concrete block. I shouted, 'Fuck!' He shouted 'Fuck!' back, and told me if I said it again he'd arrest me. So what was I gonna do?"

"Climb down from the block and walk away?"

"No. I screamed, 'Fuuuuck!' Then he arrested me."

Ian continued, "I was charged under Public Order 5.1. I had to go to court and defend myself. I read up on the laws and cross-examined the police officers."

"What was your defence?"

"I said to the policemen, 'You were at a riot. People were swearing all around. You'd obviously heard the word before and therefore couldn't be shocked by it.' The case was dismissed from court."

We finished our meal, rounded off with grainy Turkish coffee, and walked out onto the menacing Sarajevo streets. It looked like a long, cold trek back up the vertical hillside.

"You must be tired after a 13-hour drive," said Ian.

"It's the standard commuting time to work these days," I said. "I love it."

After 40 minutes' hike, we were standing among hundreds of white headstones, overlooking Sarajevo's dimly lit valley. We'd forgotten where we were staying. We didn't know the address, the phone number or even the name. The temperature was fast approaching zero.

We looked around. Endless black lanes led up the valley sides. A pack of stray dogs howled nearby. We heard a single gunshot.

"I remember it was *beside* a graveyard," said Ian, stress levels beginning to soar.

"Sarajevo has graveyards everywhere," I pointed out. "Ten and a half thousand people died here during the war."

"It's got to be up *one* of these roads!" said Ian. "We'll have to go down the hill and try another."

Ian and I marched up and down more times than the grand old Duke of York. By two thirty in the morning, we had passed the same binmen nine times, and were lost in total darkness inside another graveyard.

"Fuck!" screamed Ian. "I can't take this! You've been to this city before. Is there any chance we'll get mugged?"

I decided to be frank. "Well, my friend Dylan was left with a scar like Harry Potter after an assault here. But he did go down an alley looking for drugs."

"That's it! If we can't find it now, I'm sleeping on the street! I don't care any more!"

We walked downhill and up three more times. Finally, in a twilight-zone conclusion, the hostel door appeared. We galloped gleefully towards it.

It was locked. The manager hadn't given us a key. We rang the bell. No one came to answer.

I lay down on the cobbled street and began to curl up.

"We're gonna die out here!" screamed Ian. "Fuuuck!"

A light came on. The manager appeared in the doorway with a heavy club. "I told you not to cause me problems," he said threateningly.

"Sorry," we whispered and scampered past him to bed.

No thanks to Public Order 5.1, Ian's final 'fuck' that night had saved our lives.

11

THE SPY WHO LEFT CRICKET COLD

Zrenjaninci istražuju novi sport i spremaju se za Olimpijadu

Uče kriket od Škota

Angus Bel demonstrira kako se pravilno drži palica za kriket

ZRENJANIN - U okviru Bejzbol kluba „Bečkerek", na čijem je čelu Dragan Nedeljkov, u Zrenjaninu je zahvaljujući „izvesnom Škotlandaninu", članu Evropskog kriket saveza Angusu Belu, piscu i svetskom putniku, osnovana prva sekcija za kriket.

Na pomoćnom terenu gradskog stadiona održan je promotivni trening sa prikazivanjem opreme i pravila igre, što je nepoznatih većini Zrenjaninaca koji znaju za bejzbol, a odlično igraju banatske šore. Da je

tako, postalo je jasno kada je jedan od radoznalaca, štitnike za noge stavio na ruke, što je munjevito bilo ispravljeno. U upravi Bejzbol kluba u kojoj je i Dejan Čapo, veliki ljubitelj i promotor bejzbola na temeljima banatskih šora, imaju ambiciju da kriket sekcija preraste u ozbiljan klub i uđe u prvu srpsku kriket ligu, a 2012. godine i u državnu reprezentaciju za Olimpijske igre, jer kriket je ove godine postao olimpijski sport.

Dvadesetčetvorogodišnjeg stručnjaka za kriket iz Glazgova Angusa Bela, kontaktirajući sa britanskom ambasadom preko Interneta je pronašao Miloš Pešić, urednik sporta u listu „Zrenjanin", i pozvao ga u ovaj banatski grad. Sa Belom su se sreli zamenik predsednika SO Zrenjanin Aleksandar Marton i šef kabineta predsednika opštine Zoran Kovački.

- Mladi kad nas imaju bejzbol i kriket palice u mobilji, ali bez obzira na interesovanje najmlađih, ali i njihovih roditelja ovi sportovi... su se bez obzira na interesovanje najmlađih, ali ovaj način korišćene na pravilan način - objasnio je smisao osnivanja kriket sekcije Dragan Nedeljkov.

"Učeći Škotlandanin" je popularišući kriket već boravio na Visu, u Zagrebu i Sloveniji, gde je ova sportska disciplina pustila korenje, a obišao je gotovo sve zemlje istočne Evrope.

- Na putu za Litvaniju, u Ukrajini i Belorusiji pratila me je tajna policija jer su mislili da sam britanski špijun - poverio je Bel pripadnicima izmeđa dva zabavna palicom i kriket loptom i dodao da se ... da mu je već davno jedan australijski vrač prorekao avanturiste i promotera kriketa. **J. VOJINOV**

From the *Blic* newspaper, Serbia and Montenegro, July 11, 2005

Organising my next game had been hard work. During the planning stages of this Slavic odyssey, as I typed away in the Glasgow flat on damp, wintry evenings, a horrid setback had occurred; one that threatened my mental well-being and batting average. My emails to the Serbian cricket captain bounced every time.

I racked my brain after a day at the methadone clinic, wondering how I could schedule a match. Then an idea popped into my head. Possibly it came from great-uncle Ivor. I would Google the captain's name, find his personal or work website, and track him down. It couldn't fail.

Except my search didn't return a personal or work website. On-screen came the front page of a Serbian newspaper, with a photo of my contact in a suit. Below I found an article from *The Sunday Times*.

Serbia's cricket captain was an MI6 secret agent, who close colleagues described as "the classic gentleman spy". He helped mastermind the arrest of Slobodan Milošević and arranged an RAF jet to fly the Balkan dictator to the War Crimes Tribunal in

The Hague. And during evenings and weekends he scheduled cricket matches.

Let's think about this for a second. Not MI5. MI6. That's James Bond-level. I wondered if he bagged Milošević using a trap involving cricket.

"You available next weekend, Slobodan? Match starts at 12."

The article went on to say that the secret agent's email address had been leaked across the Serbian press. That explained my unanswered mails, then. His cover – running the Belgrade cricket team (very subtle) – had been blown and he'd since grown a beard and gone into hiding.

Another thought stung me as I read this. Somewhere in my inbox was this poor man's mobile number. Should I call him and ask where he left the kit? Best not. I searched for the email and deleted it. It was not safe to hold onto such information.

Over the next fortnight, my efforts to track down Serbia's remaining cricketers proved fruitless. I wrote to football clubs on whose grounds they had played. The football clubs laughed and told me cricket didn't exist in Serbia. I contacted the British and Australian Embassies, where I imagined cricket to be an important part of their jobs. They said they didn't have the time to play. All the evidence suggested Serbian cricket was in tatters.

A month later I received an email from a sports journalist in the city of Zrenjanin, in northern Serbia. Milos had been passed my details by the British Embassy. He wanted to found a Serbian cricket league and take his country to the London 2012 Olympics.

"This is my dream," he wrote. "For a year I am trying to organize cricket club. Zrenjanin is the city of sports, yet when I speak about cricket here, people think that I've gone nuts. All my efforts were useless, nobody wants to help me. So, you are my last hope!"

How could I refuse? I knew exactly how Milos felt, having spent much of my youth searching for people to play with in the Scottish hills. I'd have my work cut out, though. There'd be the Olympic Committee to convince that London was the most worthy venue. Then there was the fact that cricket *wasn't* an Olympic sport. It would mean campaigning to introduce another sport that doesn't quite fit, like football and tennis, where pros compete against amateurs. England versus Serbia in Olympic cricket would be like U2 taking on Belarus at the Eurovision Song Contest.

Cricket had only once been an Olympic sport, making its first and last appearance – along with croquet, tug-of-war and the obstacle swimming race, which involved diving under boats – at Paris in 1900. After Belgium and the Netherlands' last-minute pull-out, there were two teams of 12-a-side: Devon and Somerset Wanderers, and Paris.

It was an odd Olympics. There were no gold medals. The English cricketers were awarded miniature Eiffel Towers for their triumph. Stranger still, Germany came second in the rugby.

But Serbia's modern-day Olympic vision would not be realised easily. Milos had a few bombshells to drop in his next email. He said he had no ground and no equipment. He confessed to having no players and never having played himself. He had never *seen* cricket before. And he said he hardly spoke English. Bar these small setbacks, I felt we were doing great.

"Never fear, Milos," I wrote back. "I will bring you equipment. I will train you from girls and boys into men! And we will see Serbia there in 2012!"

I imagined this like a Disney film, ending in Olympic glory.

*

It was eight thirty in the morning in Belgrade and my spirits were buoyed by the announcement that London would be hosting the 2012 Games. Things were swinging in our favour. I telephoned Milos with the good news from the hotel reception.

"Where are you?" said Milos. "Why did you not come yesterday? I stayed up most of the night for you."

"Very sorry, Milos. There was a seven-hour hold-up at the border. Every Turk in Central Europe was driving back to Istanbul. We got into Belgrade at half past midnight. We're staying in a hotel beside a sex shop."

"Yes," said Milos. "The border is slow because they arrested the son of Radovan Karadžić. But why didn't you call me?"

"Sorry, I don't have a phone."

"What? You have car and no phone? How is this possible? Okay. Listen." Milos sounded serious now. "You must be here in one hour thirty."

"One hour thirty? I won't make it out of Belgrade by then. Zrenjanin's, what, an hour and twenty minutes away?"

"Yes. One hour twenty. So you must leave Belgrade *right now*. You *must* be here in one hour thirty. This is *very*, *very* important. Do you understand? Leave now."

"I haven't paid for the hotel yet! I don't know my way. Why? What's going on?"

"Every TV station, every radio station, every newspaper and every magazine will be here for you at a reception with the mayor in one hour thirty. You must leave now!"

I ran into the bedroom and screamed, "Milos has called a press conference!"

Anarchist Ian sat upright in bed. "What?"

"He's called a press conference for 10 o'clock! What am I gonna do? I haven't shaved in days! I'm not dressed! I need a cash machine! I need to pay for the hotel! How will I get out of Belgrade when I can't read the street signs?"

I picked up my deodorant stick to stem the sweating. "My deodorant's run out!" I screamed. "Aaaaaggh! D'you think I've got time for a shower?"

"Listen, man!" said Ian. "You haven't got time for shit! Get packing!"

While Ian reloaded the Škoda, I tried to get directions from the hotel staff. They engaged in a 10-minute argument with each other before tearing up their map and throwing it in the bin.

"I haven't got time for this!" I yelled, running out of the door. Great-uncle Ivor would have to go beyond the call of duty to navigate me out of this one. I just hoped he read Cyrillic.

I sprinted up the cobbled hill in search of a cash machine. It was already 20°C on Belgrade's sterile-looking boulevards. Sweat began pouring off me.

Ten minutes later, breathless, I screamed, "Where are all the bloody cash machines?"

A haggard-looking man in a red tee shirt emerged from a darkened doorway. He was a mugger, for sure, and not to be trusted.

"My friend, I will help you," he said, fiddling with an earring. "Come with me."

I followed.

The mugger seemed to be taking this leisurely. "Look, I'm in a real rush," I explained as we strolled. "I have to get to Zrenjanin!"

"Don't worry, don't worry. I will help you. Come under here." He walked beneath the canopy of an empty shop.

"Look, do you know where a cash machine is, please?"

"Yes. But first, listen."

He opened his jacket and began rolling a cigarette. "I help you, you help me," he said after lighting it.

"Sure!" Just hurry the fuck up.

"How you travel to Zrenjanin?"

"By car, but . . . "

"Car? Hmmm." He took a long draw. "I have a car . . . umm . . . Do you understand?"

"Yes!"

"Umm . . . some guys took . . . my . . . petrol . . . in the night." His head swished from side to side as though he'd forgotten his lines. "I live in another . . . city . . . and I'm stuck . . . here now . . . Could you . . . "

"Spit it out, man!" I yelled.

"Take me to your car . . . and I will . . . suck out four litres of petrol . . . to get me home?"

"SUCK OFF!" I shouted, and ran.

I found a cash machine in another hotel lobby. I tapped in my details. My card was refused. I raced back to my hotel, almost crying.

"I couldn't find a cash machine!" I said at the front desk.

"Do you have credit card?"

"Yes."

"No problem, we take that."

I paid the bill and Ian stuffed cash in my pocket. "Good luck, man," he bade. "I hope you make it."

I climbed into the sweltering Škoda. It was already ten past nine. I was about to start the car when I realised something was missing. My passport! I raced inside and found it at reception, then jumped back behind the wheel. I turned the ignition. I had no petrol. My tank had been sucked dry.

"Aaaaaggh!"

With my last teacup of fuel, I zigzagged across Belgrade and reached the Danube. A skinny young man with a goatee stood clutching a piece of cardboard by the bridge. The letters 'Zn' were marked on it.

"Zrenjanin! Zrenjanin!" I shouted from my window. The young man looked startled and nodded.

"GET IN! GET IN!" I shouted. "I need to find a petrol station and I've 35 minutes to get to Zrenjanin!" He came round to the passenger door at a gallop.

Just over the Danube, as the engine was conking out, we pulled into a petrol station. "This is a *good* car," commented my hitchhiker. I felt saddened I had to come to Serbia to hear this. But yes, compared to the donkeys and '50s tractors leading out of Belgrade, the Škoda was a miracle of modern transportation.

With us fully fuelled and flying down a potholed country lane, my passenger told me when it was safe to overtake haystacks and Ladas. "It's funny, you can't see from the right?" he said. "Okay. Go! Go! Go!" He was a lunatic co-driver. I upped the speed to 80 miles per hour in second gear at his insistence.

"You can pass anything in this beast," he said, his seat belt unclipped. "This is how to drive! When I was 14, my friends and I stole a car and drove to Montenegro. A cop stopped us and couldn't believe his eyes. 'You're crazy!' he shouted, then let us go. This is Serbia. No one follows laws. You can go faster!"

I asked if there was a train between Belgrade and Zrenjanin.

"Yes, but our tracks are 150 years old. It takes five hours by train. You can jump off and run alongside. Come on, you can go faster!"

I explained my deadline and my hitchhiker pledged to help. "We don't get many tourists here. Only Italian hunters and Romanians for the beer festival. Give me this Milos's number and I will phone him now."

After a quick conversation, my passenger said, "I told Milos we will be 10 minutes late."

Ten minutes! He had confidence in my driving. "Did you get the address?"

"No, I forget."

"We must call him again!"

"That was my last credit."

As we raced across the Great Hungarian Plain, past grass and sunflower fields, I asked about Belgrade in the war.

"I was nearly killed by a NATO bomb on the TV station," said my passenger. "I was a kilometre away. It blew me off my feet. Women and children were screaming all around. You know they bombed a hospital and the Chinese Embassy?"

The thought of a 76-day bombing campaign put my press conference problems in perspective. My passenger reckoned 2000 civilians had been killed.

"And NATO said they were freeing us. Now people are dying of leukaemia from the bombs."

An oncoming truck flashed its lights. "Police," whispered my passenger, fastening his seat belt for the first time. "We are approaching the city now. Slow down, a little."

I didn't want to be stopped and questioned. With all the cricket gear, and without a journalist visa, I was like a gentleman spy myself. We spotted a police car parked under a tree.

"There is the bastard," said my passenger waspishly. He unclipped his seat belt as soon as we were clear.

Zrenjanin was a former Hapsburg city, with grand yellow and green buildings. Other traces of its imperial past, like order and efficiency, were hard to spot. At the major traffic intersections, none of the lights worked. It was a tentative free-for-all. And among it we were looking for one man and a press conference.

"Do you know Milos? He is a sports journalist?" we asked 13-year-old girls riding bicycles on the pavement. They had no idea.

The press conference was into its forty-fifth minute and we were helplessly lost.

"Oh my fucking God!" screamed my passenger.

We cruised the empty residential back streets for a while, but there was still no sign of Milos. "How can we get phone credit?" I asked.

"We can stop at the next shop."

I pulled over by a kiosk and handed my passenger some dinars. The kiosk didn't stock the right cards, nor did its competitor opposite. "Aaaaaggh!" my passenger cried.

At the third kiosk he bought his card and phoned Milos.

Milos was waiting around the corner. The press conference had been put back to 12. Lunch, however, was waiting urgently on the table.

I thanked my passenger.

"I am happy to help somebody," he said. "This is Serbia." With that he dashed off to catch a bus.

Milos had the appearance of a friendly military man and the handshake of a judo player. He would be 37 by the time the London Olympics came around, with a vastly experienced cricketing brain. "Thank you for coming and welcome to our city," he said.

He jumped into the passenger seat and led me down a buckled mud track by a swamp. "This is where you will stay tonight," he said, pointing at his parents' two-storey home.

Contrary to what he'd written in his email, Milos spoke good English. "But I don't understand 90 per cent of what you say," he confessed. I hadn't even begun on cricketing terms.

We walked through his parents' red gates and under an ancient grape vine. Chickens roamed in cages beside the path. Milos's parents sat at a picnic table by the house, in traditional cap and headscarf. The table was spread with vegetables from their garden, yoghurt from their goat and an open bottle of home-brew.

"My father makes the rakia from these grapes," said Milos, pointing at the vine. Though not understanding English, Milos's parents nodded and cackled at the word 'rakia', signifying its potency.

Milos poured me a tumblerful of the clear liquid. "Chin-chin," he said, indicating I should down it without delay. My eyes watered and my throat blistered.

"Another," said Milos, reaching for the bottle.

"I have to drive later, Milos," I protested.

"This is Serbia. Come on." Milos placed a second tumblerful beside my plate. "We eat quickly now, then we go to the mayor's reception at City Hall," he explained. "After, I take you to lunch. Then we will play cricket!"

After two lunches and *two* glasses of rakia, I wasn't going to be fit to bowl.

There was just enough time to shower and shave before the press conference. Donning cricket wear, Milos and I mounted the steps of the palatial City Hall. In the boardroom there were firm businessman-like handshakes all round, and then I was led through double doors to a roomful of journalists. I felt like a kid. What was all this about? It looked like they were expecting a foreign ambassador. Where were the Ferrero Rochers?

"You are ambassador from the European Cricket Council," whispered Milos at my side.

"No, that's not true. I just like the game," I squealed.

"No, no. For this meeting, you *are* ambassador from the European Cricket Council." I gulped. It would require my finest acting skills to pull this stunt off.

"Whisky, Mr Bell?" offered a lady with a tray.

"Thanks. I'll just have an orange juice, please. I'm driving."

"This is Serbia!" said an official, slapping me on the back.

I plopped down on a comfy window bench between Milos and the deputy mayor. One of the radio journalists spoke first.

"We thought you would be in your forties or fifties," she said.

My mouthful of orange juice almost sank down the wrong hole and I spluttered over my shirt. I tried to regain composure. "Generally cricketers retire by the age of 40," I answered, which seemed to satisfy them.

A great deal of discussion followed, of which 'cricket' was the only word I understood and the one word no one else did. A TV cameraman hovered around the room, using a clunky home camcorder. I hoped upon broadcast this would recruit thousands of Serbian cricketers.

The room turned to me again. With my three translators, I expressed delight at Milos's plans to form a Serbian cricket team and sadness at the departure of the MI6 secret agent. I gave my full backing for entry to the 2012 Olympics.

Then the question on every journalist's mind was put forward, tentatively. "They have decided to call the cricket team 'The Lowlanders'. Is this a good name for a cricket team?" The room held its breath.

"Yes. It is an excellent name," I said with great authority. They all looked rather pleased.

There followed cries to pad up. I debated at length over reaching down my pants to put in my box, and decided against it. This was going to be on TV after all, and what if my mum saw it?

One reporter spotted the box on the drinks tray. "What is that big curvy thing?" he asked.

"It's a face mask." I held it to my mouth and inhaled deeply.

Press conference over, Milos led me on a tour of the city in the Škoda. No bombs had landed on Zrenjanin during the wars, he said, only on a nearby pig farm. However, Zrenjanin was facing terrible economic problems. Out of a population of 80,000 nearly half were unemployed.

"This used to be a major industrial city," said Milos. "And Serbia was like the United States of Eastern Europe. Now we are like the Africa."

Through the Škoda window I saw scrawny men raking through skips. Litters of puppies lay on the pavements.

"People are very nervous about work," said Milos. "Fights can break out in seconds. I was in a fight myself a few weeks ago."

I felt sure Milos had won that fight. Apart from being a regular participant in handball and water polo, he was a judo wrestler, and came third in pole-vaulting at the 1994 Yugoslav State Championships.

"It is a dangerous sport. Someone was killed when they missed the mat," he said.

I asked what had caused Zrenjanin's economic decline.

"Tito ruined us," said Milos. "And under Milošević Serbia was a Mafia state. In 1993 we had hyperinflation. My newspaper today costs 20 dinars; back then it cost one billion. People had to spend all their savings. We lost everything."

Between October 1993 and January 1995, Serbia's prices rose five quadrillion per cent. That's 5,000,000,000,000,000 per cent.

"It was like a hurricane," said Milos. "People wrote cheques for everything: for bread, for a newspaper. Shops had to accept them by law. By the time cheques were cashed, inflation had rocketed again and they were worthless."

Milos continued, "One friend went to see his girlfriend in Belgrade every Friday. They stayed in a hotel all weekend. Their cheques were cashed three days later, so he got his stays for free."

Though Serbia's economy had since stabilised and steps were being taken towards EU entry, the situation for career people like Milos was grim. He could barely afford to catch a bus to Belgrade to see his girlfriend. For a while he thought of getting out of the country and moving to Iceland. "But they don't play cricket," he said jokingly.

"They have two teams," I corrected him.

We parked and Milos led me on foot to a rotting concrete bridge. There was no road or river under it, just grass. "They diverted the old river flow because it was too stinky," explained Milos. "The Romanians were throwing in poisons upstream."

I felt quite depressed about this place. It had faced a rough run. But it was credit to Milos and those around him that they set their sights high. Forming a cricket team was a sure sign of recovery.

"Last year people were beating each other with bats. Now we want to get them hitting balls," said Milos. He had the right philosophy.

"Would you take a tour to Croatia?" I asked. "To the island of Vis?"

"Oh! This would be my dream!"

We walked into town and entered a gloomy internet café. While Milos tottered off to the toilet, I jumped on a terminal. No internet connection was possible on any PC. I followed Milos to the toilet and discovered there was no paper. "In Serbia you need connections even for this," said Milos.

We left to join the president of Lowlanders Cricket Club, Mr Beard – so named because he had a grey beard. He was waiting by the fireplace in a traditional Germanic restaurant when we arrived. Stuffed boars' heads were mounted on the walls. Business was quiet.

Milos translated for Mr Beard. "He says he wants to make a rule all players must have a beard. And tonight he will marry you with a Zrenjanin girl."

"Thanks," I said, "but I'm taken." Mr Beard had hoped I would impregnate as many local girls as possible during my stay, creating a generation of Serb cricketers.

Over many Cokes at the table, Milos, Mr Beard and I talked about the plan for Serbian cricket. Milos said that he had secured a football ground for the afternoon's game, but it would not be available every week. I suggested they take up indoor cricket.

"We have a war going on between basketballers and hand-ballers for the courts," he replied gravely. "This will be difficult."

I drew field placings on the back of a napkin, while Milos and Mr Beard squinted and nodded. As the meal progressed, it struck me that this pair knew absolutely nothing about cricket except that Iceland had two teams. A curdling sensation formed in my gut. Within an hour an unspecified number of confused people were going to be arriving at a football ground to play a complicated game which they'd never seen. We had one partial translator, and they'd be looking to me as the sole director. What in Greater Yugoslavia was I going to do?

It came to me as we assembled on the ground in football strips and polo shirts. What would Borut do? He had formed a Yugoslavian cricket team with fewer resources and less experience than me. A single-wicket competition! Borut should have patented the model. The man was a genius. I could see how he'd won twice on *Who Wants to Be a Millionaire?*

"Thank you, Borut!" This time the players would have the option of batting right-handed.

I ran to the Škoda and dug out 12 copies of *The MCC Laws of Cricket*. I distributed one to each player. "You may use these to defend yourself in court," I said. They smiled. Already they were warming to cricket, and this was the boring part.

I returned to fetch the rest of the equipment from the car. As I carried an enormous cardboard box to the centre of the field, I remembered inside it was kiddies' equipment, kindly given by

NatWest. And on the field were 11 full-grown men, aged 20 to 60, and one nine-year-old.

But none of them would *know* it was kiddies' equipment, would they? "Sure, we play with knee-high bats," I could tell them. Hell, I could even bowl wides and pretend I was good. I could convince them Scotland had the best cricket team in the world.

No. I didn't want any surprises when they made their Olympic debut. I brought two more full-size bats from the car and laid them before the gathering. They reacted as though a flying saucer had landed.

Milos had done superbly in his recruiting. No longer did people think him nuts. He had sourced the top marksman in all of former Yugoslavia, whose accuracy would serve him well in all disciplines. He had found a chemical engineer whose expertise in fertilisers singled him out as the groundsman. We had a psychologist – the Mike Brearley of the team – who, although never scoring runs himself, possessed the brain to outwit Australia. Also making the line-up was a member of the regional parliament. He would be able to cut through bureaucracy and lobby the Olympic Committee.

"My neighbour is a musician and a carpenter!" said Milos, picking up a bat for the first time. "He will make us 1000 like these!"

"And he will sing songs of your great victories!" I declared.

Best of all, here to play was the mainstay of the Zrenjanin baseball team. They'd formed three years before, yet never played a game, because they had no equipment. Once they managed to find a stick and played a game of 'šore' (sockball). It was an ancient sport from the region, traditionally played by shepherds. The bowler would stand one metre from the batsman and deliver a ball of socks. The batsman would swing with his crook and run 50 metres straight and back for a single point. The fielders would try to catch the socks and hit the batsman with them. Legend had it that local hero Mihajlo Pupin, the inventor who developed the long-distance telephone, took sockball to New York in 1874, where it lent its traits to baseball.

"You will all love cricket!" I said. "You only have to run 20 yards for a point!"

Riding on the crest of this confidence, I set up stumps and began coaching. "You pick up the bat like this . . . "

Already five pupils had hands up. "What is a bat?" asked one, bravely.

Oh boy, I thought. Where to begin? They didn't know what a run was, or a batsman, or, crucially, the purpose of a box. How to explain 'wicket' when it meant four things? As far as they knew, 'googly' was a search engine.

"This is a bat. This is a ball," I said, holding them up for all to see.

Over the next 15 minutes something remarkable happened. Twelve men who that morning wouldn't have known what cricket was if they were standing in the middle of a Lord's World Cup Final became fully-fledged internationalists. They learned how to bowl, where to stand and how to defend their stumps. After five try-outs they were swinging the ball away on a length.

With them more than ready for their first game, I spread the field as indicated on the restaurant napkin. We would rotate the field after each over. Bowlers would bowl one-over spells, and batsmen would retire on 24.

Standing at cover, I told the batsmen when they ought to run. Soon they learned to pick up cheeky byes. The fielders counteracted by cutting off wild overthrows. The very first Serbian square cut produced the greatest stop in their game's history. Milos, crouching with his camera, dived and copped the ball on his lens, thus saving four. And when a bowler, releasing off the wrong foot, tripped and cartwheeled into the stumps, he *still* managed to deliver the ball straight. I wiped a tear from my eye.

After an hour and a half, when every player had racked up a personal best, the equipment was packed away in its holdall and handed to Milos for safekeeping.

"We will train like this every week," promised Milos.

As we were leaving the field a camera crew arrived in Chelsea shirts. Milos went over to speak to the giggling journalist and returned with the news we'd have to play again. Out came the stumps and I urged the team to show Serbian television what they could do.

Somewhat weary from their debut efforts, only four players made it to the middle for the news mock-up. It looked promising for me. Now there were so few fielders, I could rattle up runs.

My stumps were flattened first ball, as I tried an arrogant whip to the legside. The bowler seemed to have forgotten if this was a good thing or not. My pupils had outstripped their master.

12
THE CRICKET AND KICKBOXING CLUB OF BULGARIA

Batting for the Bulgarian CC

Saif was a man who could smile even after a three-hour wait for a stranger at the Bulgarian border. "No problem, sir. You're very welcome. I told you, we arrange everything," he said as we shook hands at 11 at night under a lightning storm. He introduced me to his girlfriend, Katia, and her 15-year-old son, Sasho, who'd also endured the sit in the car.

"You had no problems crossing over?" asked Saif.

"Just a five-hour standstill and currency problems over road tax and disinfection fees. Nothing serious."

"Good. Okay, you will follow our car now to Sofia and you will stay in our National Sports Academy."

I followed Saif's car in the darkness. Mist swirled over the road, hiding potholes and lurking speed cops. We entered the capital's gloomy streets after midnight, and drove between the white pillars of the National Sports Academy.

As promised, Saif had arranged everything, including an apartment. "Now we must return to our home by the border," said Saif. "Rest well; and tomorrow get your bowling boots on."

Saif met me at the academy's café next morning, dressed in his cricket gear. He rushed to buy me a sandwich and coffee and sat down across the picnic table, answering every question I fired at him.

Originally from Punjab in Pakistan, Saif had been a famous actor and playwright. He moved to Bulgaria in 1994 after holidaying on the Black Sea.

"It was my dream at school to make cricket where there was no team," he said, "like Bangladesh at that time. I had never thought about Bulgaria before, but here it was possible."

Saif was now a sports equipment importer, mostly selling boxing gloves and footballs. "I don't sell so much cricket gear, yet," he said. The 'yet' betrayed his determination.

"I hear weightlifting is the second most popular sport in Bulgaria," I said. "Have you tapped into that market?"

Saif laughed and shook his head.

Official cricket began in Bulgaria in 2001 with the registering of the Bulgarian Cricket and Kickboxing Club. Training started in the February snow, and there was never any mixing between the two sports. It was just a way of avoiding bureaucracy.

"There were no other benefits of being together," said Saif, "so we went our separate ways."

Cricket, though not recognised by the communist government, had existed in Bulgaria in the 1980s, when Pakistani, Indian and Bangladeshi medical students clashed.

"When they finished their courses, they moved to other parts of Bulgaria and stopped playing," said Saif. "After the Cricket and Kickboxing Club's formation I met Mr Nikolay, Professor of Rugby here at the academy. He let us use the facilities. I started coaching kids, bowling underarm and telling them, 'Just hit the ball!' Within one week they had run-ups! Now they play tournaments. We have over 100 juniors in school!"

"Who was Bulgaria's first match against?"

"We took a train to Belgrade in 2002 and played against Serbia. They were all Yugoslavian except the captain, I think. We won both games. But we haven't heard from them since . . . "

I cleared my throat. "Umm, the captain was accused of being an MI6 secret agent. He's now grown a beard and gone into hiding."

Saif clasped his head. "What? I had no idea he was James Bond! You won't find this in Bulgarian cricket. We are clean."

Three pigeons flew off the window ledge and shat over my arm and notebook. "Oh my God! This is something funny!" shrieked Saif. He handed me a napkin.

"How many teams are there in Bulgaria?"

"Six. We have started university teams across the country. Out of 100 players, 50 are Bulgarian – not including the schoolkids. All players are graduates of the Sports Academy, mostly rugby and baseball players. The government says you cannot have a national team in Bulgaria unless the players graduated at the academy."

Saif added, "This week is our National Championship, actually. A team from Varna University is coming this weekend – all Bulgarian. Maybe you will play them. What is your programme?"

I explained that I had to leave for a few days, but agreed to shave off two days from Romania to play in Bulgaria's National Championship.

"Excellent." Saif looked at his watch. "Okay, now we must go for today's match."

Monday afternoon's friendly was Bulgarian CC versus Sofia Medical Academy. "Some players try to say it is India versus Pakistan," explained Saif on the way. "I tell them, 'No! It is BCC versus the Medicals.' If they want to fight, they can go to Kashmir!"

As we walked through the academy campus, we saw shot-putters and discus-throwers practising on either side of the path. Future Olympic sprinters were limbering up on running tracks, and tennis stars were smacking volleys against walls. Even ballet dancers were stretching on the lawns.

We reached the AstroTurf pitch under snow-capped Mount Vitosha. It was overlooked by grim communist student halls of residence. A donkey and cart moved between rusted pylons in the meadow over the fence. Both cricket teams were assembling around the rugby posts and hockey goals on the pitch.

At Saif's instructions, half a rubber mat was dragged to the AstroTurf's centre, and plastic stumps were erected. Saif won the toss and elected to bat. As our Bulgarian CC openers strode out in jeans in the gloom, rain began to fall steadily.

With five Bulgarian internationalists present, and one Pakistani claiming to have played first-class cricket, the standard was higher than the average UK village Sunday team. Helped by the lightning outfield and change in the laws (lbws had been ruled out because they caused too many arguments), Bulgarian CC rocketed along, reaching 100 for no wickets in 11 overs.

Conditions looked ideal for a personal 100. Coming in at number four, after the fall of the two Muhammads, I was given a brisk workout by the Medical pacemen. I had to fetch my own sixes from the adjacent meadow. But by the conclusion of the innings, on 191 for 3 after 20 overs, I was stranded 7 short of a half-century.

In response, Saif charged in to open our bowling. "Who needs the toilet paper?" cried the waiting batsmen, as the Medicals sprayed the first 6 deliveries for 22 runs. The smirk was wiped from their faces when, in his next over, Saif knocked over danger man Dr Dipak Thampa's middle stump.

I felt a bit sorry for our Bulgarians. They didn't appear to have much involvement in the game, which was dominated by the more experienced South Asians. With them consigned to the outfield for the most part, their greatest contribution was trapping balls under their feet. They seemed enthusiastic, nonetheless, and showed no regrets about turning from the dark side of baseball to spend their afternoons playing cricket idly in the rain. Their red ankles soon had the Medicals struggling to score a boundary.

Arguments flared in the Medical batting camp as pressure mounted. They flickered between Bulgarian and Urdu. There was debate about whether a batsman had struck a six or the ball should be declared dead because it pitched short of the rubber mat. There were cries that nine overs, and not ten, had been bowled. At one point, when the ball struck the stumps, the batsman claimed he'd leg-glanced it cleanly for four. Never was a game more serious than in Bulgaria.

"When the Medicals lost to Pakistan Businessmen, they cried," said Saif.

There were no tears after our 82-run victory, only handshakes. The Medical Academy left the field vowing to wreak revenge in the weekend's Championship.

After the game I set off by minibus to Sofia's unglamorous concrete centre. I stepped out at the train station, where wrinkled Roma women shuffled past wheeling broken shopping trolleys. Tough-looking gypsy men sat on the street swigging beer while office workers marched past, eyeing them with suspicion.

I walked beside the tram route up Boulevard Maria Luisa and entered the first currency exchange booth.

"Do you accept American dollars?" I asked the bald man behind the counter.

He shook his head. I thought this strange. "Do you accept euros?" I asked.

He shook his head again.

"What kind of exchange bureau is this? Do you accept British pounds?"

He frowned and shook his head.

"Flipping heck! Australian dollars? Canadian?"

He shook his head, more violently this time, and shouted, "LOOK! I TAKE AMERICAN DOLLARS!"

In Bulgaria people nod for 'no' and shake their head for 'yes'.

I walked further up the main boulevard and ducked into a grubby snack bar. There I asked the barman if he knew of an internet café. He nodded and stared back in bamboozlement.

"Internet," I said, typing on an invisible keyboard.

He nodded again, and returned a blank look.

"IN-TER-NET," I said. I drew a diagram of a computer on a napkin.

"No understand," said the barman. As it was a Bulgarian who invented the digital computer, I was finding this exchange just as puzzling as him.

"Internet!" I tried a final time.

"Ah! Internet!" He smiled, then nodded. "Sorry. I do not know where."

I found an internet café next door.

*

The following morning Saif led me on a tour of the Sports Academy with the broad-shouldered, mustachioed Professor Nikolay. There were 3000 students, Professor Nikolay explained. The academy attracted Bulgaria's raw sporting elite, honed their talents and turned them out with university diplomas. It had produced champion chess players, motorists, wrestlers and alpinists. King Boris III, no less, had commissioned its construction.

"His son, Simeon, was prime minister till yesterday," said Saif, as we rode a lift to the top of the tallest building.

"Why did he lose the election? Because he banned smoking in public places with three weeks' notice?" I asked. Bulgaria had the world's third largest per capita cigarette consumption.

"Maybe, maybe," said Professor Nikolay. "Many people smoke in Bulgaria, but not at our academy." He tapped the side of his nose.

It was exam season, so our classroom tour was restricted. Bouncers guarded the hallways to prevent cheats coming and going.

Back on the campus lawns, I asked Professor Nikolay what other sports he presided over. He began a long list. "Rugby, football, table tennis, golf, squash, hockey, badminton, baseball . . . "

I asked Saif what course he was studying.

"Cricket," he said, matter-of-factly.

I stopped in my stride. "You're *studying* cricket?"

"Yes. It is a five-year degree."

"You're taking a degree in cricket at a Bulgarian university?"

"Yes. We started the course last year. We have six students; boys and girls. More are enrolling next term."

"And you're studying . . . in Bulgarian?"

"Yes."

"Who teaches?"

"The professors here."

"Bulgarian professors?"

"Yes. But we hope to attract guest lecturers from the European Cricket Council, and I also help out teaching."

"And it's a Bachelor of Arts?"

"Yes."

"Because of martial arts?"

Saif laughed. "No. Actually, I am writing a book in Bulgarian about how to play cricket. I've written 100 pages so far. When it's finished it will become official course material."

"What do students do on the course?"

"The focus is on cricket coaching. How to play? What is cricket? What is front-foot drive? What is back-foot drive? What is the history of cricket? It includes some baseball, handball and anatomy."

"Is there a baseball degree too?"

Nikolay shook his head to confirm. "This started in 1998. Next year will be a big year. We will be building a cricket and baseball stadium over there." He pointed to a nearby football field.

"You're serious about this? You're not making it up?"

Both Nikolay and Saif looked confused.

"No, this is all true," said Saif.

This was astounding. Cricket, taught by Bulgarians for Bulgarians – none of who had ever heard of Andrew Flintoff or the

Ashes. If the lectures and notes hadn't been in Cyrillic I'd have signed for my master's on the spot.

"Do you offer a degree by correspondence?" I asked.

Bulgarian CC versus Medical Academy, Sofia

National Sports Academy, Sofia

11.07.2005 (20-over match, 11-a-side)

Scorer: Saif-ur-Rehman

Umpires: Musadiq (Goga), Farhan

Weather conditions: Raining

Result: Bulgarian CC won by 82 runs

Toss won by: Bulgarian CC

Man of the match: Muhammad Hanif

Bulgarian CC	R
Muhammad Hanif	67
Muhammad Arshad	41
Ivailo Katzarski	1
Angus Bell	43 not out
Ali Raza	13 not out
Saif-ur-Rehman*	dnb
Muhammad Faisal	dnb
Stanislav Stoyanov	dnb
Nasko	dnb
Paulina Todorova	dnb
Muhammad Ali Chuhan	dnb
Extras	26
Total (3 wickets, 20 overs)	**191**

Medical Academy, Sofia	R
Dipak Thampa	7
Vickram Tiwetiea	33
Prabhjot Gill*	2
Farhan Azmi	5
Aditya Sharmol	9
Prashant Kumar	14
Vineet Gill	6
Siju Kumar	7
Umer	1
Rehman	4
Abinash Rai	0 not out
Extras	21
Total (all out, 12 overs)	**109**

13
MidNiGhT EXPRESS

I was standing on the bridge over the Bosphorus. Istanbul's cricket captain, Mr Mubashir Kahn (no relation to the great Imran), was facing me, a look of terror in his eyes. The legside was packed with rush-hour traffic, honking madly. Behind me was an oil drum for stumps; beyond that, the Blue Mosque and Hagia Sophia.

Still in work clothes, Mr Mubashir focused on his spot, loosened his shoulders, trotted in and released. The tennis ball, pushed gently by the breeze from the Sea of Marmara, swung in. I charged to counteract. As the ball bounced a second time I launched it cleanly into the distance. Mr Mubashir, mouth agape, turned on his heels to watch. The ball struck a pillar, ricocheted into the rush-hour traffic, rebounded off a truck and plopped over the bridge into Asia. Somewhere in that direction was the Darts and Cricket Federation of Azerbaijan, a combination more frightening than Lillee and Thomson.

Mr Mubashir Kahn had just become the first man to be hit between continents. I shook his hand, and awarded him a cricket bat.

"Now, let's get out of here," he said.

We darted from the scene.

*

I abandoned the Škoda at the academy and Saif escorted me by minibus to Sofia's central train station. After hearing from Swedes gassed between Krakow and Budapest, and from Aussies who woke to find holes in their pockets in Zagreb, I decided I'd book a private cabin on the night train. The last thing I wanted was to wake in Istanbul penniless, and find my pants on the wrong way around.

"You will be safe," said Saif. "Any problems, please call me. Do you want me to wait till you leave?"

"No thanks, Saif. I don't want to hold you up. I'll be fine. What can happen?"

"Okay. I'll see you in a few days."

Saif departed and I walked out onto the smoggy, hot street. I bought a tram ticket and rode up the main boulevard in search of an internet café again. My schedule was tight, and Yahoo! was key to pulling the plan together. The email I most wanted was waiting in my inbox, from Turkey's cricket supremo.

To: Angus Bell
From: Professor Syed, Bilkent University, Ankara

Dear Angus Bell,

We have been waiting for the final confirmation of your visit. In couple of hours we should be able to finalize who will receive you at the station. I will try and meet you in Istanbul myself. So please check your email, if you can. We will give you all the information. Or you can call me and find out about the arrangement.

Best regards,
Syed

I logged off and left to return to the train station.

As the tram doors closed, every passenger in the carriage surged forward. Within 10 seconds, 15 well-dressed men and women were huddled around me, pushing with intensifying force. My backpack tipped and I fought to stop myself tumbling onto the shrivelled babushka beside me. There's no need for this. There was a large space behind the mob. I clung to a pole with increasing strain and battled to stay upright. The shoving grew and my legs buckled.

"For fuck's sake! What are you playing at?" I shouted. "Move back!"

I felt three sharp tugs at my money belt. Oh God. My money, my passport.

"GET OFF, YOU BASTARDS!" I screamed. I doubled over and burrowed backwards, swinging my backpack into bodies. Now, more than ever, I needed Mr Saif and his martial arts skills.

The tram screeched to a halt and I tumbled to the floor. The doors opened and I saw my teenage muggers flee. The mob returned to their seats and pretended to read newspapers. I stood up and spun in circles, arms outstretched, ready to attack. Every passenger had been in on it. I reached down and felt my money belt still attached to my waist. This was merely a two-minute tram ride. I shuddered at what I might face on the midnight express.

I cowered under my blanket in the darkness, the slow grind and whistle of the wheels keeping me awake. Though alone in my '70s compartment, I was taking no chances. Paranoid about theft and rape, I lay in bed with a cricket bat on either side of me. I had stuffed my camera and money belt down my boxer shorts.

I drifted in and out of consciousness in the early hours, woken frequently by the neighbouring compartment's ghetto-blaster. Bill Bryson's summation in *Neither Here Nor There* rang frighteningly true: "If you can imagine a man having a vasec-tomy without anaesthetic to a background accompaniment of frantic sitar-playing, you will have some idea of what popular Turkish music is like."

My bladder pulsed, so I slipped out from under my blanket and slung on my backpack. I crept into the shaking corridor to find a toilet. As I tiptoed between the narrow carriages, I came face to face with four Roma men unscrewing panels and stuffing plastic bags with white stuff in them into the gaps. I did a double take. The men looked at me and motioned with their fingers I should keep quiet.

I held up my hands. "Oh boy. I ain't seen nothing," I said. "I'll stay in my room and piss in the sink." I returned with haste to my chamber and sealed the door. I pulled the blanket over me. For the rest of the night I dreamed of John Hurt being buggered in a Turkish prison.

At 6.45 a.m. there was a rap on the door. I shot out of bed, semi-naked, cricket bat in hand. When I opened the door my money belt and camera slipped from my boxer shorts, landing with a thump on the floor. The uniformed Bulgarian border guard examined the scene. He looked at the cricket bat warming in my bed and said, "Gym work, yes?" He shaped to lift a dumb-bell.

I nodded, and he collected my passport.

An hour later we shunted forward 20 yards and stopped at the Turkish checkpoint. The guards turfed me out of bed and sent me to the platform to buy a visa. The visa man wouldn't accept Scottish notes.

"But it's ten pounds!" I said.

"This is not pound," he stated again and again. I dipped into my dwindling supply of US dollars, normally reserved for bribes. He happily fixed a magic sticker in my passport.

Back on the train, progress was slower than usual in that we weren't moving at all. Three hours evaporated, my patience fading faster than my dollar supply. The stillness was broken by a woman's scream, followed by heavy thuds down the carriage.

I peered from my door to investigate. Those same plastic bags I'd seen being stuffed behind the panels in the night were now in the hands of customs guards. Twenty passengers were being led away on the platform in handcuffs. A sniffer dog padded past me in the corridor and I went to pet it. Then I realised this might not be a good idea. What if narcotics had been concealed in my compartment?

It was time to abandon post. I made my way to the far end of the train. Almost every compartment was empty. Two-thirds of the train had been implicated in the drug run.

"What's happening?" I asked the conductor, who was parading around in a string vest as though he'd lost hope of ever leaving.

"They find 350 ecstasy pills," he said. "The gypsies, they say, 'But the pills are white! Ecstasy is green!' The Bulgarian guards take some pills and leave rest for Turkish police. Now we wait on fingerprint man from Istanbul. That is still five hours away." He let out a grunt.

By the time the midnight express pulled into Istanbul, I had three hours till my return journey. I looked for a payphone and called Professor Syed.

"What happened?" he asked. "We sent people to find you. You are in Istanbul? I am still in Ankara. I will get someone to meet you."

Within minutes a small Pakistani man whisked me away from the station. As we picked our way through the busy streets, between carpet shops and grilled-fish vendors, we saw a beggar with no legs crawling with his hands in slippers.

I was taken to a house above a sports shop. There, confused cricketers had gathered, headed by the mustachioed Mr Mubashir Kahn, a sports importer extraordinaire and captain of Istanbul's cricket team.

"So, we heard something about a bridge from Professor Syed in Ankara," said Mr Mubashir. "What is your programme?"

"It's quite simple. I just need someone to bowl at me on the bridge, and I'm going to smack them from Europe into Asia."

Mr Mubashir's face, along with those around him, drained of colour. He was hesitant in his response. "There is a problem. Since a few years now, you are not allowed to walk on the bridge, only with special government permission. This is because of all the suicides. It can take weeks to get clearance, and there are police *all over* the place. For how long you are here?"

"Three hours."

"I am sorry, my friend, it is not possible . . . "

I felt like I'd been struck by a Brett Lee bouncer.

"Look, I don't care if I get arrested, but I have to do this. I've planned it for two years! What if we were to *ask* the police?"

"When Michael Jackson asked permission to see the throne at the palace, they told him no. Not even him. He was so angry he cancelled his concert and left right away. I don't think asking will work. They are very, very strict about this bridge."

"There *has* to be a way."

"Perhaps we could take a boat across and you can hit me on that."

"See! There is a way!" I leapt to my feet and grabbed the bats.

"Okay. I will fetch the tennis balls."

As Mr Mubashir drove through rush hour, joined by two teammates, he looked like a condemned man. We talked about the state of the Turkish game. His players were forced to drive six hours to Ankara to play against its three supermarket-sponsored teams because they had no ground.

"We leave work on Friday, drive there and play Friday, Saturday and Sunday before coming back."

Mr Mubashir was a sponsor of the national handball team and he had some startling statistics about baseball bat sales in Istanbul.

"They are among the biggest sellers here. You can find them in every market. But there is no game! Nobody plays. It is only for beating people! Hah! Maybe I will introduce cricket bats for this." He was a shrewd businessman.

The traffic thickened and Mr Mubashir accelerated through the gaps, tooting like a Turk. "Change of plan. We will go to the bridge first and ask the police. Maybe because you have come all this way they will allow it, but I am not sure."

One of Mr Mubashir's biggest wishes was to raise awareness of Turkish cricket.

"But I don't know how to do this. Have you any ideas?"

"You could break the world record for the longest non-stop cricket match," I suggested, "like that French team, and then the one in Australia. Play for 27 hours."

"Hah! No problem! My team, they play cards all night. This is easy! We will do 28 hours!"

We neared the bridge and tension gripped the carload. An ice cream vendor knocked on the window and jogged after us. Mr Mubashir bought four Magnums.

Dry land disappeared and we zipped over the Bosphorus. All eyes darted from the windows. As we touched into Asia, a convenient parking bay appeared. There was no sign of any police.

"I have never seen this!" exclaimed Mr Mubashir. "Quickly! We must go!"

Whistling to avert suspicion at first, then bolting, we made our way along the disused pedestrian strip, crouching as though a sniper hid in the girders.

"Okay, this is far enough, I think," called Mr Mubashir, 20 paces behind.

"We must go further!" I said, continuing towards the centre, where a blue oil drum lay in wait as stumps.

I turned at the oil drum and practised my lofted drives. Mr Mubashir loosened his arms and approached. His teammates took up positions at wicketkeeper and slip. What if I missed? There wouldn't be a second chance at this. Match rules applied, and the stumps were enormous.

It was all over in a minute. As we sprinted back to the car, its engine still turning, my gracious opponent was breathless with excitement.

"This is amazing!" he cried. "I have never seen this place empty! Every day it is crawling with police! The whole time you could see in my face I was afraid. It was your fate! The power of your concentration, coming thousands of kilometres! When you told me, I knew it was impossible. I think it was the rays coming out from your brain!"

14
A MAN ON MY CHEST

A Lada powered by sunflower oil

Back in Sofia, after an identical whipping of the Medicals, I slept soundly ahead of the crucial Varna clash.

The apartment was filled with sunlight when I awoke. As my alarm hadn't sounded yet, I guessed it was nearly nine. I showered, kitted up, and was about to leave for the game when I glanced at my watch. It was one o'clock in the afternoon. I was three hours late for the match. My alarm, and the opportunity of a large score before lunch, had failed to rouse me.

I bolted to the ground faster than Mr Mubashir fled the bridge over the Bosphorus. Reaching the AstroTurf, I found it deserted. I wondered if we were playing elsewhere.

I discovered Saif relaxing at the campus café.

"What happened?" he asked.

I had slept through the entire match. A National Championship match. I'd never missed a game in my life, but Bulgaria does strange things to a man. I apologised, and took this as a sign to move on.

I drove out of Sofia, guided by a Lebanese petrol station owner. He said there was no other way I'd find my way through the signless, potholed suburbs.

The road east took me between wooded hills, sunflower fields and rows of abandoned factories. Families sat on sofas under bridges. Slim teens in Gucci shades gathered beside collapsing tower blocks. It was as though the cast of *The O.C.* had been plucked up and deposited in South Wales.

I reached Veliko Târnovo, once Bulgaria's capital, and cruised up its vertical medieval streets. As I scoured for a room, I experienced a haunting flashback from my previous visit.

I had tried to come to Veliko Târnovo by train on a backpacking escapade two years previously. Fighting cramp, I sat with teenage skinheads and babushkas in a smoky carriage. At every stop they assured me, as did the conductor, that Veliko Târnovo was just a little further. I kept checking my map and scratching my head. The journey should have only taken a few hours.

After eight and a half hours, when I had given up hope, the train pulled into what looked like an oil refinery. Piles of sulphur lay exposed on the ground. The platform sign read, 'БУРГАС'. It looked a little short of lettering. Every passenger prepared to alight. I asked again if this was Veliko Târnovo. The skinheads and babushkas cackled as they stepped out. I scrambled through my guidebook for a translation of the station sign. I discovered I was in Burgas, at the end of the line. I'd overshot Veliko Târnovo by 200 kilometres.

It took me two days to backtrack. (Remind me never to pick up a Bulgarian hitchhiker.) I caught the last bus on a Sunday north from a grotty town called Sunny Beach and arrived in Varna at midnight. I showered in the town fountain and bedded down for the evening on the beach. Next morning I would take the train to Veliko Târnovo.

For cover on the beach I constructed a shelter out of four parasols. I looped the poles through my bag straps. It was the most comfortable night's sleep of my trip, until four in the morning, when I woke to find a man straddling me.

"Hi!" I said, confused.

"Huh?" replied the fat bloke with blond highlights.

"Hi!"

He looked irritated and slipped away. I didn't think anything strange of our meeting and fell asleep again.

It was daylight when I saw the big man again, this time with a mate from one of the all-night beach bars. They began dismantling my shelter to get at my backpacks. I sat up in my sleeping bag, watching them. They stared back, but continued while we each figured out what to do. Then the pair dropped the third parasol and traipsed off. It began to pour.

I arrived in Veliko Târnovo, in even heavier rain, at eight in the morning, carrying all my worldly possessions on my back. I checked at the tourist info stand and found my train didn't leave for Bucharest till midnight. As my budget had been blown by the extra days of travelling, I had no choice in the meantime but to beg.

Begging in Bulgaria is tougher than it might sound. Ever the entrepreneur, I believed my best chances lay in begging for services rather than hard cash. I trawled the streets looking for hotels listed in my guidebook. I relayed my woes at each front desk and asked kindly for a shower. The receptionists spared me no charity. I was turned away like a criminal every time.

In the final hotel, the receptionist nodded her head like everyone else that day. As I turned to leave, a Yorkshireman boomed across from the restaurant section. "Go on, give 'im ten leva from us! Put eet on our bill! You can't be goin' round without mooney, lad!"

But I didn't want money; I wanted a shower. Nevertheless, I accepted this offer gratefully. It might prove a powerful bargaining tool for the remainder of my afternoon. Now I could rent a shower.

"D'you want a piece of cake?" asked my rescuer. "'Ere you go."

I sat with the man and his wife, and gobbled up my first meal in two days. "We're joost 'aving a party to celebrate our new 'ouse," said the Yorkshireman. "We bought it after watching *A Place in the Sun*. Say, is that a cricket bat sticking out your bag?"

I pulled my bat from my backpack and handed it over. "I take it everywhere," I said.

The Yorkshireman stood up and practised his backlift and forward defensive. "That's the one thing we'll miss 'ere," he lamented. "That and me granddaughter. We've got ski slopes, Roman ruins . . . but no bloomin' Bulgarian cricket!"

*

Rather than pay a babushka ten leva for a shower now, which, incidentally, I did after my cake last time, I scored a whole room. It smelled of stale bread and overlooked Veliko Târnovo's river-loop gorge and ruined fifth-century citadel.

I feared for the residents of this pleasant town. English estate agents had popped up all over the hill, thanks to programmes like *A Place in the Sun*. It was attracting a mixed crowd. As I sat in a restaurant, scoffing omelette and quaffing tap water, 60-year-old Pam and Craig fae Greenock at the next table were giving two Bolton newcomers a rundown on what to expect from the region.

"Listen!" said fat, balding Craig, spitting as he spoke. "This place – Bulgaria – is wonderful. Ah came oot the pub here in the dark wan night, pished, and fell doon a pothole. Ah smashed a' ma teeth oot. Now, how much d'ye think it wid cost me fer a new set o' teeth back in Scotland? Eh? How much?"

Craig wouldn't let anyone else answer. "Aboot a grand, aye? Well, let me tell you ..." He thrust out a finger. "Here in Bulgaria, fer a whole new set o' teeth ... " He opened his mouth and his new set nearly popped out. " ... It cost me 200 quid. Two hundred! Ah'm no jokin'. Magic!"

Pam nodded and stroked Craig's arm. Craig continued. "This place has cul'ure. Back home, ballet is just fer *mincers*. Oot here, yer mannie on the street goes to ballet, and he's no necessarily a mincer. It costs two pounds for a show. *Two pounds*!"

"Ah'm full o' cul'ure, right? Ah went tae see the oldest piece of gold in the world in Varna. Ah said, 'That is shite! Whit am ah payin' fer? That's fuckin' tiny!' It's aboot the size o' a postage stamp, right? But then ah went and read up aboot it. Ah went back tae see it. Ah said, 'See you, ah've seen yous twice!' That, my friends, is cul'ure."

No one in earshot could draw breath before Craig was off again.

"And whit am ah gonna do back in Greenock? Sit on a dead man's chair, sipping tea? Ah can dae that in Bulgaria, by Christ. How many bags o' Tetley's did we bring back, Pam?"

"Six thousand, dear," said Pam.

"Six thousand!" echoed Craig.

He put his arm around the Bolton man's wife.

"A'right, darlin'?" he whispered.

He took her hand and planted a long kiss on it. The Bolton couple didn't react.

"Ah have irritable bowel syndrome," continued Craig, after dropping the hand. "Since ah've come tae Bulgaria, ah've no had the shites. Well, ah take that back. Maybe twice. But back in Greenock it wiz every day. Why do ah no have the shites here? Because the food is grilled. Su-perb! There's nane o' them preserva'ves or wit ya call them."

Craig saw me looking over and included me in his next bit.

"Another great thing. The yoghurt here cures ma bad breath. Ah tell yous, this place cannae be beaten. It's fuckin' paradise!

"The only bad thing," said Craig, "the only wan, is if you're a criminal. They put rapists in wi' thieves an' drug dealers here, wi' only a hole in the floor fer yer mornin' shower and shite."

I envisioned living here with Pam and Craig. They would come around to my house every night, telling these same stories till they got pished, fell over and smashed a' their teeth oot in a pothole. Yes, Bulgaria was a wonderful place. Until you got toothache, appendicitis, or neighbours like Pam and Craig.

*

I set off next morning for the Black Sea. If memory served me correctly, it was like Blackpool with Russians. It was where Skegness swingers bought timeshare. Still, I was compelled to return – not to see the oldest piece of gold in the world (after all, that wiz shite) – but because Varna had an all-native cricket team. Granted, they were currently on the other side of the country, engaged in the National Championship in Sofia. But by visiting their town I could pay homage and heal old travel wounds.

A two-lane motorway led to Varna. Every motorist drove on the hard shoulder because the legal lanes shredded tyres quicker than the 'Kitchen Wonder'. I veered onto them only to overtake donkeys and tractors running on their final pistons. In the country of the Trabant, the Škoda was king, I thought. Then a Lada powered by sunflower oil overtook me. I turned purple with envy.

Near the coast, the sky turned purple, too, from industrial plant emissions. I steered away from the chimney stacks and beach apartments of Varna and took the country back roads to Zvezditsa (or ЗВЕЗДИЦА on the rare signpost). As there was only one shop and a goat in the square, I believed the 700 residents would know the whereabouts of a youth hostel run by a young English couple in their village. Not even when armed with the street name and number could they hazard a guess. I began to think I'd be sleeping on the beach again.

Mercifully, I stumbled across Gregory's Backpackers by early evening. It was only eight kilometres from Varna, but those eight kilometres had taken me another two hours. I parked the Škoda outside the white gate and staggered in under the grapevine.

The hostel was full for the first time in its history, said the nice proprietors. I collapsed on a leather armchair.

"You're joking, right? I've driven for six hours. Can I pitch a tent out the back?"

A stranger called over from one of the computer terminals. "I'm sorry. Did you say you came by car?"

I turned to see the man. Who would have thought, in an eastern Bulgarian village, I'd run into another international cricketer?

15
TRANSYLVANIAN TOOTHACHE

Transylvanian transport

Mike was an Irishman who'd played cricket and rugby for Rhodesia.

"Zimbabwe?" I asked, as we sped past a dead dog every mile towards the Romanian border, together with his Dublin colleague, Peter.

"No, Rhodesia it was then," said Mike.

"How come you played for them?"

"My father sent me there at 19. When I landed at the airport, with £25, I got offered a job on a tobacco farm. As I'd played cricket back in Dublin, I joined the local club. And from there I ended up in the Curry Cup."

In a glittering career, Mike had spanked Mike Proctor for six and once knocked Graeme Pollock's off-stump out with his third delivery.

"That was back in the days when fielders smoked in the outfield," he said.

I asked if he'd ever seen anything paranormal on the cricket field. Mike thought about it for a minute, then answered, "I once saw two fielders knocked unconscious with one shot . . . It was in South Africa. The ball glanced off short leg's head, then struck square leg on the forehead. Both collapsed out cold and had to be carried from the field."

Mike was a real-life Prester John. He went on to buy his tobacco farm and became a horse-breeder and racing driver. He'd survived a snake bite and five car crashes. "One was at 120 miles per hour," he said. "I was annoyed at that. I broke a finger." At 67, retired from rugby, he was still not a man to mess with.

"You should've seen him yesterday," said Peter in the back, a broad grin on his face. "A gypsy tried to steal his wallet in Varna. Mike caught him. He smacked the guy in the face, and the thief and his five mates ran off like pack animals. It was hilarious!"

"I'd say the punch was about 70 per cent there," said Mike. "I got the little shit's ID card too."

Mike was able to provide invaluable advice on self-defence as we drove. "If two people are attacking you, you kick the fuck out of one of them. Break a bone and the fight's over."

We reached the remote Bulgarian–Romanian border, and stepped out of the car to allow an inspection. The guards opened the boot. My cricket gear was spread across it, hiding bottles of rakia, whisky and Croatian wine. Mike, standing over the guards, saw my bat and picked it up. He practised some lofty strokes. It looked like a toothpick in his hands.

"Come on, bowl at me," he said. The guards turned to watch.

I bowled a low full toss with a tennis ball. Mike smashed it over the fence into no man's land. The guards laughed.

"Sorry about that," said Mike. "We'll buy you another ball in Bucharest. I just needed a feel again."

Through the barrier, we came to a single tree-lined, cobbled avenue. Beyond lay flooded plains. Five bony Roma workmen were hammering in new cobbles, with one hammer between them. I wondered if the EU had pumped billions into connecting Sofia and Bucharest in this manner.

We guessed Bucharest lay to the right, but after 15 minutes a sixth workman said we were heading for the Danube delta.

"So it was left at the border," said Mike crossly. "You'd think they'd invest in a fuckin' sign."

Immediately beyond the border post again, the road stopped on the banks of the brown Danube. "We're trapped!" cried Peter. "What the hell are we supposed to do?"

"Look, there's a tug coming," I said. "Maybe we cross on that."

"Christ, it's like the Congo," said Mike.

The tug and its platform neared. I ran to buy a ticket from a hut. Romanian currency was confusing, having just had four zeros knocked off. Thousands of old lei were blowing over the dirt ground. A pirate lookalike in the ticket hut happily accepted a wodge of my euros and US dollars.

The tug and its platform took us alongside green islands populated with wild horses. We passed a gulag-like housing estate on the banks. Inside its courtyard sat a wingless passenger jet, which Mike reckoned was more housing.

We rolled off the platform on the Danube's far bank and second-geared along a causeway. The potholes were deep enough to bury old dishwashers in. Soon the right-hand lane became so ploughed up that both flows of traffic drove on the left.

Rural Romania was a grimy time warp. Gypsy caravans dotted the fields, with shelters pieced together from agricultural sacks. We passed linear bungalow villages, where even the horse and cart looked like a recent development. Kids swam in rivers while nodding donkeys pumped oil on the horizon. "This place is fucked," observed Mike accurately.

Mike seemed to have done a lot in his life, so I asked him if he'd ever killed a man.

"Sure. Lots of them," he answered coolly.

"Army?"

"Volunteer. I went into the Congo in 1960 after Belgium's pull-out."

"You *volunteered*?"

"The United Nations refused to do anything. I drove in with a convoy to get refugees out."

"From Kinshasa?"

"No, Elizabethville, as it was then. We bought our weapons at the border. We had to sign for them, and were told we'd be billed at the end, would you believe?"

"Who was in the convoy?"

"Just a bunch of guys."

"Backpackers?"

"A few. Some Australians. They would only get the basic rifle. Those with training got machine-guns, grenades and explosives for blowing up trees that had been felled for ambushes."

"Were you nearly killed?"

"Sure. Lots of times. Gangs were running from village to village, hacking people to pieces with machetes. In one house I saw a butchered mother and her children. There was a lot of blood . . . and flies. That made me vomit. You can't help it. Then we had showers of poison arrows coming down on us. We lost a lot of men that way. One little nick on your finger and you'd have about a minute and a half to live."

"What do people do when they know they're about to die?"

"They talk a lot. They pass on messages. They're generally pretty hysterical."

"And how many refugees did you save?"

"Over 90. I went back in again after."

Mike had stared death in the face and shrugged it off. I felt sure he'd save us in a Bucharest carjacking.

Peter, meanwhile, at 40, was engaged in his own equally terrifying battle. He had cancer.

"Before this trip the doctors gave me a two per cent chance," he said without a trace of concern. "I was diagnosed with seven tumours on my liver. They operated, but it was unsuccessful. They got six, but couldn't get the other."

Peter spoke positively. "That's why we're making this journey," he said. "I'd never done anything like this before. If I'd stayed in a hospital bed, I'd be dead now. I've got to go back for a scan in August. Hopefully, the tumour won't have grown, or spread, because my liver has been operated on too much. If it has developed, then my options are some more drug cocktails or, as a last resort, a liver transplant."

Both Peter and Mike had balls of lead. They looked at life in a way most of the rest of us, fortunately, couldn't.

"Where are you off to after Romania?" I asked.

"We're meeting a guy in Kyiv this weekend," said Peter. "Then we're thinking about going to Chernobyl and Moldova. What's the radiation going to do to me?"

"So you'll be getting your visas in Bucharest?"

"No. You don't need visas for Ukraine or Moldova now," corrected Peter, "because of the Eurovision Song Contest."

It had opened up the world in a whole new way, just like the fall of the Berlin Wall.

"Thank God," I said. "I needed a visa for Ukraine two years ago. I had to arrange accommodation beforehand. I mixed up the day and month on my application, and got grounded in Romania for weeks!"

By late afternoon we had reached Bucharest's nightmarish tower suburbs. The city was once called the Paris of the East, I guess on account of its drivers.

"Fuck! I can't work a bloody thing out if they don't have street signs!" screamed Mike, tossing the map on the floor. "Every damn building looks the same! Look at them. They're 20 years past their life expectancy!"

Horses and carts with number plates wove among the murderous rush-hour crowds. There were no lanes; traffic was six cars abreast. It was a 60-mile-per-hour free-for-all over a treacherous surface. The blood drained from my face as cars on either side slewed in front without warning. It looked like there'd shortly be no Škoda for shady bastards to pilfer in the night.

We were psychologically damaged when we reached our hostel two hours later, though astonishingly the Škoda remained unscratched. "This hostel'd better be good," warned Mike, "or you're a dead man."

I approached the desk inside.

"Hi, we have a reservation."

The girl looked at her book, then led us down a broken staircase to the basement. The walls were dripping with condensation. We entered a TV room. Four topless hippies were smoking spliffs, parked on a bench around the walls. It reeked of feet.

"These are your beds," said the receptionist.

"Where?" I asked.

She waved her hand at nowhere in particular.

"The benches?"

"Yes."

"How do we know which is our bed?" asked Peter. "And how do we get into bed if people are sitting there watching TV?"

"Ask them to move," suggested the girl.

"How many people will be in here tonight?" I asked.

"Seven or eight."

This may have been a conservative guess. Four more mattresses were leaning against the wall.

"It's 10 euros each," said the girl. I almost choked. The sweat-soaked sheets looked as though they hadn't been changed since the last full-moon party. We'd be sleeping head to toe while dreadlocked dudes pumped wind onto us all night.

We checked in upstairs and left for a beer at the pub.

"I'd rather sleep in the car," confessed Peter after a large draw on his pint. Mike and I nodded.

"I think we should drive on and find another hotel. Don't worry about it, Angus, we'll take care of it," promised Peter.

"Let's just grab our stuff and walk out that shithole," said Mike.

"What happens if they call the police?" I asked. "We checked in and never paid."

"They'll need to get through me first," said Mike.

Next morning we stepped out of our new hotel onto Bucharest's searing, dirty French boulevards. A pack of stray dogs was waiting for us in a street-wide, shin-deep puddle.

"Don't feed one or you'll have a thousand following you through the country," I warned from experience.

Stray dogs were the legacy of former President Ceauşescu. He outlawed shooting them because he felt pity for them, and even made his dog a colonel in the army. He had a hospital bulldozed when a cat, brought in to catch rats, scratched his dog's nose. Now 50,000 stray dogs roamed Bucharest's streets, biting up to 80 people a day.

We rounded the corner to see where Ceauşescu made his final speech on the balcony before fleeing by helicopter. Bullet holes still peppered the nearby buildings, showing where soldiers opened fire on protestors.

Next, we marched towards the People's Palace. It had been built exclusively for Ceauşescu and his wife, Elena. The bastard razed one sixth of the capital to make space for its modest 1000 rooms, and in doing so nearly bankrupted the country. Now it looked like a Hilton hotel missing the sign.

With heatstroke threatening, Peter, Mike and I decided to drive north to the mountains of Transylvania.

"So, where's your big cricket match?" asked Mike when we reached the Škoda.

Shamefully, there would be no scheduled cricket action in Bucharest, or in Romania. I'd heard of games played at the American International School, of knock-arounds at orphanages and of others involving priests. Indeed, during the 1880s cricket leagues had flourished between Bucharest, Odessa and Constantinople. But my only Romanian contact had fallen through just before I set out on tour.

"I will be on holiday at that time on a summer camp," he wrote. "I have lost contact with the cricket activity. Sorry."

Was this a 13-year-old I'd been coordinating with for over a year?

We motored out of Bucharest and traversed the plains into the conifer-covered mountains. The roof spires took on a more Gothic design, and thunder clapped above. I would have felt safer with a cricket stump in my hand for a stake. There were villages here where even today they dug up their dead at night and hatcheted them to pieces, believing them to be vampires. In one far-flung corner of Romania, an Orthodox priest had recently crucified a nun to death, claiming she was possessed.

We entered ski capital Braşov before sunset. This Saxon city had a special significance for me. It was here I first met my girlfriend, Candy.

I came to Braşov in 2003 to negotiate the purchase of a donkey. Some people thought this was strange until I explained that people rode the Inca trail on donkeys all the time. Given the number of donkeys in Romania, it was natural to want to cross the Carpathian Alps on one. And then I discovered I'd screwed up the dates on my Ukrainian visa and was grounded here for weeks.

I realised my funds wouldn't stretch far in a 13-euros-a-night hostel. I certainly couldn't buy a 200-euro donkey, as quoted by a farmer. I decided I had to get a job. In fact, I had to *beg* to get a job, *illegally*, in a country tens of thousands were trying to get out of in order to find work.

I explained my situation to Braşov's Korean-American hostel owner. He said the front desk was already overstaffed, by people who spoke four languages. I countered, saying that my niche lay in gardening. (I'd been an organic gardener in Edinburgh for a fortnight.) The owner was impressed. I was assigned the task of plucking up weeds and scooping dog dirt by day. By night, I restocked the beer fridge. I would not be paid. Instead I would be given a mattress on the floor, or first claim to the sofa when the hostel was overbooked.

I toiled hard in the heat and afternoon showers, hoping for a good reference for my CV. Then one day a dark-haired Québecoise arrived by car from Belgium and spied my rippling torso and mucky hands in the garden.

When she said she was a chocolate heiress by the name of Candy, I was won over. She was the girl I'd suffered years of celibacy for. I washed my hands before shaking hers.

That night it was imperative I put on a good show, given the tiny window of opportunity. I showered, shaved and put on my crumpled best to woo her. I was transformed from a grubby bushman into a suave, French-speaking Scotsman. I skipped to the shop and purchased a bottle of Burgundy with which to ply her.

After dinner I pulled out my trump card, recounting my tales from Australia's hotel from hell. I talked about the dwarf I lived with, who was straight from prison and stole dummies from babies. For the first time a girl listened without screaming and running away. In fact, Candy believed my stories. Most people thought *I* was the lunatic. I knew I was in with a chance.

*

Any doubts Mike and Peter might have had about my hostel choice were banished as I now led them into my former workplace. They kicked off their shoes and sat with a beer apiece on the first-floor balcony, overlooking Braşov's wonky, tiled rooftops and wooded hills. They wouldn't get such comfort on the night train to Ukraine and Moldova.

Rather than sleep on the floor or sofa this time, I shared a dorm with several potential new passengers. I set about cross-examining them. The first was an Englishman, who looked like a Soho pimp. He admitted he'd slept in the stalls at Birkenau death camp after missing his bus.

My second roommate was a Swede. He'd travelled all this way to see wolves.

"I just want to see wolves, you know? Wolves. I'm going up the mountain tonight. Do you want to come? Maybe we'll sleep up there?"

"There's bears up there!" I pointed out. "Eight mushroom pickers were mauled by one with rabies last year!"

My third roommate was a Canadian, also oblivious to the dangers of wild animals in these parts.

"I got bitten by a stray dog yesterday," he said, "but I figured I don't wanna go to hospital. I wanna make Budapest on this trip."

"What if it had rabies? You've got to get to the hospital now, or you'll die!" I said.

"I don't care, man. I really wanna see Budapest. The hospital's an inconvenience."

It looked like I'd be travelling alone to Ukraine.

*

Two days later, after Mike and Peter's departure, I woke with swollen glands. I had a feeling in my mouth like I'd been chewing on glass in the night. It was Day One of the Ashes. The last thing I wanted was to miss the action because of an appointment at the Romanian dentist.

I darted groggily through Braşov's cobbled old quarter, dodging rabid strays. I asked a man trying to sell one shoe if he knew a bar with Sky Sports. I'd been told the Queen's Arms (renamed for legal reasons) was the surest bet.

I reached the Queen's Arms entrance. Clutching my cheek with one hand, I felt my way down the banister to the basement. I could hear supporters' screams on the other side of the door. A wicket must have fallen! Were the Transylvanians Australia or England supporters? I knocked frantically on the door to be let in. Again, I heard shouts.

"Hurry up!" I cried.

A half-naked man with a ponytail opened the door. Behind him I saw a dimly lit room full of bare-topped truckers. One or two were leather-masked; all were moshing to AC/DC. I could see no TV, nor any cricket action. Never had I glimpsed so much chest hair.

"Cricket!" I said breathlessly. "The Ashes!"

The half-naked man clasped a hand around my face and pushed me back two steps. "Sorry. There is no Alice in Wonderland here."

He slammed the door. I could have cried.

I mounted the steps and asked the first teenager on the street for directions to the Opium Bar.

"Opium?" he said. He slapped his veins and pointed back down to the Queen's Arms.

With no Ashes action, the pain in my mouth doubled. I staggered into the nearest photo shop.

"Do you know a good dentist?" I asked at the counter.

"Yes, I know a good dentist," replied the shopkeeper. As he opened his mouth he revealed an entire front set missing their centres. It looked as though a Black & Decker drill had been applied to his teeth. The edges had rotted silvery-grey. It reminded me of a Bosnian building.

Fuck me, I thought. I grabbed the counter to steady myself. "I think I'll wait and see how I feel tomorrow."

As I turned to leave, I felt a sharp twinge.

"Give me the address and phone number, please."

I took a taxi and found myself heading deep into Ceauşescu's suburbs. They made Manchester's worst sink housing estates look attractive. The taxi driver stopped and pointed at a tower block doorway.

"You mean it's in someone's house?" I asked.

The taxi man shrugged.

I entered the tower block as though a mugger was ready to jump me. I rapped on the first door. No one answered so I tried opposite. A teenage girl wearing a face mask and an apron appeared.

"Hi. I phoned about an appointment earlier."

She beckoned me into a blue room – the reception and surgery combined. She motioned me to sit in the dentist's chair. It was like a medieval instrument of torture, held together by rope. The lady dentist raised the chair with a foot pump.

"Umm . . . I'm experiencing some pain at the back right . . ." I began.

The dentist lowered her face mask. "Sorry. My English . . . very . . ."

"Limited?" I said.

She nodded. "You have to . . . speak slower . . . not use . . . big words."

"Like anaesthetic?"

She made an advance for my mouth with a mirror and a scraping tool. My eyes flitted around the room. There was no toy box in the surgery, which I felt aggrieved about. The walls were bare but for a poster of a smiling, white-toothed model.

"I see," said the dentist. "You have hole in . . . what is word?"

Oh God, oh God, oh God.

"Gum," she continued.

Relief washed over me.

"And there is . . . food in it. You have very good teeth."

"What kind of food?" I asked.

"Hmm. Pizza, maybe? I clear hole."

Now I could relax and enjoy the experience.

"Is that poster advertising teeth whitening?" I asked.

The dentist looked over and nodded.

"How much does it cost?"

What was I saying? I'd got off lightly, all things considered, and now I was enquiring about cosmetic surgery.

"I wouldn't . . . recommend it," said the dentist.

"Don't undersell yourself."

"I *really* wouldn't recommend it."

I admired her honesty.

The dentist approached the chair, this time carrying a syringe. The needle looked as crooked as a Romanian carrot. I squealed, though no sound came out. She put the syringe into my mouth. I felt a sensation in my gum, but never having had a mouth injection, I couldn't say whether the needle had been plunged. My mouth burned and I tasted bleach.

"I squirt," said the dentist. "Now spit."

The assistant brought a bucket.

"Horrible, yes? We do it again . . . Spit."

Operation complete, I rinsed my mouth and leapt from the chair.

"I give you note for pharmacy," said the dentist. "You need antibiotics for lumps in neck."

"Thank you. How much do I owe you?"

She shook her head. "No charge. I didn't do anything."

After the agony of England's first-innings batting collapse, I realised there was little I could do to help them. I needed to focus on my own recovery. I held net sessions outside the hostel with orphaned street kids, and followed the dentist's antibiotic course, abstaining from (too much) alcohol.

The two-month watershed for this trip was nearing and my powers of observation were waning. My clothes smelled, I missed Candy, and I was in danger of looking at architectural masterpieces and thinking, 'Yeah, whatever.' I understood how professionals must feel on tour. It was no wonder some ended up in titty bars.

Driving through Romania and into Ukraine would be a dangerous business. I pored over the map and saw my distances were doubling in direct proportion to the road surfaces worsening. I wanted an immediate end to the trip, but I then remembered I had a mission to complete.

From a cricket perspective, my itinerary was mouthwatering. Coming up shortly were four matches in seven days. It would test all my powers to reach that 100.

16
TROTSKY WAS A UKRAINIAN CRICKETER
(OF SORTS)

'A posh area', Kyiv

The Škoda began tearing up the miles on its final leg. Zipping north through Romania, I passed oxen pulling carts and crop fields no bigger than snooker tables. Recent flooding had devastated the region, leaving shops without walls and rivers running through people's kitchens. Newspapers had reported Romanians were donating crockery, lipstick and fancy-dress costumes to the relief cause.

After more environmental taxes, I left the Romanian check-point and crawled forward to the Ukrainian post.

'Attention! Entrance is allowed 1. For lack of: cultural values, poisonous, virulent, radioactive, explosive substances, weapons, ammunition, drugs and psychotropic substances, precursors', read the sign.

Was cricket an English cultural value? Would I be in trouble for having intent to play? Best not declare it, I thought. Precursors were a concern, though. I had no idea if I was carrying these or not. What if the guards found some in my boot?

"Do you have a lot of guns?" asked the lady guard.

What did she mean by *a lot*? Were five or six acceptable? I shook my head. She lifted the barrier.

Ukraine – cradle of Slavic civilisation – both fascinated and terrified me. I'd first entered the country in the back of a van chartered by a man with gold teeth. It was a sign of prosperity in Ukraine. Poked and ridiculed by my fellow peasant passengers, I thought I was going to be mugged and shanghaied to Moldova, where I'd wake in an ice bath, minus a kidney. When the man with gold teeth set me down in Chernivtsi with only a five-euro note in my possession, I discovered a place where wheels fell off moving SUVs and houses collapsed as buses drove past.

This time the drive into Ukraine was a pleasant experience. I passed melon vendors and overtook a donkey, a horse and cart and a Mercedes with blacked-out windows. Shortly I reached the cobbled streets of Chernivtsi.

All the menace seemed to have lifted within two years. The city was like a mini-Vienna. New shops with fancier goods had sprung up, fresh paint gleamed on the baroque stonework and the once-crumbling balconies had been replastered. I checked into a *studenti* squat and crashed out in my lumpy bed.

After a 13-hour coma, I was woken by a fight in the corridor between a floorlady, a businessman and a prostitute. I left them pointing fingers at each other, and wandered outside to catch a trolleybus to the city centre. One hundred and fifty babushkas packed on board, sandwiching me as we bounced down the street like a space hopper. The conductress sat on a high chair at the back, feeding lines of change and tickets along the bus.

Escaping the crush, I trekked up and down Chernivtsi's steep avenues, admiring the Austrian churches, a Soviet tank and the pillared, green Opera House. Babushkas squatted on the pavements beside bins, selling wonky carrots and potatoes from cardboard boxes. I came across a Viennese square dug up into World War One-like trenches. I was about to head back to the hotel when a girl shouted, "Angus!"

I spun around to see Nadya, a graduate friend I'd met on my previous trip. She'd been a journalist back then and wrote a piece for the *Chernivtsi Times* about my visit to Ukraine.

"Nadya!"

"This is unbelievable! I have school friends for five or six years and I have never met them on the street! What are you doing in Chernivtsi?"

"I'm heading to Kyiv to play cricket. I stopped to say hello. I was going to track you down at the newspaper office today."

Nadya lowered her eyes. "I no longer work there."

"What? You said you'd never quit!"

"I know, but a businessman we featured came to me and threatened, 'You are on the last step to death!' I was too afraid. I resigned. Our editor was beaten in his home five times, and summoned to court 48 times some years ago ... But now I am a state official. I am the main specialist in the Department of Information on Policy and Press!"

"Congratulations!"

"Oh, it's not that great. The pay is only $60 a month."

Nadya had to return to the Department of Information on Policy and Press, but we agreed to hook up after work.

We met again in the Hard Rock Café – not part of the Hollywood chain, just an admirable rip-off. There was a concert on stage, but we were the only audience within the vast, gloomy hall. I asked Nadya about Ukraine since the Orange Revolution.

Nadya shook her head. "I am disappointed. I expected great change, but many bad things still happen. Many corrupt people are still in power."

I asked if she'd taken to the streets after the rigged presidential election.

"Yes! But first I was going to university. I could see people looking nervous. In class I said, 'People, you can sit here and you can sit here for your lives! We must do something! Think about your future!'"

Nadya said, "We formed a student strike committee. In Chernivtsi 40,000 protestors gathered on the street, even though the temperature was below zero. We got the boys to guard the square because there were no police. They were all in Kyiv, ready to fire on protestors. We camped out every night and organised food for people. Employers donated many supplies. We would not accept the election result and we would not leave till we had free elections."

Ukraine's 2004 presidential election campaign involved tricks Saddam Hussein would have been proud of. Besides the poisoning of the favourite contender, pro-Western Viktor Yushchenko, whose handsome face turned to mince as a result, some polling stations issued voters with disappearing ink, while others recorded 105 per cent turnouts.

I remembered Baltic Adventurer Julian from Estonia telling me he'd voted in Ukraine's 1994 election on holiday. He went to the polling station with a friend. The officer gave him a slip and told him who to vote for.

Nadya continued, "They poured acid into ballot boxes, bribed election officers, exploded a bomb in the market, then blamed it on Viktor Yushchenko. State employees were threatened with losing their jobs if they voted for Yushchenko. They even used subliminal messaging on TV."

I felt for Nadya and her proud countryfolk. In the West we had democracy, and hardly anyone voted. In Ukraine they risked their lives just for the chance.

The next morning, before leaving Chernivtsi, I was torn between two camping excursions. To the west lay the Carpathian Mountains, heavily populated with bears, wolves, boars and lynxes. To the east was lovely communist Transdniestr, a Mafia breakaway region of Moldova, where holiday homes come cheap. I decided I would make for Kyiv after lunching in Transdniestr because it was in another country, and it's not every day you get to do that.

I motored through single-street bungalow villages, where peasants sat on grass verges selling tomatoes. Others bicycled along swinging Hugo Boss bags. The region was painfully poor, but each village boasted a monumental church topped with gold domes.

As it turned out, I was refused entry to Moldova. Customs were unaware Eurovision had brought down their visa requirements. I consoled myself by saying lunch would have been crap anyway, and drove on.

From the Ukrainian-Moldovan border I had little idea where I was going. I couldn't read the road signs and my map was useless. My only hope of finding Kyiv was a plastic compass stuck by a suction cup to the windscreen.

A smell of creosote blasted constantly through my air vents as I journeyed north-east. Wrinkly peasants were selling kippers by the roadside; smoked, perhaps, by diesel fumes. I passed cities where cows grazed beside factories and every window was broken. Then I stopped to buy lunch in a village shop. The shopkeeper handed me my loaf and banana in a yellow Sainsbury's bag.

'A penny will be given to you each time this bag is re-used in Sainsbury's', it read. Where on earth was the nearest Sainsbury's to southern Ukraine? There wouldn't be one for 2500 kilometres.

At the end of the next village I stopped to pick up a family of hitchhikers. When I pulled over, a babushka with metal teeth began babbling through my window.

"Kyiv! Kyiv!" was all I could say in return. I unlocked the passenger doors and a blonde girl sat down in the back seat, carrying a Hugo Boss bag and a shoebox. The rest of her family remained on the grass, shouting at me.

"Kyiv! Kyiv!" I said, and sped off.

It was not long before I heard chirping and clucking in the back. I looked in the mirror and saw a hen flapping out of the Hugo Boss bag. The shoebox was full of chicks.

At the next town, my passenger signalled me to set her down. I pulled over and she grabbed her chicken by its feet and slung it back in the bag. She held out a two-hryvnia note and I waved it away.

Kyiv was the third largest city in the former USSR. Driving into it alone without a map was a challenge I relished. I made my way to the packed train station and went inside the main building. Military music was playing through the speakers. I found a payphone and called my contact.

"Hi, Thamarai. It's Angus."

"Who, sorry?" replied the polite Indian man's voice.

"Angus – from Scotland. I was in touch by email about playing cricket here."

There was a pause.

"And you are in Kyiv?" He sounded shocked.

"Yes."

"Really? You made it here? Oh, man. Where are you now?"

"The train station."

"Okay, okay, you need to take a taxi."

"I have a car."

"What? You have a car? You drove all the way to Kyiv? Oh, God, oh, God, oh, God . . . You know, this is the worst time! I am stuck in three meetings this evening. If you can make it to the New Bombay Palace restaurant, I will meet you there. Everybody knows it. Okay?"

"Okay."

I found the New Bombay Palace sitting on its own in the centre of a spaghetti junction. If I'd been told it was beside a giant stainless steel statue of a woman brandishing a sword and shield, known as Tin Tits, I might have found it in less than three hours.

Inside, I was whisked to a high-backed throne by a waiter in full Indian servant dress. Kama Sutra carvings hung on the wall and England versus India from 1979 was being screened on the telly.

A small, round man wearing a shirt, a moustache and a gold watch appeared.

"Welcome, welcome! Great to meet you," said Thamarai. "I simply cannot believe this, that you have come all this way to play cricket! This is amazing! So, you are an official from the International Cricket Council, yes?"

"Umm, no. I'm just a bloke who likes cricket."

"Right, right." Thamarai nodded. "Can I get you something? Something to eat? Something to drink? Chai? Samosas?"

Thamarai signalled to the waiting staff, who hurried into the kitchen.

"Okay, I am very busy right now. I apologise. This is the worst day. I must return to meetings now, but I will see you afterwards. If you want anything, just ask, please."

I sat watching the cricket, eating samosas and sipping herbal chai. They were like sporting and culinary heroin. When Thamarai's meetings concluded, 20 Indian businessmen entered the room. They each shook my hand and gave me expensive business cards.

"So this is Angus, a freelance professional cricket writer," announced Thamarai. "Can you believe it? He drove all the way from Scotland via . . . where was it?"

"Montenegro."

"Oh, man! And he is going to be playing cricket with us this Saturday and Sunday!"

"Just Saturday," I said. "Sunday I have a game in Gomel."

"Oh, man!" said Thamarai.

The businessmen left and Thamarai led me in his green Škoda to the supermarket. He bought me bananas, muesli and two celebratory Stella Artois, then checked me into a hotel.

"Unfortunately, there is no hot water," he said at reception. "Sometimes you have to pay extra for this. In this hotel it is normally included, but they are fixing the pipes. There will be no hot water for one month. The price is 30 euros per night – but it is a nice room. You won't find anywhere cheaper."

I tried to work out how many books I'd have to sell to afford this, but soon lost count. It would do. I could always sleep in the car on my return home.

After Thamarai had inspected the room to ensure there were no cockroaches, he said, "Okay. Tomorrow I will send my driver to pick you up. If you have any problems, here is my card. Please, call me any time."

I was collected next morning and delivered to Thamarai's office at Unique Pharmaceuticals. A gold cup, almost as large as Thamarai, rested on the bookcase.

"Ah, this is our tournament trophy!" he announced, grinning. "Excuse me. I will fetch you a cup of chai."

I sat down at the boardroom table and flicked through a copy of the *Kiev Post*. There was a distressing article about the murder of Ukraine's junior rugby coach. He'd been run down the previous week. When he stood up and shouted at the driver, the driver got out and shot him four times at point-blank range. Twice in the head. Sport was a dangerous business in Ukraine.

Thamarai reappeared with the tea.

"When are you playing in Belarus?"

"Sunday."

"Oh, it is a shame you will not get to play in Ukraine as well."

"Sorry?"

Thamarai put his hand on my shoulder. "I am afraid I have some very bad news. You see, it is India versus Sri Lanka on Saturday, and it is being broadcast on television. There hasn't been any cricket broadcast for five months, so the guys are very excited. They have arranged to watch it."

"Could we play a short game afterwards?"

"Maybe, but I am not sure. I just want to keep your feet on the ground. Already I am feeling very guilty about this, but there is not much I can do. I will speak to the guys and see."

Thamarai produced a plastic bag containing a new cricket shirt, a tracksuit and a tee shirt. The logo 'MacCoffee' was printed on them.

"I brought you these," he said. "They are from our last tournament. Take them, please."

Thamarai sat down at his desk, which was buried under paperwork. I asked him how he came to work at Unique Pharmaceuticals.

Originally from Madras (now Chennai), he moved to Kyiv from Moscow in 1997 to set up the company. It now had a $10 million annual turnover from selling throat lozenges and a cough syrup called Dr Mom.

"Have you fallen ill since working here?"

"Actually, I don't think I have."

I asked how cricket started in Kyiv.

Thamarai talked passionately about it. He said, "I helped form the first club in Moscow in '95. When I moved here I wanted to do the same. It was a way of bringing people together. Now we have three Kyiv teams."

"Are you a batsman or a bowler?"

"Actually, I am a bit of an all-rounder, but I don't do much on the field now. I mainly coordinate the Exotic XI. Cricket is not my best sport, you see. Back in India I played hockey at national level."

"What was Moscow cricket like?"

"Oh, man, it was incredible! There were some very fine players, mostly pharmaceutical workers and traders. Now there are many ambassadors involved. And the Russians, they had a similar ancient game called lapta."

I made a note to follow up on this.

"How many other cricket teams are there in Ukraine?"

"Let me see . . ." Thamarai counted on his fingers. "There is one in Kharkiv, one in Donetsk, one in the Crimea . . . about eight altogether. There are various breakaway leagues, too, in many cities and universities, but this," he shook his head, "is not proper cricket. They play with tennis balls wrapped in tape. This is not cricket for me."

"And you use proper balls?"

"Well, they are softer because we have no sanatorium."

"Who plays?"

"Mostly we are medical students, engineers and corporate businessmen, but . . . oh, man! You should have come during one of our tournaments! It is simply amazing! We have 400 people in the crowd!"

Thamarai shook with excitement.

"Four hundred!" I said.

"Yes, it is like a big festival! We play 25-over games in a stadium. We have a DJ, advertising boards, medals, the lot!"

"Corporate hospitality?"

"Yes. That too. Business deals are being made. Families go wild in the crowd, there is cheering! Here, I'll show you some photos of our last tournament." He produced an album from his desk and began flicking through.

"Are there ever fights?"

"Oh, many! There are a lot of threats made . . . mainly over the Duckworth and Lewis method for rain interruptions. The prize is big, you see. Each team must pay $500 to enter."

"Five hundred dollars!"

"Yes. We have a $500 award for each man of the match. A $1000 award for man of the tournament. There are $2000 for the winning team, and another $1000 for the runner-up."

For a moment I considered becoming a professional cricketer in Ukraine.

"How much does all this cost?"

"Last tournament cost $10,300."

"How do you afford all this?"

"We get big-business sponsorship. We are due to go to sponsorship negotiations right now, actually, if you would be interested in coming."

Thamarai's driver took us across the River Dnipro, past its once-radioactive beaches, to the far side of sprawling concrete Kyiv. He dropped us at a shopping mall where Thamarai and I took the lift to a sports clothing store on the third floor. There Thamarai introduced me to three more Ukrainian-Indian cricketers, including the store manager, who'd played with Thamarai in Moscow.

We were led to an office in the attic. Most of the furniture and files were still packed in boxes. Chai was brought by the store manager's secretary to smooth the way for negotiations.

"Each tournament has to match the previous, at least, or better it," began Thamarai. "Here is a breakdown of our proposed fourth tournament costs."

He handed the store manager a spreadsheet. The store manager cast his eye over the figures and nodded.

"You can see we want to raise tournament prize money to $5000 this time. To compensate some of this, team entry fees will rise to $1000."

I felt giddy at these figures. It was like going into my parents' mail order business as a kid on a day off from school. And all this for a Ukrainian cricket competition. I sipped my chai and tried to act grown up.

"So, how much sponsorship do you want?" asked the store manager, leaning back.

"Ten thousand dollars," replied Thamarai coolly. The two other men in the room nodded. I also nodded.

"Ten thousand dollars?" repeated the store manager, flexing his fingers and puffing out his cheeks. I thought for a moment he'd have us chased from the building with dogs.

"For example," put in Thamarai hastily, "last time we were sponsored by three-in-one instant coffee-maker, MacCoffee. They donated $5000. The players drank their coffee at drinks breaks, all clothing carried their logo. We erected a podium and advertising boards with their brand. We can guarantee people will come and see your brand. Last time we had 400. This time I think we can get 600 or more. Maybe we could put your logo on every bat sticker."

The manager flicked the costing sheet with his finger.

"Okay. I will make some phone calls, and see what I can do. I will call you back with an answer tonight."

"Excellent," said Thamarai, smiling.

We all stood up to shake hands.

I spent the afternoon wandering around Kyiv and arranging my Belarusian visa. Ukraine's capital was as fond of its gold domes as it was of gold teeth. Although ploughing ahead with Western reform, Soviet signs remained. Shoulder pads were popular among women in the 35–50 age range. When combined with bleached hair-buns and ghastly pink lipstick, it was enough to put me off the traditional pork fat dipped in chocolate.

Ukraine's path to a fully-fledged market economy was evidently a struggle for many citizens. Gold-medallist Olympians now drove taxis. The metro steps were packed with headscarved babushkas attempting to sell meat and berries. It was said some of them did their picking in Chernobyl-affected areas, where cucumbers could grow to the height of cricket stumps.

I walked into an internet café and decided to research the ancient Russian game of lapta, which Thamarai had mentioned. Could it have had a hand in shaping cricket? Google provided some intriguing leads.

Lapta sounded like Serbian sockball without the socks. It used a hard ball and dated back to Mongol rule in the fourteenth century. Even Trotsky had played lapta. In Max Eastman's biography *Leon Trotsky: The Portrait of a Youth*, Trotsky showed the author where he played lapta with other inmates in a Moscow prison courtyard.

Could Trotsky, with his lapta skills, have become a professional cricketer? I wondered. I did another Google search, and rubbed my eyes.

Up came an article titled *The Secret Life of Leon Trotsky* by Robert A Elias, a mystery writer and Professor of Politics at the University of San Francisco. His article had been published in *Nine: A Journal of Baseball History and Culture*.

Elias had been visiting Trotsky's Mexican residence, where Trotsky was found with an ice pick in his head, when he noticed a Cleveland Indians' baseball pennant in the corner of the study. Using his investigative skills, Elias made an extraordinary discovery.

Trotsky had been a lapta whizz in his native Ukraine. He went on from his school side to become a semi-pro pitcher for the region. His vision, other than Marxist revolution, was to see lapta as Russia's national sport. Even Lenin said, "Anyone who wishes to understand the Russian soul had better learn lapta", wrote Elias.

As Lenin's right-hand man, Trotsky often squabbled with Stalin over their favoured lapta teams, claimed Elias. Then Stalin gained control of the party. Trotsky was arrested and eventually banished from the USSR. It was believed he went to Turkey, but Elias had discovered something different; something that turned history on its head.

He argued that Trotsky had in fact slipped secretly into the US, where he hid away on an Iowa farm. He forged paperwork to obtain a birth certificate and changed his name to Harold Arthur Troyavesky.

It just so happened that at this time an ageing baseballer named Hal Trosky emerged on the scene. Elias's investigations found his background information to be sketchy. It was known only that he came from Norway, Iowa – where Trotsky was said to be hiding – and that he mingled a great deal with Eastern Europeans. Elias's findings suggested Leon Trotsky and Hal Trosky were one and the same.

Even at an age by which most players would have retired, Hal Trosky became a star hitter, though his cross-handed batting baffled everyone. Everyone, that is, except Cleveland Indians scout Cy Slapincka, a man of Czech and Russian descent. Elias wrote, "Hitting cross-handed was standard practice in Russian lapta", and Slapincka would have known this. He signed Hal Trosky on the spot. The Russian revolutionary had broken into Major League Baseball.

In his first full year with Cleveland Indians, Hal Trosky was labelled 'the next Babe Ruth' by American League President William Harridge. But for his age, he looked destined for the Baseball Hall of Fame. As soon as the season ended, Trotsky was to pop up across Europe and Mexico, only to return for the next baseball season under his secret identity.

Elias cited a *New York Times* article published on February 17, 1935, which reported that the Soviets were planning to make baseball their national sport. Trotsky was involved in the scheme. When Stalin learned of this, heads rolled at the Ministry of Sport. Stalin "launched a counterproposal to make ice hockey, and not baseball, into the Soviet national game".

Stalin then set out to kill Trotsky, not because of the baseball plan, but because he was a political threat. Elias's most extraordinary claim was that Trotsky's ice pick murder in 1940 was in fact faked to throw off Stalin.

After the staged murder, Hal Trosky was to play a couple more baseball seasons before retiring and returning to his Iowa farm.

"For a short stretch, he was one of baseball's greatest players", wrote Elias.

Even after his playing days, Trotsky remained involved in the game. He pushed for the professional women's league and scouted Latin America for the White Sox. In a final twist, long after his real death from a heart attack, Hal Trosky's farm was used to film *Field of Dreams*.

I spun around in my chair. I wanted to share this incredible discovery with the Ukrainian teenagers in the internet café. This was phenomenal. I reread the article and printed it out. I began writing to Mr Robert A Elias at the University of San Francisco to congratulate him.

But wait, I thought, the pointer hovering over 'Send'. This smacked of something familiar. Yes. It smacked of Howard J Wall at the Department of Economics, Birkbeck College. I needed to check the facts.

Another Google search revealed Hal Trosky had indeed been a great baseballer for a few seasons. And Trotsky *had* played lapta in a Moscow prison courtyard. But could the head of the Red Army really have gone on to play Major League Baseball? The next Babe Ruth?

I rewrote my letter to Robert A Elias. "Is this a clever spoof?"

"No," he wrote back. "I'm afraid it is a spoof. I've had a number of people believing it, however. I'm curious about your research on lapta. What are you investigating in particular? Take care, Rob Elias."

I would never believe anything by American academics again.

Thamarai was driving me to the game in his Škoda.

"Oh, man. This is a huge event!" he said. "All our wives are on holiday. We haven't seen a game for five months. Everyone will be there!"

"Do your wives approve?"

"Oh, they're fine with it. But last night we were at the casino till four. It's typical weekend fun. Though if I'd left at two, I'd have been happy." Thamarai laughed.

"How much did you lose?"

"One guy lost $2000, then won it back. I stopped after losing 500."

We reached a cluster of Lego-brick tower blocks between leafy parkland.

"This is a very posh area, like Southall in London," said Thamarai. "There are a lot of Indians living here."

We parked beside an Opel that had been set ablaze. It was missing half its windscreen, its bumper and lights. Thamarai led me into one of the towers and we took the lift. At the top we were beckoned into an apartment thick with incense.

"Welcome, please," said our barefooted host.

Five Ukrainian-Indian cricketers were spread out on the pink sofas, dressed in shorts and tee shirts. India versus Sri Lanka was on the TV.

"Oooh, very, very, shaky, shaky, Yuvraj!" commented one player at a loose stroke.

"Well batting!" said another, as the next ball was hit for four.

Conversation switched quickly to Urdu. I could only latch onto words like "bowling", "vicketkeeper" and "excellent".

"I'm sorry," said one player, when he caught my glazed look. "Do you speak Urdu?"

"Some Punjabi," I said.

"Really?" asked Thamarai. "What can you say?"

"It's not polite. I'd rather not . . ."

Everyone sat upright. "Go on. Say it!"

I told them all the Punjabi I knew. "My black mum gives me strength", "Did you drink your mother's milk, or somebody else's?" and "Your mother is a whore".

They liked that.

"My God! How did you learn this?" asked Thamarai.

"From the cricket field."

Lunch was ordered from the New Bombay Palace. Shortly, potent tubs of pilau rice, palak paneer, romali roti and dal makhani arrived, along with a bright mixed pepper salad. I spooned a helping of this onto my plate and took a large bite.

It was raw chilli. My eyeballs and throat seared. I gasped for air.

"What is it? What is it?" cried Thamarai, leaping to his feet, running around the table. He looked ready to perform the Heimlich manoeuvre.

"Oh, God, oh, God, oh God!" he screamed.

I couldn't speak. I went into a fit of violent hiccups on the floor, pointing at the chilli salad.

"Coke! Quick, man!" ordered Thamarai.

The bottle was passed down the line, and Thamarai poured some into my mouth. It was like antivenene.

By the time the hiccups had eased, late in the first innings, we were each curled up on the sofas. India's batting had been so boring that we all fell into a snooze. The players had waited five months for this.

We awoke to see Sri Lanka's fans setting fire to newspapers in the stands after their team's three-wicket victory. It was not the result the Ukrainian-Indians wanted. Indeed, some even felt

Kyiv's Exotic XI would have fared better.

I had one final question for Thamarai. It was central to my mission. It had been the word Ukraine, after all, which had sparked this trip. Was it a coincidence, or was it for deeper, more mystical reasons?

"Thamarai, could I play for Ukraine based on being Ukrainian in a previous life?"

The players looked at the chilli salad again, then at each other.

"I don't know," answered Thamarai. "What are the rules? Maybe the ICC would know."

Thamarai gave the matter some more thought, then added, "Maybe you'd need a psychic in court to prove residency."

17

INSPECTOR MORSKi

A Belarusian tourist coach

Near the Belarusian border a policeman pulled me over.

"Bloody hell!" I screamed, bringing the car to a halt. "I wasn't speeding!"

The officer approached and I rummaged for my licence. He walked to the passenger door and tapped on the window. I lifted the lock. He climbed in and sat down. There would be no speeding fines; this policeman was trying to get to work.

The officer didn't speak any English. He didn't even speak Ukrainian. Only Russian.

"This is magic!" I said. "There's no way I can get booked with you in the car."

After five miles, crossing villages where the communist flag still flapped proudly, I set the policeman down.

At the end of the next village I was hauled up again. But this time the policeman had a speed gun. In my push to make today's game, I'd been going 10 kilometres per hour over the limit. This could be costly, I thought. My supply of foreign currency was critically low and all my Ukrainian cash had been spent. I looked in the mirror and saw a skinhead being forced into the back of a squad car. The officer arrived at my window and saluted.

"Good morning, officer," I said. "I'm sorry. I'm in a hurry to get to a cricket match in Gomel."

"Huh?"

I handed over my car papers and licence.

"Pivo? Pivo?" asked the officer, shaping to tip a bottle down his throat.

"No, I don't have any beer," I said. "But I *do* have some other stuff in the back which you might like."

I got out of the car and dug around in the boot for some miniature whiskies and Serbian brandy. I did this conspicuously because I didn't want him confiscating my entire stash.

"There's the stuff!" I said, laying a hand on two bottles.

I turned. The officer was looking back at his car. A thought struck me. Maybe he'd been asking if I was *under the influence* of beer. Not, could I give him some? And now I was about to show him I was on the brandy and Scotch. As he turned to face me again, I tossed the bottles over my shoulder.

"Look, buddy," I said, glancing from side to side, reaching into my pocket. "Here's five euros." I held it out. "Shall we call it quits?"

The officer looked back at the skinhead in the car, then at the moist five-euro note in my hand. He took it, stuffed it in his pocket and returned my licence. With another salute, I was free to go.

Getting through Belarusian customs was like sitting every A-level exam, changing a driving licence address, renewing road tax, registering with a new doctor, opening a British bank account and applying for a sex change all in one. And this had to be done in Russian.

For four and a half hours I queued, filled out forms, made dishonest declarations, paid dollars and sought tertiary approval for every sheet of paper. The sweat dripped uncontrollably throughout.

Documentation complete, I waited in line in the Škoda for an hour while the engine overheated. Upon reaching the front of the queue, I was given a "this-is-the-Belarusian-car-only-lane" look by the guard, followed by a "why-didn't-you-read-the-sign?" I was ordered to the rear of the neighbouring queue. When I got to the front again, the guard wasn't happy to see the forms I'd filled out were in Russian. He sent me back to the office to find English versions and redo them.

I was in no fit state to bat when I cleared customs. I floored the accelerator and sped between birch forests. I had no idea if today's match was still on. By twenty to four in the afternoon, having set out at seven that morning, I entered Belarus's second largest city. Gomel had been a popular holiday destination before clouds of radioactive material descended upon it. It was made famous in 2004, when thieves stole a portable loo while a man was inside with his pants around his ankles.

I passed rows of warped wooden houses with intricate shutters and window frames and found a statue of Lenin in the square. I asked a babushka sweeping the street with birch twigs for directions.

I reached my contact's apartment block and knocked on his door. Instead of the Belarusian cricket captain, though, a lady wrapped in a towel answered.

"Umm, is this the flat of Kaushal?"

"Huh?"

"Kaushal the cricketer?"

She shut the door in my face.

"Fuck," I muttered. "What the hell am I going to do now?"

Then I noticed this was the wrong apartment.

"My goodness, come in, please," beckoned Kaushal downstairs at number two. He and his red-haired wife, Irina, hastened me into a cramped, antique-looking lounge and sat me in front of the telly.

"We were very, very worried," said Kaushal. "I called the border to ask if you'd come through, but they told me they could not give out personal information. They said the average delay was five hours. You must be exhausted. Please, you can take a shower before we play our game."

I apologised for being so stinky and happily took up the offer.

Kaushal was a Nepalese heart and lung surgeon and a lecturer at Gomel's State Medical University. When he wasn't performing spontaneous pneumothorax operations, he devoted all his energies to developing Belarusian cricket.

"I am from the greatest cricketing city of Nepal," he said. "I came to Belarus to study medicine, and then I met Irina, on the Minsk cricket field."

"Was she impressed by your batting?"

"I had just been bowled, but she didn't know what that meant at the time."

"Now I know most rules," said Irina, with an ironic pout of the lips.

Even after my shower I was so sapped of energy that I could hardly speak. But time was short in Belarus. My visa only allowed me 48 hours. I continued my questioning while Irina brought tea and prepared a Nepalese dinner. Kaushal recounted Belarus's colourful cricket history.

There were currently six teams in the country, all but one in the capital, Minsk. More teams could be assembled if needed.

"Back in 1997–98 we had 10 teams," said Kaushal. "It was the uprising of cricket in Belarus. Many players were illegal immigrants then because the captain – a fat man who could hit a six at will – was a chief trafficker."

"So the players were fleeing political oppression and lack of opportunity and coming here."

"Yes," said Kaushal. "We even circulated a Belarusian cricket magazine in those days."

It outsold *Wisden Cricket Monthly* and *The Cricketer* together.

"Are most players Indian and Nepalese medical students?"

Kaushal nodded.

"We have tried to introduce the game to Belarusians, but it is not easy. We had some television news coverage a few years ago, and we hoped it would attract people, but only Indian and Nepalese students play. I have begun writing an explanation of cricket in Russian to attract more Belarusians."

Kaushal showed me his notes and diagrams. Fielding positions were marked in Cyrillic. Wicketkeeper was 'Кипер', fielder was 'Филдер' and no ball was 'Ноу бал'.

"Once, in April 1998, we arranged a big tournament in Minsk. Two days before the start, the temperature dropped to minus six, and one foot of snow fell. We had to play through it."

Kaushal switched the TV from a singing Bollywood clown to the news. Belarus's President Lukashenko was delivering an important parliamentary speech.

"The news begins with him every night," explained Kaushal. "You can see him 24 hours a day on television."

President Lukashenko was a collective-farm director, who won the election in 1994. He enjoyed his post so much that he decided to change the law and keep himself there. Meanwhile, political opponents simply vanished – victims of secret kidnapping gangs, shrugged the government – or were imprisoned.

Lukashenko was a wonderful leader, though, according to himself and the news. His state-run economy made Belarus the envy of the West. Most famously, he promised his people, "You will live poorly, but not for long."

On-screen, Lukashenko sat at the front of parliament at a high desk while his government looked on and listened. "He is like a teacher in school," said Kaushal. "All the other ministers are his pupils. He is the only one who ever talks."

Belarus was in for a special treat this evening. There was a live link-up between the president and a collective-farm committee. Kaushal translated. "He says to the farmers, 'What are you doing? Other regions are producing more milk and grain. You are not doing it right. I will show you, otherwise I will cut your supplies.'"

President Lukashenko's marvellous ideas for boosting crop production included awarding TVs and carpets to successful farmers. His big fancy, which was taking longer than planned, was to reunite Belarus and Russia, with him at the head of it all. Vladimir Putin was not so enthusiastic about the idea.

"We wrote to the president to get help for cricket," said Kaushal. "I am hopeful we will get something, because he is good with sports and sports funding. At the moment we have no ground. We have to play on concrete with tennis balls wrapped in tape."

Kaushal stood up and went to take his rubbish bags out. He opened his front door and a man stepped inside the flat. He addressed Kaushal in Russian. Kaushal seemed nervous in his responses. Through a narrow gap in the door I glimpsed a broad-shouldered man in jeans and a polo shirt.

I quietly rebagged my notebooks, sound-recording equipment and camera, and crouched behind a chair. The strange guest continued to bombard Kaushal with questions. This was Belarus's modern-day secret police – the KGB.

I wondered if I'd been followed. Had he spotted the car outside with GB number plates? The KGB man took a step nearer the lounge and Kaushal, with his back turned, half closed the door. He was trying to protect me. At any moment the KGB man could walk into the lounge and find a foreigner, without a journalist visa, playing hide-and-seek behind a chair. Kaushal answered everything directly until the man left 10 minutes later.

Kaushal re-entered the lounge, looking shaken.

"What did he want?" I asked.

"He asked me if I was a foreigner, if I had registered with the police. He wanted to see my passport."

"You're not in trouble because of me, are you?"

"No, no. He didn't know you were here. Sometimes we get questioned like this."

I'd been in Belarus only a few hours and already I wanted out. Now I understood why Ukrainians were scared to come here.

After dinner Kaushal, Irina and I left to round up the cricketers.

"When you were late because of the border, my players, they kept phoning me, asking, 'Sir, what do we do?'" said Kaushal. "I hope they are still around and willing to play."

"Why do they call you 'Sir'?"

"They are my students at the university. They are afraid to swear or smoke in front of me, in case they get lower marks."

We reached a housing estate and Kaushal parked and entered a tower block. He emerged minutes later with a gang of excited Indian and Nepalese students, dressed in tee shirts, work shirts and chinos. We clambered into separate cars and drove onto a disused car park between tower blocks.

There were head-high weeds, fist-sized rocks and patches of torn tarmac across the surface. A green former toll building stood at the edge, its door broken open. Twin industrial chimney stacks puffed on the horizon.

"Okay, this is the pitch," said Kaushal, hurrying proceedings along. He produced four tennis balls wrapped in blue insulating tape and two poster-sized scoresheets. At his instructions, the students hammered stumps into a ruptured dirt strip.

Radiologist Rama won the toss and put Dr Kaushal's XI in to field.

"Please, Angus, bowl the first over," insisted Kaushal, as the batsmen walked out with short, light bats designed for hitting tennis balls.

There was little difficulty in making the ball spin on the car park. Unfortunately, the ball turned so much it had no chance of reaching the stumps. The Belarusians, used to these conditions, taught me a powerful lesson. My first over was blasted for 4, 6, 6, 6, 0. Finally, the bastard was caught beside a tree, a foot short of another 6. These had been monstrous sixes too. It took many minutes to find the ball among the weeds.

I was sent to the outfield to think about my disastrous start. Rama's team flayed every ball and sent clouds of soil into the air each time they scrambled a run. I started to feel drowsy. I was in danger of falling asleep. It was no fault of the Belarusian cricketers; they were engaged in a mad frenzy in front of me. But it had been a long day, and a long tour.

Dr Kaushal's XI looked to have performed commendably in the field when we learned our opponents had only mustered 89. However, there were another 59 extras to add, including 30 wides, making our target a stiffer task.

Opening the batting, Kaushal showed exactly why he was a professor and everyone else was his student. He looked to be leading us to a comfortable win when disaster struck. The combination of Asif and Waqar proved deadly. Coming in at number three, I attempted a cover drive off Waqar's first ball and missed by several seconds.

"Ooh! Classical player!" someone called out, flatteringly, on seeing my follow-through.

Classical player or not, my dreams were shattered next ball as Waqar produced a rapid inswinging yorker. I was bowled for nought, second ball, in Belarus. It doesn't get much lower than that.

Despite continued resistance from the doctor, who top-scored with 17, we collapsed to a painful 50-run loss.

After the game, I mingled with the teams by the boundary.

"Do you have any unusual club stories?" I asked.

They shook their heads.

"Ever seen any violence on the cricket field?" I asked.

Five players spoke at once.

"Oh, yes!" cried one above the others. "In April a drunk man came to watch our game here! He was shouting at us! He came on the field and pushed one of us, so we ran over and beat him! We hit him on the head with the bats!"

Eight players were nodding and smiling more broadly than they had at any point in our game.

"What happened then?"

"He sat down on the boundary. He was bleeding. He watched us finish our game."

"Were the police called?"

"Not that time. That happened a few months ago during the big tournament in Minsk. Some of us were not selected, so we were playing our own game here. A man tried to steal our necklaces on the boundary."

"Was he a transvestite?"

"No, no. He was just trying to steal them. So we beat him too! Then another man was driving past and saw this. He stopped to rescue the thief. So we attacked him also! We destroyed his car! We dented the panels and scratched the paintwork! This man," the teller pointed to a lanky, grinning teammate, "he was the hero who threw bricks through his windows!"

"Yes! I broke them all!" said the teammate, receiving pats on the back.

"And the police were called this time?" I asked.

"Yes, the driver phoned them. We were all taken to the station."

I walked over to Kaushal, who was loading stumps into his car.

"Were these guys arrested for beating people on the pitch?" I asked.

"Oh, yes. It was during the Minsk tournament. I got a call from one of them in jail saying all six players not in the squad had been arrested. They were a little annoyed at being left out, you see. They said, 'Hello! Sir! Please help! We are all in the police station and cannot communicate! Please help us!' I told them, 'What can I do now? I am about to go into bat in Minsk.' When I got back after the weekend I arranged bail and sorted everything out."

I found it strange that these players were afraid to swear or smoke in front of their teacher, but not afraid to commit assault and battery under him, or ask him for bail. Fortunately, it didn't affect their university grades.

I returned to the huddle of players. They'd recalled another run-in with the law. The green ex-tollbooth beside the pitch, which served as a pavilion, possessed a dark secret. The week before, a corpse had been discovered inside it.

"The police came to question us here, but we told them we knew nothing."

"This is like an episode of *Inspector Morse*!" I cried. "Was the weapon a pair of scissors?"

Next morning, after a night of tenpin bowling in town, Kaushal and Irina delayed heading to work to see me off.

"Which border do you have to leave by?" asked Kaushal after an enormous fried breakfast.

"The far end of the country, typically, between Minsk and Vilnius. I have till midnight."

"If you have any problems, just ask someone to reverse charges to my cellphone, okay? And I will sort it out. But don't worry. You will have no problems. I will lead you to the right highway. It is 300 kilometres to Minsk."

I was humbled by Irina and Kaushal's hospitality, but I wondered how I'd manage to convince a stranger to let me borrow their mobile phone and reverse the charges in the event of difficulty.

The highway out of Gomel was empty but for a few crows. I hit and killed one. The route took me across a vast, birch-forested steppe dotted with farms and lodges. Soft-toy stalls occasionally sprang up beside cornfields. As I neared concrete Minsk, the radiation and fuel levels dropped.

By the time I hit Minsk's ring road, I was in some trouble. There were no road signs and my petrol tank was showing empty. I was about to crack when I took a slip road at a guess and spied a rare petrol station. My problems were over.

I inserted the petrol nozzle into my tank, but after several minutes not a drop of fuel had come out. I glanced at the other motorists, who looked back at me and pointed to the kiosk. I had to *guess* an amount of fuel and pay before receiving it.

I approached the kiosk and withdrew from my pocket a wad of Belarusian rubles which I'd been given as change for my road-tax fee on entry. The babushka behind the counter shook her head. The notes were worthless. I waved a bank card, then a credit card, and the woman shook her head again. There were no cash machines and no means by which I could buy petrol.

I stormed back to the car. The woman in the kiosk got on her tannoy and shouted at me in Russian. All the other drivers stared and shouted too. I threw the petrol nozzle back into its pump and screeched out of the forecourt.

After another spin around the ring road, it was the same result at the next petrol station. The engine began to jolt as I wound around and around helplessly. I started to hyperventilate. I considered my fate. My visa would shortly be expiring. I would be trapped on a ring road in a totalitarian state, with a broken-down Škoda, without a word of the language (except 'wicketkeeper', 'fielder' and 'no ball'), unable to reach the one man who could help me – the Belarusian cricket captain – who was, in all likelihood at that moment, at the other end of the country performing a life-saving heart operation. The tour would end in disaster. There would be no hundreds scored against Lithuania or Poland or anyone else – except, maybe, my Belarusian jailmates. Not even great-uncle Ivor could get me out of this one.

At the third petrol station, I played my last hand. I took my one remaining five-euro note and my final five-dollar bill and gave them to the lady in the kiosk. She nodded and hand-pumped enough petrol to get me out the forecourt and, hopefully, the country. I left her my wad of Belarusian notes as a tip.

There were still 150 kilometres, through fields and forests, to the border. I stuck strictly to the speed limit, unable to risk a speeding fine. When the barrier at last came in sight, I leapt in my seat. Over there was Lithuania, the EU and safety. A place where I could buy much-needed fuel and withdraw cash.

Cars were slewed across the road in all directions as people fought to get out. "Lukashenko!" was yelled in anger every sentence. I parked and walked confidently to the post with my 30 signed documents. The guard sifted through the pile before returning them and saying something in Russian. The line of people behind me shouted and waved a piece of paper.

"Banka! Banka!" they cried, pointing back down the road.

The bank was a hut at the edge of the woods with a boy with a cashbox. He wanted two euros seventy for a signed chit, which I would need to get through the barrier.

"Umm, do you accept credit cards?" I asked.

The boy shook his head.

"Is there a cash machine near here?"

"Niet."

"Listen. I'm really sorry, but I don't have any money."

The boy shrugged.

"Is there any chance I could just get the piece of paper, please? I don't know what else I can do."

He beckoned the next person to the window.

I bit my tongue and paced back to the car. I scrambled around its floor and found a two-euro coin. I raced back to the bank. The boy with the cashbox was unmoved. He wanted two euros seventy.

"Please!" I begged. "It's 70 cents. I *have* to get out of this country *now* or I'm going to be arrested. I have absolutely no money and no petrol. *Please!*"

"Get your family to help you," said the boy flatly, waving me aside.

I wanted to break the glass and rip out his intestines. But I had to calm myself and think quickly. I turned to the queue, hot veins rising from my neck.

"Please! Can someone give me 70 cents?"

They chuckled, shook their heads and pushed me out of the way. I was going to jail. There was nothing for it. I had to stage a hold-up.

I regained my place at the head of the line by force.

"LISTEN ONE FUCKING MINUTE!" I screamed at the boy. "I HAVE HAD IT! I HAVE NO MONEY! GET IT? NOW TAKE SOME RESPONSIBILITY ONCE IN YOUR PETTY LIFE AND HELP ME OUT, BECAUSE NO OTHER FUCKER HERE CAN! GIVE ME THE FUCKING PIECE OF PAPER!"

For the first time he looked scared, then mumbled, "No."

"I AM NOT FUCKING *MOVING* TILL I GET THAT PAPER! IF YOU NEED THE MONEY, ASK THESE PEOPLE!"

He addressed the line. The first man, visibly shaken, paid the 70 cents.

"Thank you. Thank you very much," I said pleasantly, as though nothing unsavoury had happened. I snatched my paper and marched back to the first post. Everything was in order. I was to be let through. I returned to the car and discovered I'd lost my keys.

A babushka waddled up. She pointed back to the bank. Yes, I had left them in there.

When the barrier lifted and I cruised through, I thumped my steering wheel.

Then I arrived at a second barrier.

I was *still* in Belarus. I rushed to the next booth with my papers. A mustachioed lady with shoulder pads shook her head. I didn't understand what she was saying. The people from the bank queue were laughing. A Lithuanian girl was summoned to translate.

"She says your road tax expired at one o'clock today. It is now seven o'clock, so you must pay 10 dollars."

Ten dollars! Seventy cents was hard enough. I showed my empty wallet. "I have no money. Please! How can my road tax expire at one o'clock? You can't get through customs in that time, let alone drive from Gomel. Do you accept credit cards?"

"Ten dollars," said the guard.

"Can't you just change the one to a seven on the form, please?"

The guard shook her head.

I threw my wallet on the ground and slumped down. I wanted to cry but couldn't. "I don't care any more! I just want out of this horrible country! Arrest me! I don't care! I have no money!"

The guard said something, which the Lithuanian girl translated. "She says there is a bank back there."

At this, a tear formed.

The Lithuanian girl's father approached. After a rundown on the situation, he smiled and said, "My friend, I am a seaman. Here, I will pay for you." He handed 10 dollars to the guard.

I rose to thank him, apologising profusely and shaking his hand.

"No problem, my friend," said the seaman. "Just be careful. There are another four barriers to go."

Dr Kaushal's XI versus Rama's team

A disused car park, Gomel, Belarus

31.07.2005 (15-over match, 11-a-side)

Result: Rama's team won by 50 runs

Toss won by: Rama

1st Innings

Rama's team		R
Asif	b Deepak	8
Gabriel	c Deepak b Angus	34
Rama*	st Nirav b Angus	12
Bhupender	run out (Dr Kaushal)	1
Waqar	run out (Angus)	8
Abed	not out	16

Upul	b Nirav	0
Rajiv Goyal	b Angus	0
Javedc Bali	b Nirav	0
Deepak	c Pratap b Angus	9
Pravin	b Sashank	1
Extras		59
Total (all out, 14.4 overs)		**148**

2nd Innings

Dr Kaushal's XI		**R**
Dr Kaushal*	b Asif	17
Jimic Javed	b Asif	6
Angus	b Waqar	0
Nirav	b Asif	1
Pratap	run out (Waqar/Asif)	4
Sashank	c Bhupender b Waqar	13
Deepak	c Goyal b Javed	3
Balic Pravin	b Asif	5
Jindad	run out (Upul)	3
Subram	b Waqar	5
Avand	not out	0
Extras		41
Total (all out, 14.1 overs)		**98**

18
PUMMELLING THE POLES

The Wiejce Palace Hotel cricket ground

It was morning in Vilnius's old town hostel. I had escaped Belarus. I phoned Deputy Ambassador Keith at the British Embassy.

"Hi, Keith. Is all still good for tonight?"

"Yes, we've got people lining up for the game. About 17 so far."

"Do you want me to recruit players from the hostel?"

"You can do. Phone me back with the names. I'll have to register them at the military academy."

"No problem. So, I'll meet you at the embassy later?"

"Looking forward to it. Can't wait to play some cricket!"

While Scotsman Keith was confirming diplomatic availability, I entered the hostel kitchen, where red-eyed backpackers were munching cornflakes and checking emails.

"Anyone want to play cricket tonight?"

"What?" everyone cried.

"Cricket in Vilnius?" said a Canadian. "No *way!*"

Even the Australians were sceptical.

I explained Lithuania would be stripped of its cricketing virginity that evening, and there were five places up for grabs. Every hand in the room shot up.

After signing the lucky five, I went out for a tour of the capital. Vilnius was another glorious world heritage site, which, thankfully, Stag, Scum and Dodger hadn't yet reached. Every cobbled square had baroque cathedrals and frescoed arches. The only drawback was a Christian group singing, "We are climbing Jesus' ladder, ladder!" on a balcony.

Tucked away inside a river loop I found the breakaway Republic of Užupis. After Lithuania's independence from the Soviets, this neglected corner of the city had declared itself an independent state. Founded by artists, it now boasted an embassy in Moscow and a 12-strong army. It had a flag for each season and its own constitution. Beside the entry bridge stood a sign showing the Mona Lisa, a 40-kilometre per hour speed limit, a red warning triangle about driving in the river, and a be-happy face.

I crossed into Užupis's quiet lanes, avoiding a hypodermic needle on the pavement, and went to see the constitution.

Užupis's laws were written on three shiny metal plates on a wall. As I approached, a large tour group was studying them. The constitution started off sensibly. Point number two was: 'Everyone has the right to hot water, heating in winter and a tiled roof.'

Point number three was a little strange, though: 'Everyone has the right to die, but this is not an obligation.'

Thereafter it descended into animal obsession.

'10. Everyone has the right to love and to take care of the cat.'

'11. Everyone has the right to look after the dog until one of them dies.'

'12. A dog has the right to be a dog.'

'13. A cat is not obliged to love its owner, but must help in time of nee (sic).'

Did the cats and dogs agree to this? I wondered.

Lost in Vilnius's traffic, we were 40 minutes late for the rendezvous. The British Embassy was off the map.

"Christ! I can't take the stress!" cried my co-passenger, a Québecois, who'd been shot at in Afghanistan and arrested in Sudan. "I don't wanna miss this cricket! Did you know it was the only sport the Taliban permitted?"

My squad had an impressive CV. I was driving an American kidnapped by Nepalese Maoist rebels, an Aussie who hadn't played cricket since being hit by a train, and some Melbourne girls whose ex-boyfriends played county cricket. They would bond well with the diplomats, I was sure.

Deputy Ambassador Keith was waiting at the embassy in his whites when we arrived. He, too, had amassed an impressive line-up, including Spaniards, Swedes, Hungarians, two Lithuanians and the British Ambassador, who wore an England shirt.

"Great, you made it!" said Keith. "Thanks for kicking my arse and making me put on this first game. I've been meaning to do it for years."

The team procession left from the embassy gates and shortly entered the Lithuanian Military Academy. There were drill-sergeants and uniformed squads hopping through tyres. In the centre of the grounds was a tiny, uncut lawn.

"Well, it'll do for our first game," said Keith. "We'll just try and get everyone used to the rules."

Keith pulled several clean kitbags from the boot of his car and opened them by the pitch. Lithuania was the best-equipped club in the whole of Central and Eastern Europe. All 22 players gathered around, some trying to fit pads on upside down.

Keith was a skilled director. He'd taught Scottish country dancing in the Mozambique civil war. He explained today's match was to be a single-wicket tournament. It would not be easy to pierce the field, as there would be 20 fielders throughout.

The British Ambassador bowled the first over and demolished the Danish Vice-Consul's stumps first ball. This being the first game, no one knew how to react, so the Danish Vice-Consul was given another chance, and another. I was pleased to discover that the British Ambassador was a gifted cricketer. I believed this to be the most important role of our Foreign Office.

After spanking a quick-fire 52 not out in my innings (Lithuania's first half-century) and becoming the only man in history to give away 12 overthrows in two balls, I stood at slip and chatted to Keith, who was keeping wicket. He was a member of the Loire Saumur Strays, who'd played on the island of Vis. Under their banner he'd graced a number of the world's most obscure cricket fields.

"We took a tour to the land of the midnight sun in northern Sweden," he said, "and played on Arctic tundra from eight o'clock in the evening till six next morning. People were sound asleep in the field. The temperature went from twenty-one degrees to two and back again. I wore four jumpers at one stage."

"Did you go drinking after?"

"We went white-water rafting, then played another game. I didn't sleep for five days."

Keith took a catch, then continued, "Another time we went to an island off Helsinki and played the Finnish women's team. The game was inside a ruined castle, where the walls were the boundary."

"Do you play in the UK?" I asked.

"We had one match on the Isles of Scilly. I'll never forget. There were only two surnames in the opposition."

"And Mick Jagger is your club chairman?"

"Yes. He's actually a useful spin bowler."

Our game petered out after everyone had had a bat or two. Like a dog who'd tasted blood, Lithuania would surely come back for more.

"I think we'll have another game before winter, then look at holding more fixtures next year," said Keith. "But we've got to get Lithuanians running it. I'll be reposted in a couple of years . . . Anyway, where are you off to next?"

"Poland. The match is this weekend."

"Any idea what they're like?"

"All I know is they're pure-blood Poles, men and women, and they play single-wicket six-a-side. They were beaten by Slovakia and bowled out for 10 by a Slovenian village. It's my final game, so I'm desperate to score a ton."

Keith chuckled. "Just make sure you bat first."

*

I raced across the Polish plains, my arms tingling with pins and needles and my gut throbbing like I had a hernia. As I drove, I did push-ups in my chair to improve circulation. There would be time for recovery after Sunday. Did the Poles play on Sundays, I wondered, this being one of the most Catholic countries in the world? Were they aware cricket was played here, during World War Two, inside the drained moat of a castle-cum-prisoner-of-war camp?

Sun had buckled the road surfaces, making the Škoda bounce like a Ukrainian trolleybus. It was little wonder Poland came only second to Russia for European road deaths. I did admire their tennis court tramlines at the side, though, and pulled into them frequently to let vodka-fuelled maniacs past.

I looked out onto fields of dead grass, stork nests on chimneys and the occasional hitchhiking soldier. I passed villages with wooden churches, square farmhouses and giant plastic dinosaurs.

Soon I found myself chanting the lyrics to Solomon Grundy. He'd had a hell of a week, Solomon Grundy: born on Monday, christened on Tuesday, married on Wednesday, died on Saturday and buried by the end. I had to hand it to the fella. But he didn't score 100, did he?

"Get a grip on yourself, man!" I shouted. "You're singing nursery rhymes!"

I wondered what great-uncle Ivor in the passenger seat must have thought of all this.

Poland held special memories for me. My brother and I came here towards the end of our ill-fated 2002 road trip, joined by a curly-haired Kiwi chef named Brendan. We were the only guests in a 1000-bed hotel at the foot of the Sudeten Mountains, where the walls and carpets were as stale as the proprietor's breath. After watching *Highlander*, dubbed by a drunk, on the TV in our room, we set out to go discoing in town.

At the bar grandparents shuffled with toddlers on their feet, while the singing, backed by an '80s keyboard, sounded like a cat with appendicitis. We returned to the street and asked a taxi driver to direct us to the best nightlife in town.

We began winding into the mountains. After 20 minutes our taxi steered onto a mud track running through a pine forest. Beyond the gloom I could make out a concrete bunker and two cars.

"It's Wednesday night," I said. "There'll be no one here!"

Joe le Taxi approached the bunker on foot. The door was unbolted and a heavy peered out. The men shook hands and signalled us to follow. They led us along a corridor to a brightly coloured dance chamber with only a barman in it.

"This is shit!" I said.

We sat down on a leather sofa and ordered a beer. It was the most expensive in Europe. Le Taxi watched us from a bar stool, grinning. Then five girls, wearing only G-strings, strutted in.

The barman flicked a switch and techno started blasting around the room. A girl leapt on stage and began swinging from a pole. Before I could say venereal disease, a second girl had mounted Brendan's chest.

"Come on, guys. Hurry up with your beers, yeah," I said shyly, looking at the floor. A third girl approached and tried to rip apart my rugby shirt.

Unmoved after 30 minutes, I noted concern on the management's faces. Fearing someone might pull a gun, I marched to the exit. I must have been drunk, or drugged, because I was harbouring thoughts of joyriding the taxi. Through its window I saw the meter was still running. No longer 16 zlotys 50, as on arrival, it now read 40 zlotys. I raced to fetch the others.

Before we reached the door again, leaving the girls looking miffed, Joe le Taxi had run ahead of us and started his motor.

"No. You see, we're going to walk," I said, demonstrating with my fingers. It took several attempts till he understood. Then the matter of 45 zlotys arose. We were leaving the country in a few hours and had spent nearly all our money on beer.

"You're getting 16.50, pal," I said. "That's what the meter said when we got here." Le Taxi looked at my last few coins and his face reddened. Brendan and Doug were heading off down the mud track.

"Poliska! Poliska!" threatened Le Taxi, picking up his brick mobile. I placed the money on his roof and walked away.

"Ruuuun!" I screamed upon reaching the others. We began sprinting. A car approached on the main road, and we dived into a ditch. It wasn't Le Taxi, so we clambered out and continued, laughing like schoolgirls. We didn't know where we were, or our address, but this, we agreed, was the highlight of the trip.

There was a screech of tyres. A crazed Le Taxi swung out from the woods in pursuit, headlights on full beam.

"Quick! There's a taxi coming from the other direction! Wave it down!" I shouted.

Except it was the police.

"This isn't going to look terribly good," I said.

It had been a cruel pincer movement. Four large-jowled men got out; one dressed in army gear.

"Dzien dobry," I said. "Do you speak English?"

"Yes," answered the chief.

I pointed at Le Taxi. "This man, he bad man. We ask for night club. He took us to venereal-ridden brothel. His meter said 16.50 on arrival. That's what we paid him. He wants 45 zlotys. But we didn't ask him to wait."

It was Le Taxi's turn to explain. We stared at him, hoping his case would crumble. There was much giggling by the police. We also laughed, without understanding. Joe squirmed and was ordered away.

"We will take you back," said the chief.

Two officers were abandoned on the hillside and we were motioned into the back of the police car. I felt like a criminal.

"Can I be handcuffed?" I asked.

The chief shook his head, and answered, "You should have got that back at brothel."

*

After 10 hours at the wheel, frequently recalling my lucky escape last time, I neared my destination. The cricketers were based in Lubuskie, near the German border. To ensure I took the correct road, I pulled over and checked my notes. I was dismayed to learn I had no specific address, and even more alarmed to find Lubuskie was five times the size of Luxembourg.

"Shit!" I cried. "Okay, don't panic."

I would find an internet café and sort this out.

I turned down a tree-lined avenue, where people were selling mushrooms on car bonnets. In the first town I found an internet café. "Do you know the Polish cricketers?" I asked at the desk. The owner eyed me as though this was some secret code and denied all knowledge.

I bought a phonecard and dialled the number on my contact list. After many rings it went to voicemail. I explained I'd arrived in the area for our match, but didn't know the address and start time. I said I'd call again later.

I logged onto my email account and sifted for clues among my Polish correspondence. They were so reliable, the Poles, always replying within a few minutes. I noted with furrowed brows, though, that in recent times their emails had dried up.

Back when I planned this trip and Poland cancelled its May date, I proposed playing on August 4, 5 or 6. They said they'd schedule it. I sent them an update from the road and they mentioned some players might be away for parts of August. It didn't matter if we were five-a-side, I said, as long as we played some form of cricket. "Will contact you on Saturday after our practice session with a definite answer," was the last thing they wrote. That had been over a month ago.

I rejected all thoughts of the match going on without me and vowed to track down these Poles in time. It was only Thursday afternoon, after all. I trawled their website and saw three of their teams were based near Gorzów Wielkopolski. A quick Google search revealed there was a youth hostel in the town. Perfect, I thought. Next, I examined a photo of the cricket ground at the Wiejce Palace Hotel. I searched for the hotel's website and sketched its location. Then I fired an email to my contact.

To: Polish Cricket Association
From: Angus Bell
Subject: Here in Lubuskie

Hi, Polish cricketers,

I have arrived in Lubuskie. I am staying in the youth hostel in Gorzów Wielkopol-ski. I have only a phone number for Simon – no answer yet, and an idea that you play in the grounds of the Wiejce Palace. I am desperate to meet you and hand over some kit. Please, please reply to this email as soon as possible, thanks.

Angus

I found email addresses for the other teams on the Polish cricket website and sent them each an optimistic mailshot.

To: xxxxxxxx
From: Angus Bell
Subject: Urgent call for cricketers!

Hi. My name is Angus and I've just driven 7000 miles to play cricket with you guys and give you some kit . . . I got in contact through the Polish cricket website over a year ago. I am staying in the youth hostel in Gorzów Wielkopolski. I have a phone number for Simon but have been unable to reach anyone. I have no address of any contact, and am absolutely desperate to meet some Polish cricketers . . . Please, please email me asap and let me know how I can get in contact. Thank you.

Best wishes, Angus Bell

Gorzów Wielkopolski was a town of dirty-faced buildings, with street names I couldn't begin to pronounce. I stopped to ask directions at a petrol station. There were four nuns inside and two men with guns. The latter got in their van and escorted me to the youth hostel. There, in its gloom, I went straight to bed; the sole resident. Tomorrow would be spent tracking down cricketers.

In the morning I staggered to an internet café and logged into my inbox. No new emails had arrived. Surely one of the Poles had seen my message by now?

I breakfasted on a baguette while I drove and went in search of the Wiejce Palace Hotel. Someone there would know the cricketers and the match's start time.

The 30-odd-kilometre drive took me past brick farmhouses and through boar-infested forests. At the end of a cobbled avenue, I came to a grand eighteenth-century building with a red-tiled roof and white walls. I parked and lifted the last of the equipment from my car. I carried two pairs of pads, a helmet, six cricket bags and a sack of MCC juggling balls across the cricket field to reception.

"Hi. I'm trying to find the cricketers who play here. I don't have an address. I can't reach anybody on the phone number I have. I've got some equipment for them. Do you know when the game is this weekend?"

"No problem," said the friendly young manager. "I have their phone numbers. Where have you come from?"

"From Scotland, via Montenegro and Istanbul. I've been playing cricket in every country as I go."

"What? And you drove all the way out here to the middle of the forest to play cricket with Poles?"

"Yes, it's the final match."

"Great. Please, have a seat. Can I get you some complimentary tea or coffee?"

When the manager reappeared three minutes later with a silver teapot and tray of biscuits I'd almost fallen asleep in a chair.

"You look kind of tired," he said. "That's quite understandable. I will phone the cricketers now."

He spoke for a minute, then passed his mobile to me. It was the lady I'd been in touch with by email for a year and a half.

"Hi," I said. "Sorry, I didn't have your address, so I came to the ground to track you down. How are you?"

She spoke quickly. "We can't organise any cricket now. Simon organises all our games, and Simon is in England now. We don't really play cricket in summer. You should come back in winter."

The Poles don't play cricket in summer. Of course they don't. Why would they, when they can play in the February snow? I exhaled deeply, understanding. The hotel manager was studying my face, hoping for good news.

"Would it be possible to meet some of you, please?" I asked. "To hear your stories?"

"Well . . . I'm working right now," said the lady on the phone. "I can't . . . All the information is on our website."

"I have some kit to give you. What should I do with it?"

"Thank you. That's kind. If you leave it at the hotel, I will pick it up next week."

What else could I say?

"Bye."

I left my kit with the manager. He apologised on behalf of his country and shook my hand. I trudged back to the car, a tear forming in each eye. Just like much of my youth in the Scottish hills, here in Poland there was no one to play with. My international career was at an end, and I hadn't made 100.

I reached the Škoda and had one of those moments you're said to experience before you die. Tour memories flashed back. There was Jason and his team of Stoli-fuelled Baltic ice warriors, and the story of the Prague fielders without fingers. I saw the cheering Slovak gardeners and the game beside Lenin's statue in Hungary. I remembered the photo of 13-year-old Borut in his pads and flares in an Alpine meadow, and the happy wine-makers of Vis hitting balls into the Adriatic. I recalled the fear and the ecstasy on Mr Mubashir's face on the bridge over the Bosphorus. Then there was Saif and his cricket degree, the Zrenjanin City Hall media circus . . .

After several minutes I wondered about my tour batting average. Yes! What if that had reached 100? Surely that would count for something? There'd been plenty of not-outs to aid the cause. I tore a page from my map-book and penned down my scores.

On the ice in Estonia there'd been 40 n.o. and 0 n.o. In Slovakia I scored 52 n.o. In Austria I made 38. In Bulgaria 43 n.o. and 42 against the Medicals. Then there was 24 n.o. in Serbia. Zero in Belarus – hard to forget, that one – and in Lithuania 52 n.o. Wasn't there a transcontinental six, too, carried out under strict match rules? Total: 297 runs ÷ 3 = *oh no* . . . 99.

Ninety-*EFFING*-nine! I had needed just 3 runs against Poland to average 100. Bradman, in his final Test innings, needed 4. It seemed like fate. With more than 1000 miles to go, it was time to take this roadshow home.

19
PSYCHIC REVISITED

I see dead people – the psychic Harley Monte

I was back in Montreal with Candy. Eighteen months previously, the psychic had foretold of great paperwork to enable my return. Was it coincidence I'd since gone through Canadian immigration? It had not been a pleasant experience. The booklets took five months to complete. I was forced to undergo X-rays in hospital. They made me take HIV tests and visit my local police cells for fingerprinting. Now the psychic's prophecy was almost complete. Only one task remained on my part.

You're going to be seeing me again.

It was predestined, so I felt I had to. Besides, my six-month psychic check-up was now long overdue. Another quick Google search tracked down my man. He was a safety goggles salesman by day and a shaman by night. I noted down the psychic centre address. There was nothing he could do to stop me.

I was laughing as I rode the sweaty underground to Metro Guy-Concordia, then marched down Boulevard de Maisonneuve. I realised psychics were a bit like crack-pushers outside primary schools, giving you that first fix for free. But as I climbed the orange steps of the Spiritual Science Fellowship Centre, a terrifying thought pricked me. What, if after all these efforts, the psychic announced, "*Man*, I was *only joking*!"?

'Please remove your rubbers before entry', read the sign on the door. I knocked and approached reception.

"Bonjour. I'd like to see Harley Monte, please."

"Great," said the friendly lady. "Does he know you're coming?"

He bloody well should do. He's a psychic.

"Yes. We discussed it 18 months ago," I said.

"Oh . . . did you fix a time?"

"No."

"Well . . . I think he has a cancellation right now. Would that suit?"

We were sitting in the dull light of the old library upstairs in the psychic centre. It had all the makings of a Professor Trelawney lesson.

"I'm Angus, we met before," I said. There was no flicker of recognition in the psychic's eyes. "I guess you meet a lot of people, huh?" He nodded, placing crystals and tarot cards on the table.

I set up my digital voice recorder and browsed the bookcases. *Life on the Other Side: A Psychic's Tour of the Afterlife* leapt out at me.

"I haven't read that travel title," I said. "I suppose you've read every book in here."

"No. I don't read books; ever."

"Why?"

"I don't have the time. Besides, I can pick a book up in my hand and know what it's about."

"From reading the back cover?"

"No. From the vibration."

The psychic smiled and sat down opposite me.

"There's a couple of things that I do to begin. One of them is your power numbers. If you give me your date of birth . . ."

"Sixteen, nine, nineteen-eighty."

"Hey, happy birthday!"

"Hey, thanks, buddy!"

Gawd, I sounded like Sheena Easton.

"Okay, if you add the one and the six, that makes your power number seven. Seven is luck. It's no coincidence that casinos use it all the time. You're a very lucky person. However, luck is relative, and if you don't believe in it, then you're not that lucky."

I didn't believe in luck at all.

"If you had the number eight, then you'd be someone who goes from high to low." He drew a figure eight. "See the shape of it? The top circle is high, the bottom one is low. Every once in a while you'd have to *squeeze* through that vortex connecting them. And that's tough."

This was the best (and, at 90 Canadian dollars, the most expensive) maths lesson I'd ever had. I wondered if all women were eights and if they squeezed through that vortex once a month.

"But you're a seven," continued the psychic. "I'm not saying go out and buy a Lotto ticket, but there's been a situation going on which you're going to have to really call on luck to make it work. You've set a game plan that doesn't quite make sense in regards to the situation. You have to rethink your schedule a bit. You're going to have to bring your goals a little closer."

Had I been over-optimistic with my early plans to leave my call centre and make radio and TV documentaries? With no training, funding or equipment?

The tarot cards were spread on the table and I was given a crystal to hold. "This is the library stone," said the psychic. "This stone contains the sum total of all the knowledge of the universe. When I need an answer, I put my hand on it, and it gives me the answer."

At the psychic's request I lifted three cards and handed them to him in the order they were picked.

"Are you in antiques?" he said.

Oh no.

"What's coming to my mind is an image of a beautiful red settee. And when I ask what it means, I get the feeling it's part of a set. A stage set. I don't know if you have anything to do with acting or directing, or it could be writing, but I think you're going to be in theatrics. The only thing that's puzzling me is that if this is theatre, there should be other actors there. But there's no one else around."

The psychic looked at the second card.

"Okay, you've been doing *a lot* of travelling, so in a family situation you've been all alone. Here we have a card of a man going off travelling, and he's leaving everything behind."

He studied the third card.

"I should be seeing your name in print. But for some reason that hasn't happened yet, not on the level it's supposed to.

There's an opportunity in two and a half weeks to present your project, whatever it is."

I wanted to drop my crystal and give him a high five. I knew he'd prove genuine again. I'd been a fool to doubt him for a moment. Now I could shed my lead apron. It might make him cut to the part about naming a publisher.

"It's a book," I said.

The psychic nodded. "Great! All I'm asking for is a free signed copy."

What's the fucking point if he's not going to read it? I thought.

"The spirit will help you write it. The spirit has helped you write before. Listen to what they're saying when you're in front of the keyboard, and it will all fall into place. When you go off and do your research . . . " He broke off. "It's almost as if you already *know* what you're going to write. Man, look at this card with the swords after a battle. You're picking up all the spoils! Man, it's divinely given! Three more cards, please . . .

" . . . There *should* have been celebrations here, but they haven't happened yet. And that indicates to me you needed to make a change. As I said, in two and a half weeks there's an opportunity to present your work. And within four months, four months, the deal will be signed. *Man!* Get ready for more work . . . "

I prayed he didn't mean at another methadone clinic.

There was a rap at the door.

"Okay, we're almost out of time," said the psychic. "We've got time for one more question. So, if you send your thoughts out to the universe I'll try and answer it."

Again, what do you ask the man who can see the future? I knew what it had to be. It was predestined.

"I averaged 99 this cricket season and didn't once get close to three figures. *When* will I get that 100?"

The psychic looked flummoxed.

"Ninety-nine? I don't know what that is, but . . . haven't you gone far enough?"

WHAT IS CRICKET?
AN EXPLANATION BY DR KAUSHAL TIWARI
Что такое КРИКЕТ?

Это Английская игра, которая в настоящее время очень известна в Австралии, Индии, Пакистане, Новой Зиландии, Зимбабве, Шри-Ланке, Бангладеше, Ю. Африке, Канаде, Непале, Шотландии. Уже начали играть в эту игру страны Западной Европы.

В каждой команде 11 человек. Играют с помощью биты и мяча. Игра проводится на травяном поле (обычно 80x60 м), в середине которого устанавливаются 2 «калитки» (Wickets), на расстоянии 20 м друг от друга.

Одновременно одна команда «В» делает «Филдинг» (Fielding) и другая команда «А» делает «Бэттинг» (Batting). Т.е. команда, которая делает Филдинг разрушает бросками мяча калитку команды противника, игроки которой защищают её, отбивая мяч битами (Бэттинг). Игроки, которые делают филдинг называются "Филдерс", которые делают баттинг называются "Бэтсман". Тот который бросает мяч – Боулер, а вратарь – Кипер. После того как, игрок от команды Баттинг ударит мяч, он по возможности бежит между калитками и набирает очки (Runs). При попадании мяча на калитку и ещё в случаях, когда игрок от команды Филдинг ловит (Caught) мяч в воздухе, то противник т.е. Бэтсман (человек с битой) уходит с поля и его заменяет другой игрок этой же команды, до тех пор покка не сыграют все (все 11 игроков). Игра бывает органичена колличеством бросков. 6 бросков мяча составляют один Овер (Over). Часто игра бывает от 30 до 50 Оверов. Если команда бросала органиченное колличество оверов, то независимо от того сколько игроков осталось в команде для Бэттинга, игра останавливается. Потом команды меняются ролями. Очки, набранные при этом, являются окончательным результатом этой команды. Другая команда стремится набрать больше очков, чем противник и при успешном наборе выигрывает. Если же набрать большее количество очков не удается, то выигрывает первая команда.
Англичане говорят: «Крикет - игра джентельменов.»

Каушал Тивари

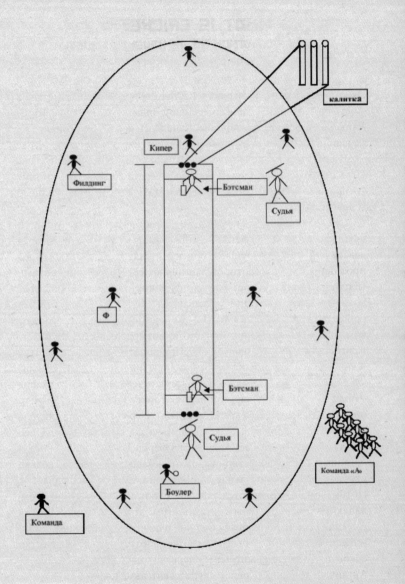

калитка

Кипер

Филдинг

Бэтсман

Судья

Ф

Бэтсман

Судья

Команда «А»

Боулер

Команда

ACKNOWLEDGMENTS

Unparalleled thanks go to:

Everyone in this book, in particular: Jason Barry, Julian Tall and Baltic Adventures (www.balticadventures.co.uk), Leo and Simon Rawlence, Vladimir and Anna Chudácik, Andrej Souvent, Borut Čegovnik, Brad Eve, Alasdair Green, Tessa Fras and the British Embassy in Zagreb, Ivo Scepanovic, Oliver Roki, Milos Pesic, Saif-ur-Rehman, Nikolay Kolev and the Bulgarian National Sports Academy, Mr Mubashir Kahn, Professor Syed, Peter O'Byrne, Mike Roche-Kelly, Thamarai Pandian, Kaushal and Irina Tiwari, Keith Shannon and Harley Monte the psychic.

And also, in no particular order: The Scottish Arts Council for their financial support, Richard Holdsworth and Louise Kent of the European Cricket Council, Island Crickit (www.island-crickit.co.uk) and NatWest for the donated kit, the Crowin family and La Cabosse d'Or Chocolaterie for the chocolate, Gigi Thibault, John Barclay, Laura Garland and the MCC, Christopher Martin-Jenkins, Sir Tim Rice, Shannon Hurst Lane, Sascha Stokes, Mark The Roadworrier, James Wills, the Wylies, Megan Valsinger-Clark, Ron Grosset, Richie Benaud, Istvan Soos, Ruslanas Iržikevičius, Ed Symes, Richard Scott, Dave Bidini, Paul Daniels, James Mawson, Lee Bailey, Ed Craig and John Stern at *The Wisden Cricketer*, Sambit Bal, Andrew Unsworth, Paul Ash, Mike Stanger, Brad Boxall, Matt Thacker, Jeff Booth, the British Embassies in Belgrade, Vilnius and Budapest, Chris Butler, Chris England, Stewart Ferris, Owain Llyr, Norman Drummond, Hugo Rifkind, Scott Gray, Sandy Wolofsky, Geeta Nadkarni, Sean Mccutcheon, Anurag Dhir, David Gutnick, Jim Morrison, Peter Clarke, Catherine Elkin, Amelia Clark, Malcolm Clarke, Lenny

Henry, Derek Pringle, Andre Louis, Stuart Archibald, Mark Rickards, Jerome Starkey, Andy Barr, Ben Freedman, George and Terry at Gregory's Backpackers in Zvezditsa, Susie O'Neil, Ann Smith, Rob Pain, Sam Reid, Niall Marshall, Sir Dennis Landau, Jim Cumbes and Lancashire County Cricket Club, West of Scotland CC, Simon Dardick, Ben Heywood, Mike Bailey and Mahendra Mapagunaratne.

I'd also like to single out: Barry Hyland, Angus Wolfe-Murray, Andy Searle, Allan Lynch, Malcolm Mckenzie, Rob Middlehurst, Euan Thorneycroft, Gemma Harries, Nick Davies, Stuart Fortey and my family (Candy, Gillian, Catriona, Douglas, Mum, Dad) for making this happen.

Oh, and of course, the ghost of Great-Uncle Ivor.

I will name my first six children after you all.